SPLASH

BOB TABOR

ACC ART BOOKS

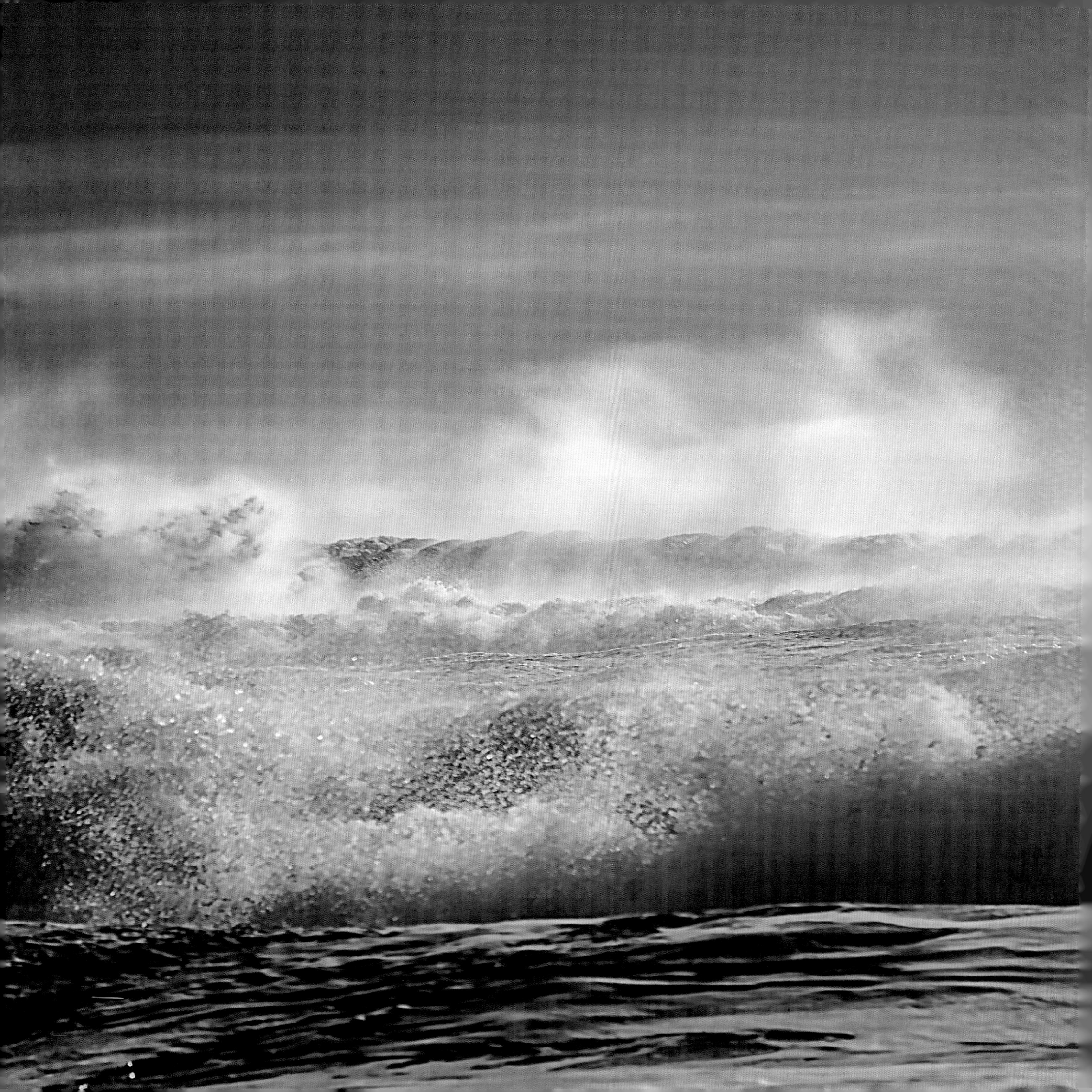

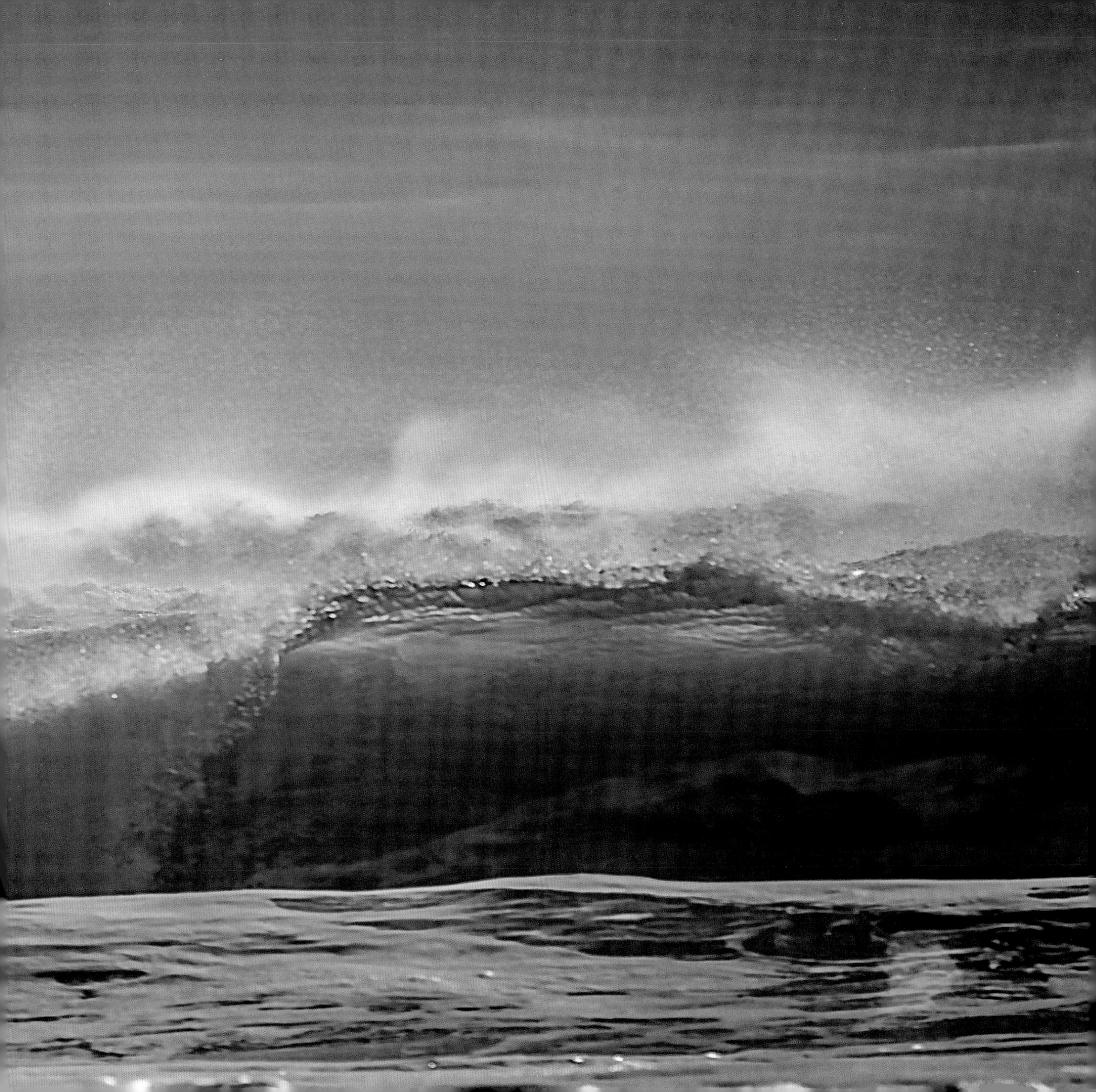

ISBN 978 1 85149 922 9

British Library Cataloguing-in-Publication Data:
A catalogue record for this book is available from the British Library.

Book design by Ray Benjamin

FSC
www.fsc.org
MIX
Paper from responsible sources
FSC® C124385

Printed in China for
ACC Art Books, Sandy Lane, Old Martlesham,
Woodbridge, Suffolk, IP12 4SD, UK
www.accartbooks.com

ACC ART BOOKS

Dedicated to:

My newest grandchild
Harrison Nash,
joining
Noah, Logan, Julia and Sam.

My wife Randi and children
Ilene, Jessica and Seth.

Ray Benjamin for his continuing
contribution to realizing my
artistic vision.

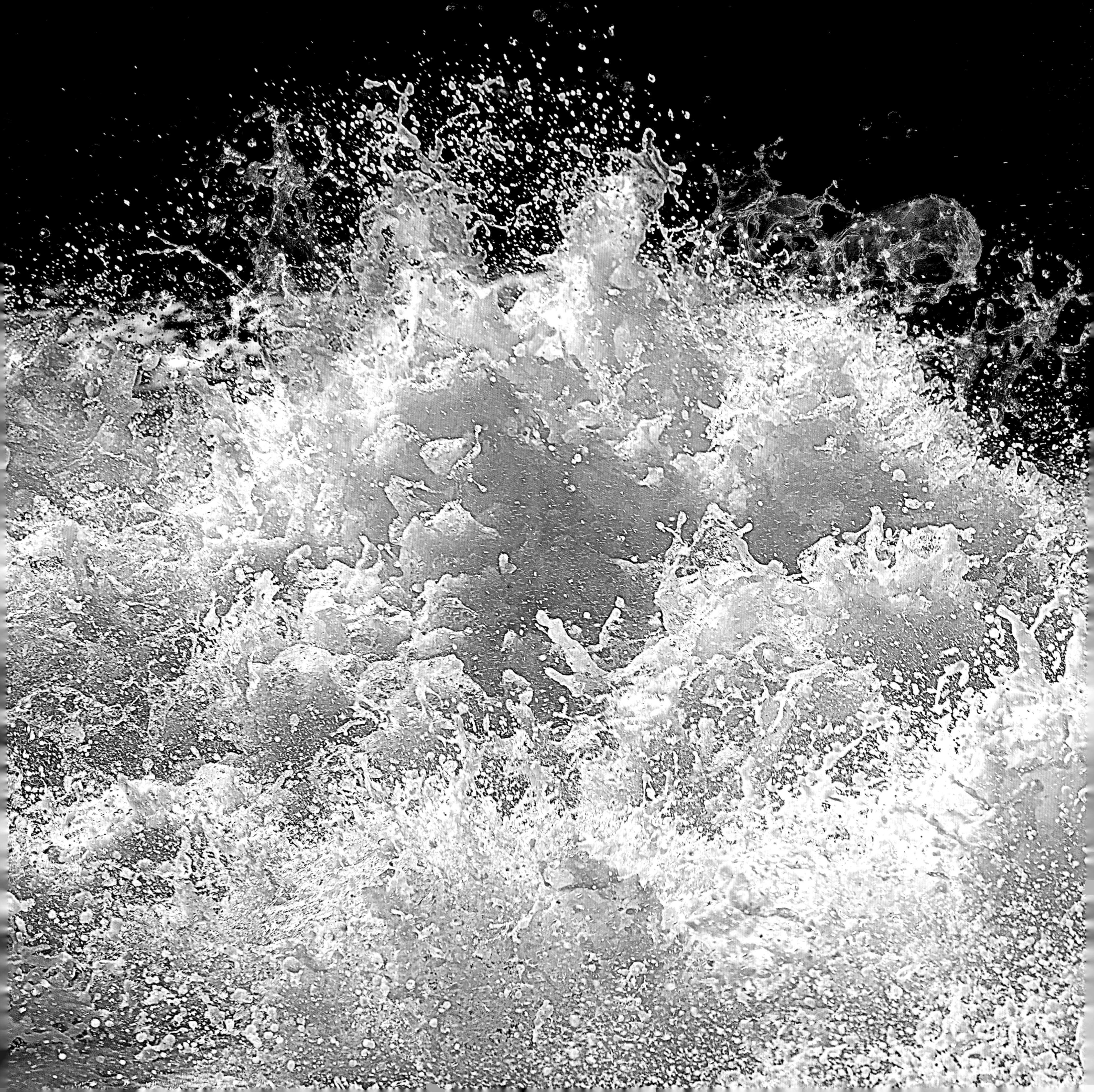

Foreword

I have known Bob Tabor a few years now; we met by chance at an exhibition in Bridgehampton, NY. We were struck by all the ideas that we had in common and how the ocean was such a force in both our lives.

The way in which a human interacts with his or her natural surroundings is always an inspiration to me, and growing up in Africa, one is automatically drawn to people who understand nature. Bob has not always lived with nature, so it's even more incredible to see how his work with horses and the ocean, two powerful forces, are so well understood and captured through his keen eye.

The mighty form of our four-legged friend and the life of a particularly wild wave are both striking examples of how this gentle man can capture power and beauty at the same time.

Bob will tell you that he fell into this life of making art by chance, although his background as a traditional Madison Avenue add man gave him the ability to see beauty. Moving from the humdrum advertising world into the art world, with its critics and experts, is in itself a lifetime achievement.

So, what is very important to understand is that Bob is always discovering and looking for new inspiration. When we started our friendship over cups of coffee, discussing our work and how we could collaborate, we toyed with the idea of bisecting pictures and using the medium to recreate new ways of looking at Bob's ocean photography. We tried taking the wave and turning it inside out or creating a mirror image of the work, or just using the texture of liquid to make art. Suddenly, we had created cathedrals of waves that moved backwards and liquid sea moments captured in outer space. Stunning.

Watching Bob bring the ocean to another level was very inspiring and so unexpected, as he initially went away saying that these conversations were terrifying and most uncomfortable for him. Well, if this is what terrifying and uncomfortable conversations can do, let's keep talking.

Bob has created a series of transformational photography moments that are both moving and stunning. I look forward to working together and knowing this kind man for many years to come.

Mark Zeff
MARKZEFF Architecture + Interior Design

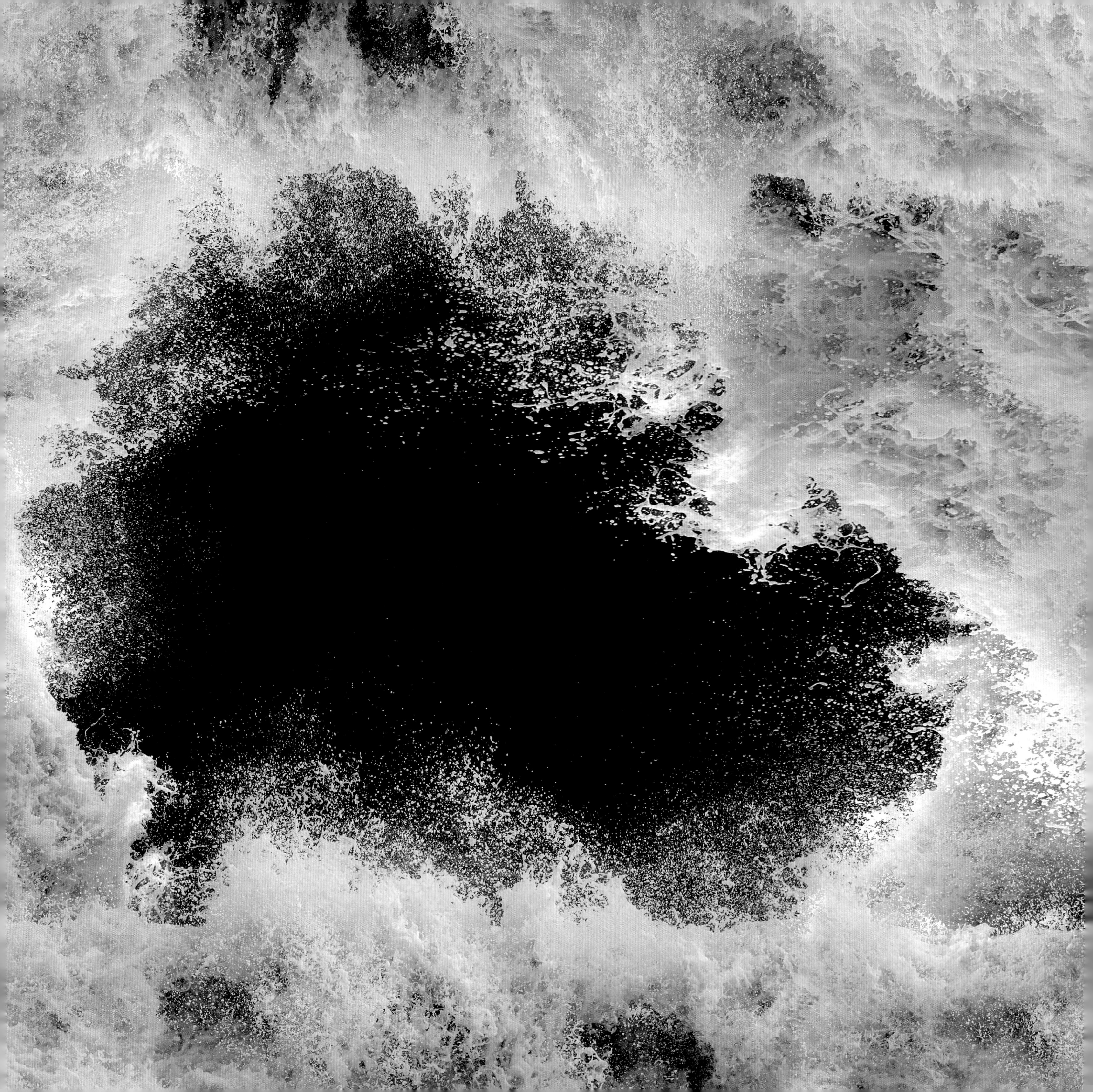

Introduction

I love photographing the ocean. Its smell, sound, energy and lyrical beauty mesmerizes me. This inspires and carries me to a state of mind that transcends time and place.

In my *Splash* series I focus on the power of the sea. The most natural way I can share my feelings is to create images that visually interpret my experience.

Part of my approach is to break down the physical elements of the crashing waves. I crop in on a section of the powerful and energetic fluid surf, losing the horizon and all reference to scale. I then manipulate these isolated pieces to create unique images that reimagine the power and beauty of the ocean.

I hope my new collection awakens your senses and helps you experience this amazing natural resource on a deeper emotional level.

Bob Tabor
New York City

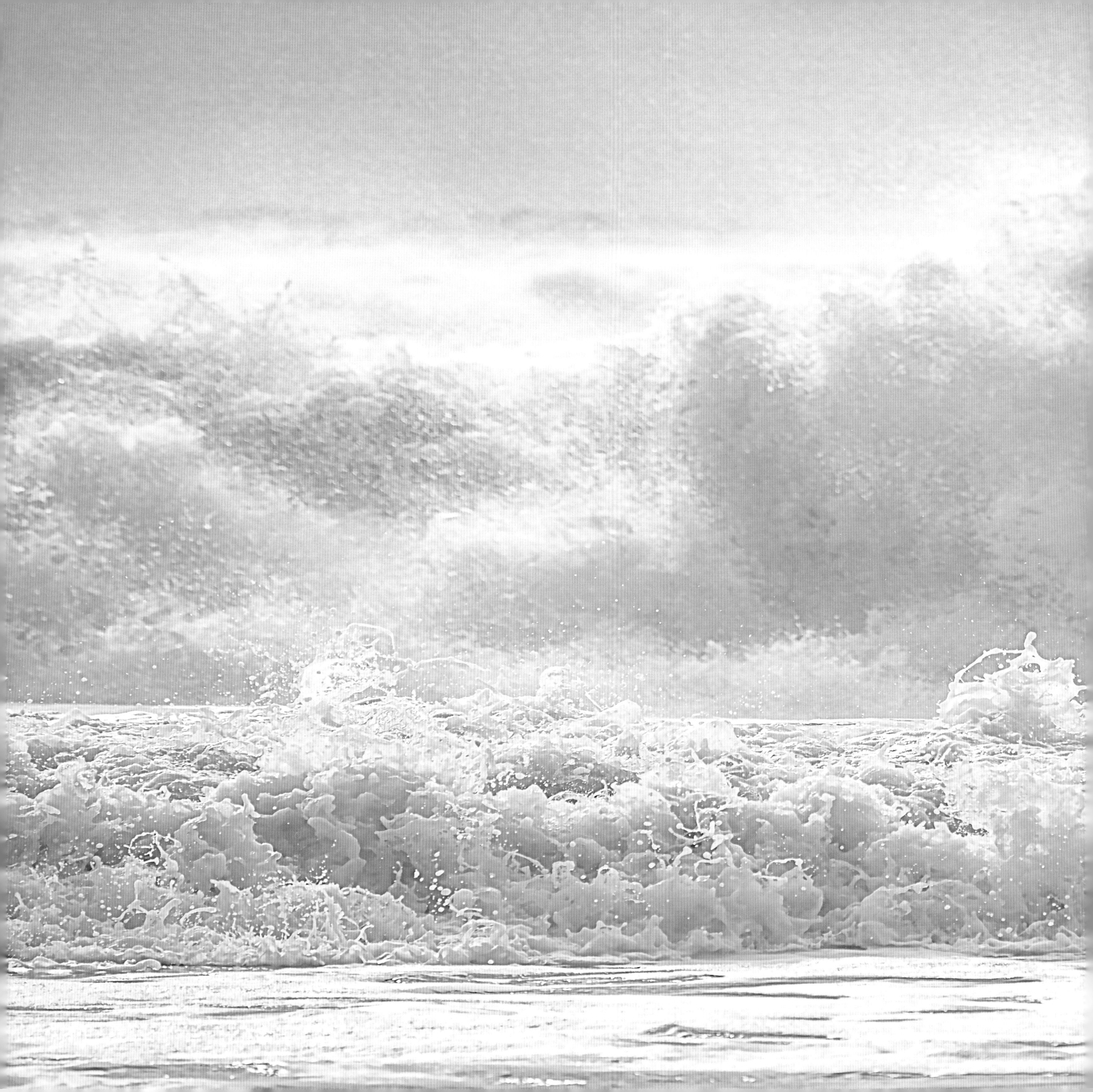

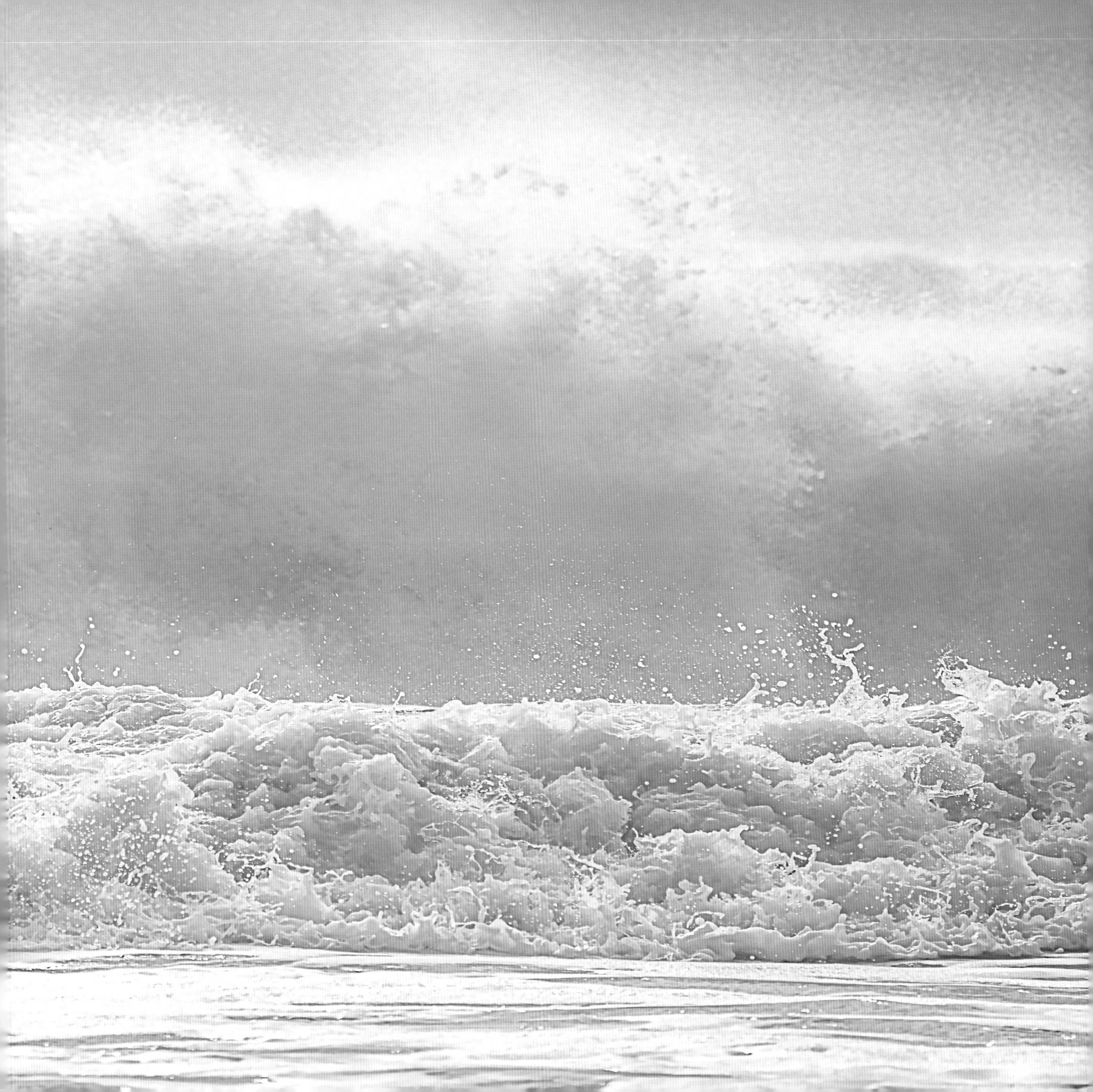

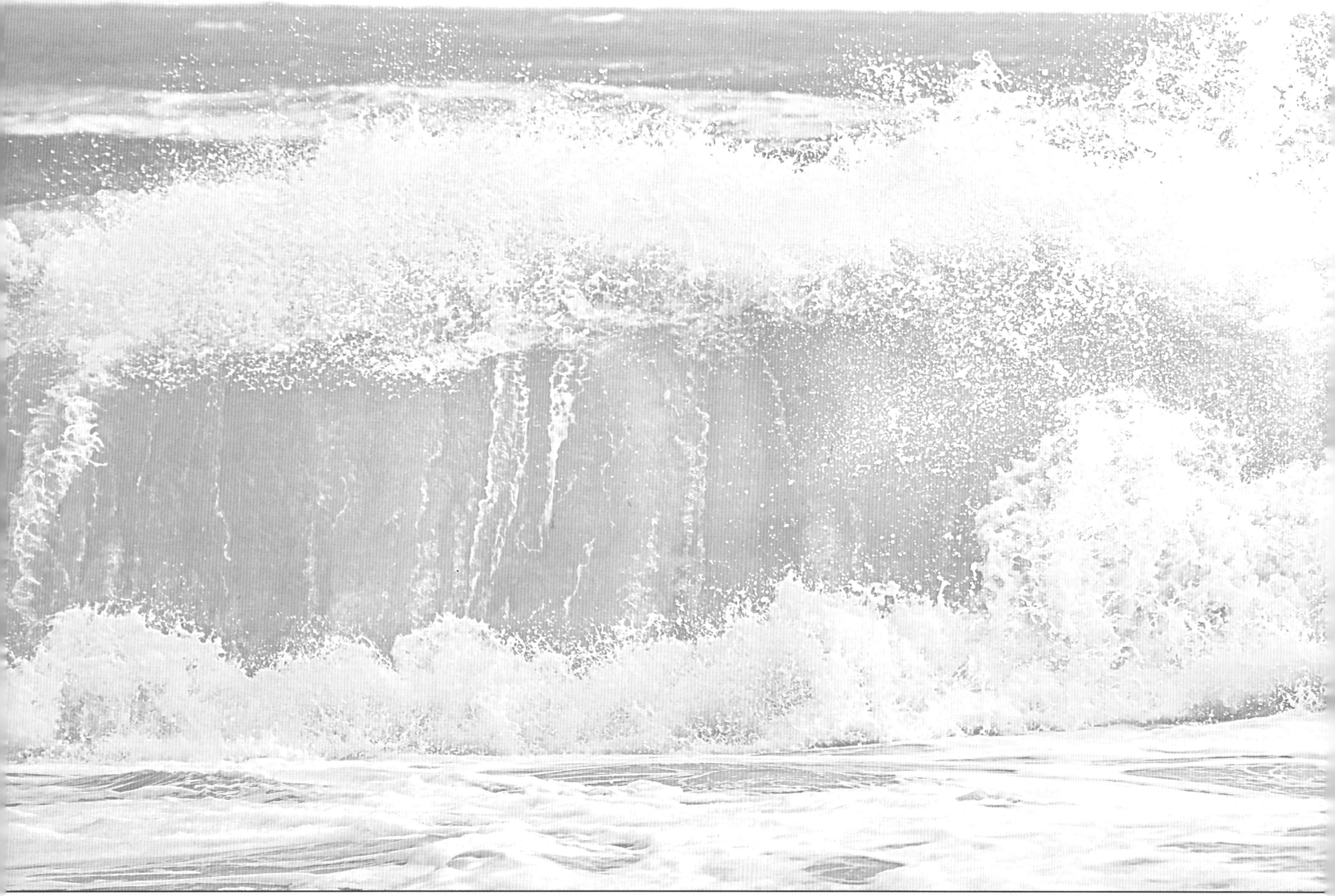

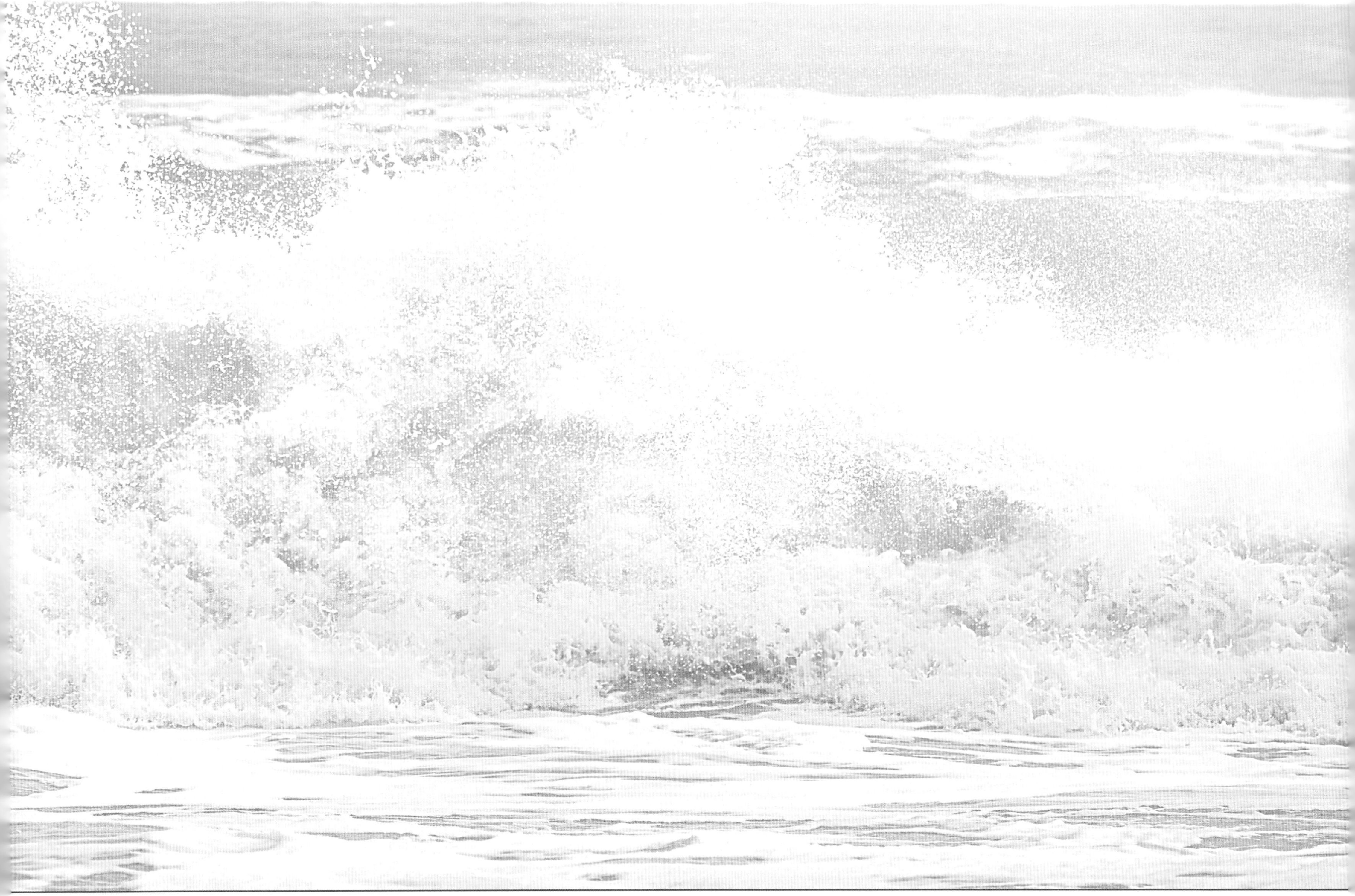

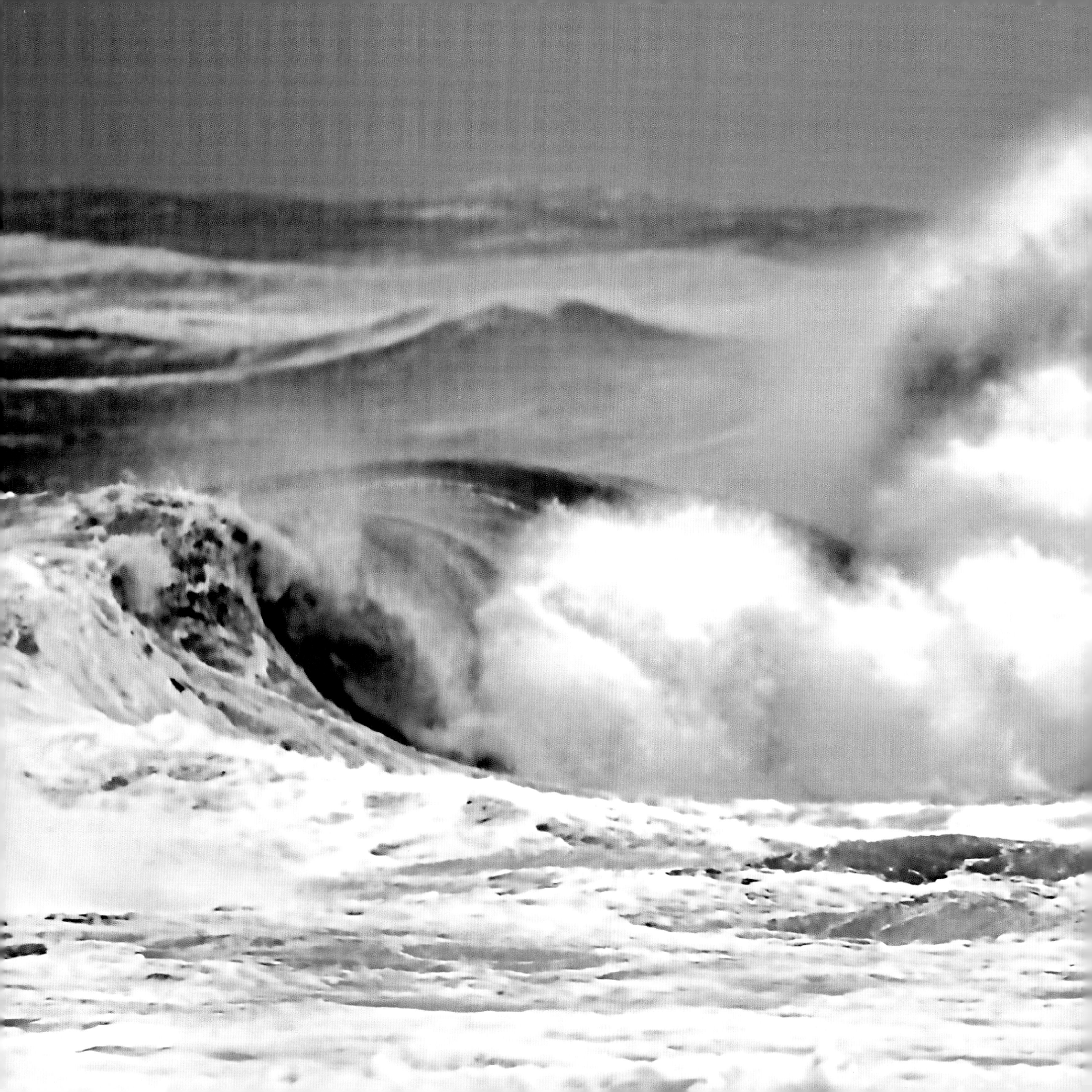

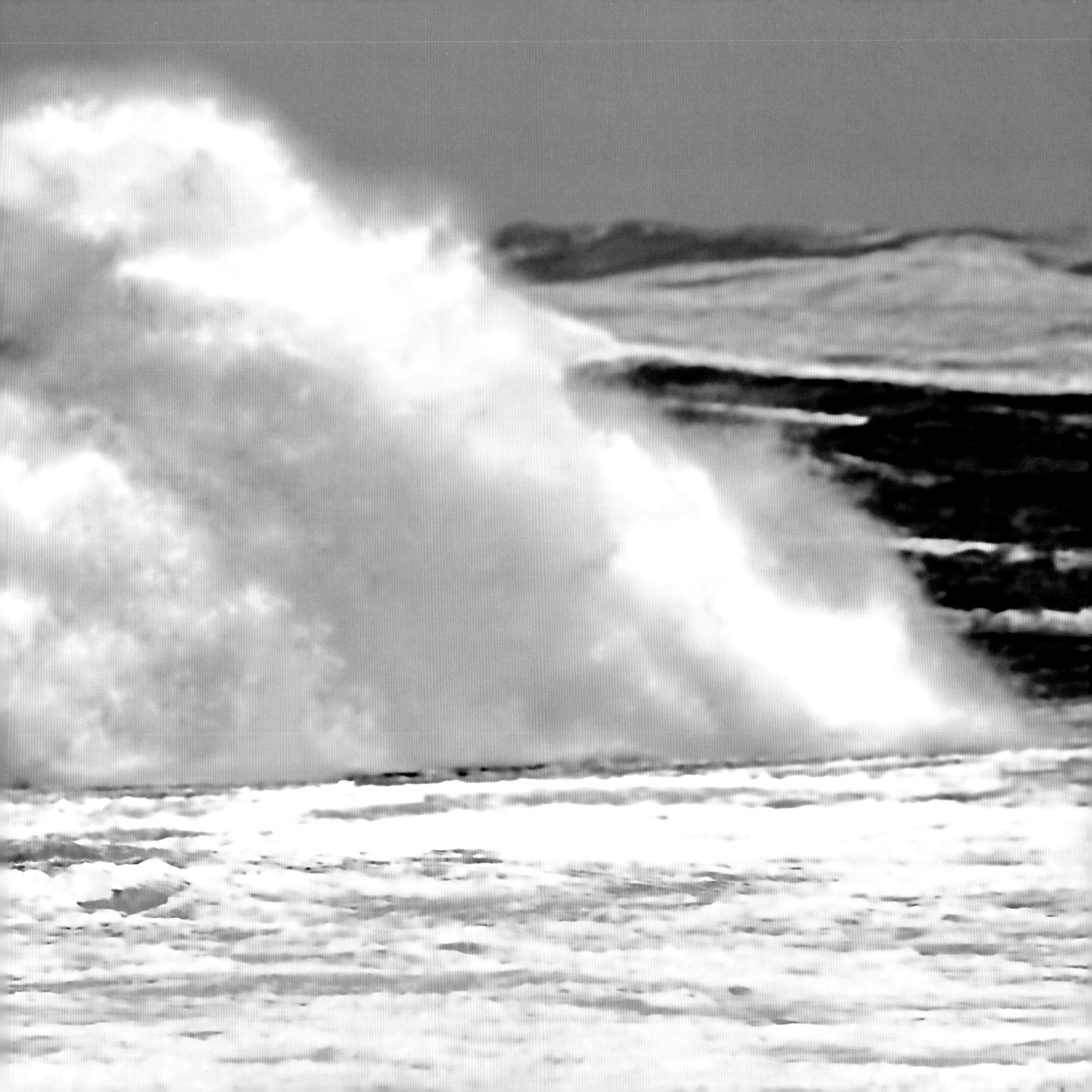

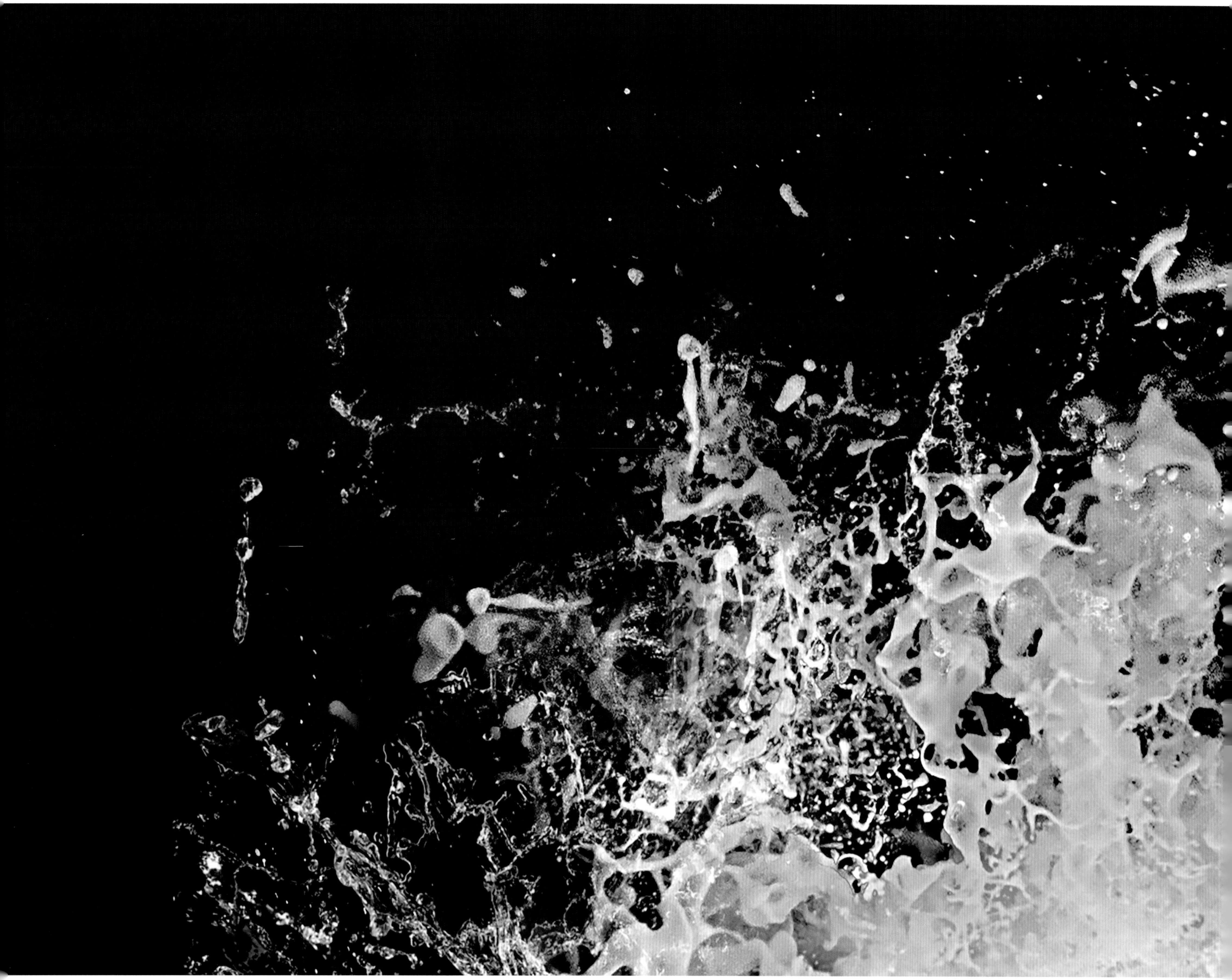

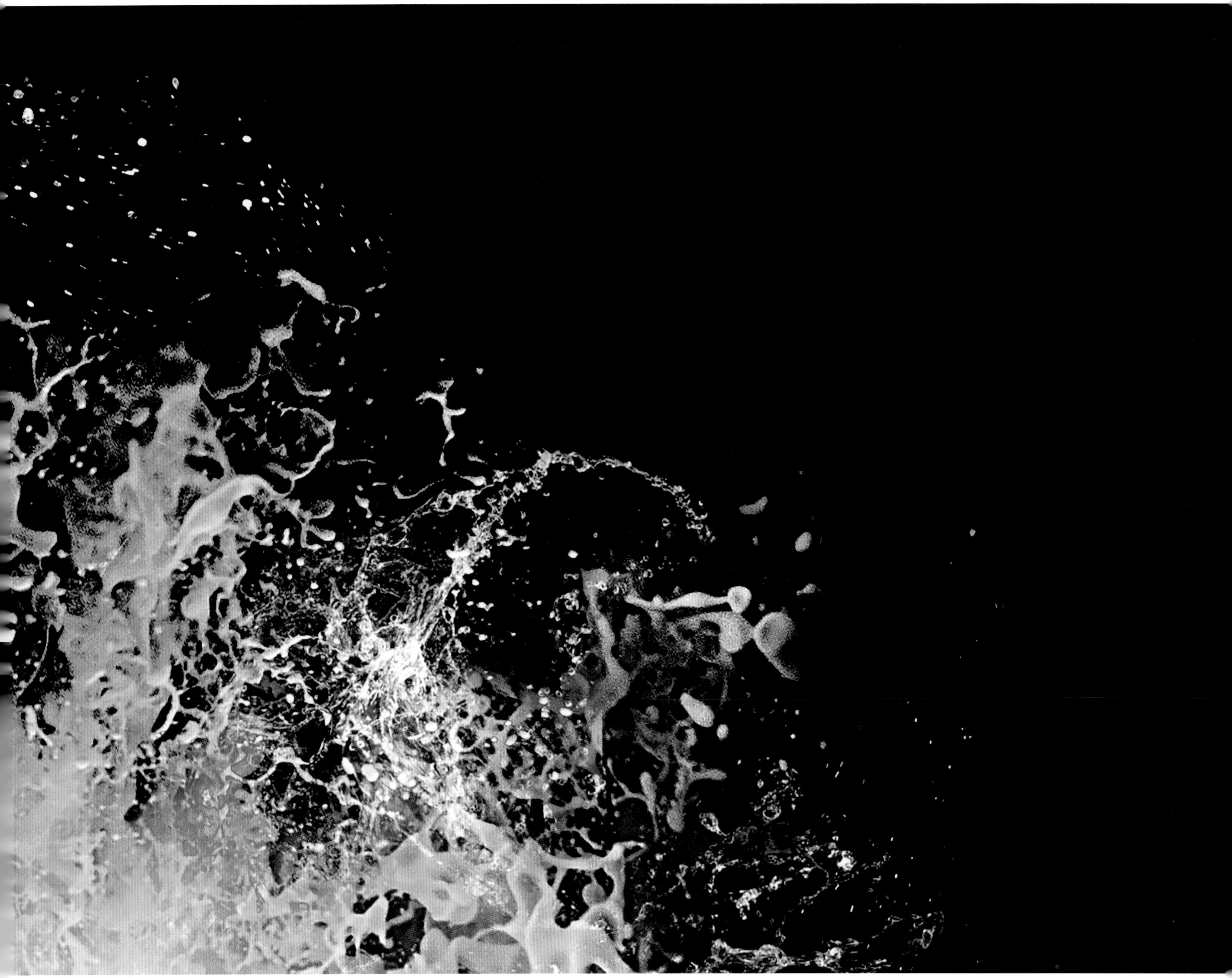

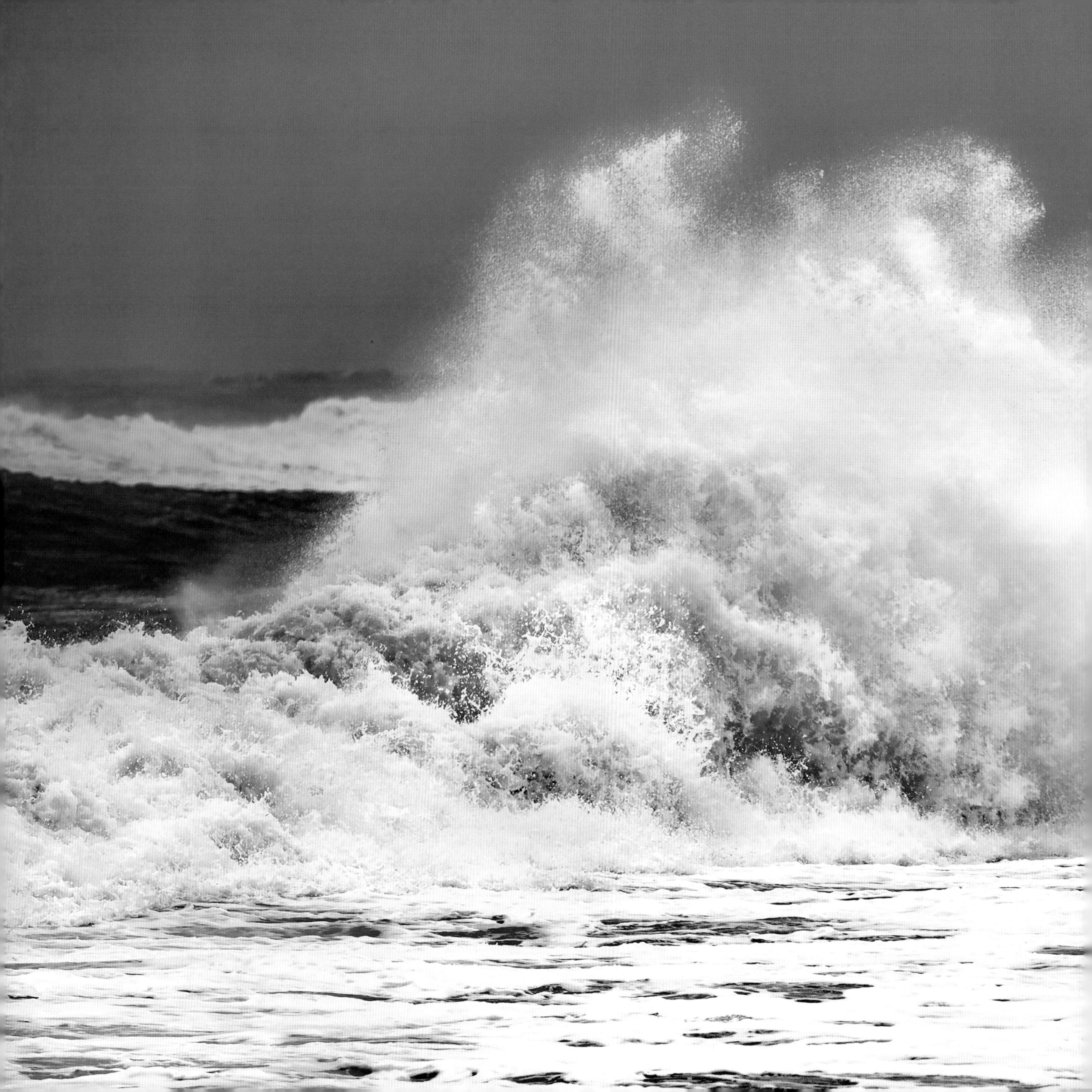

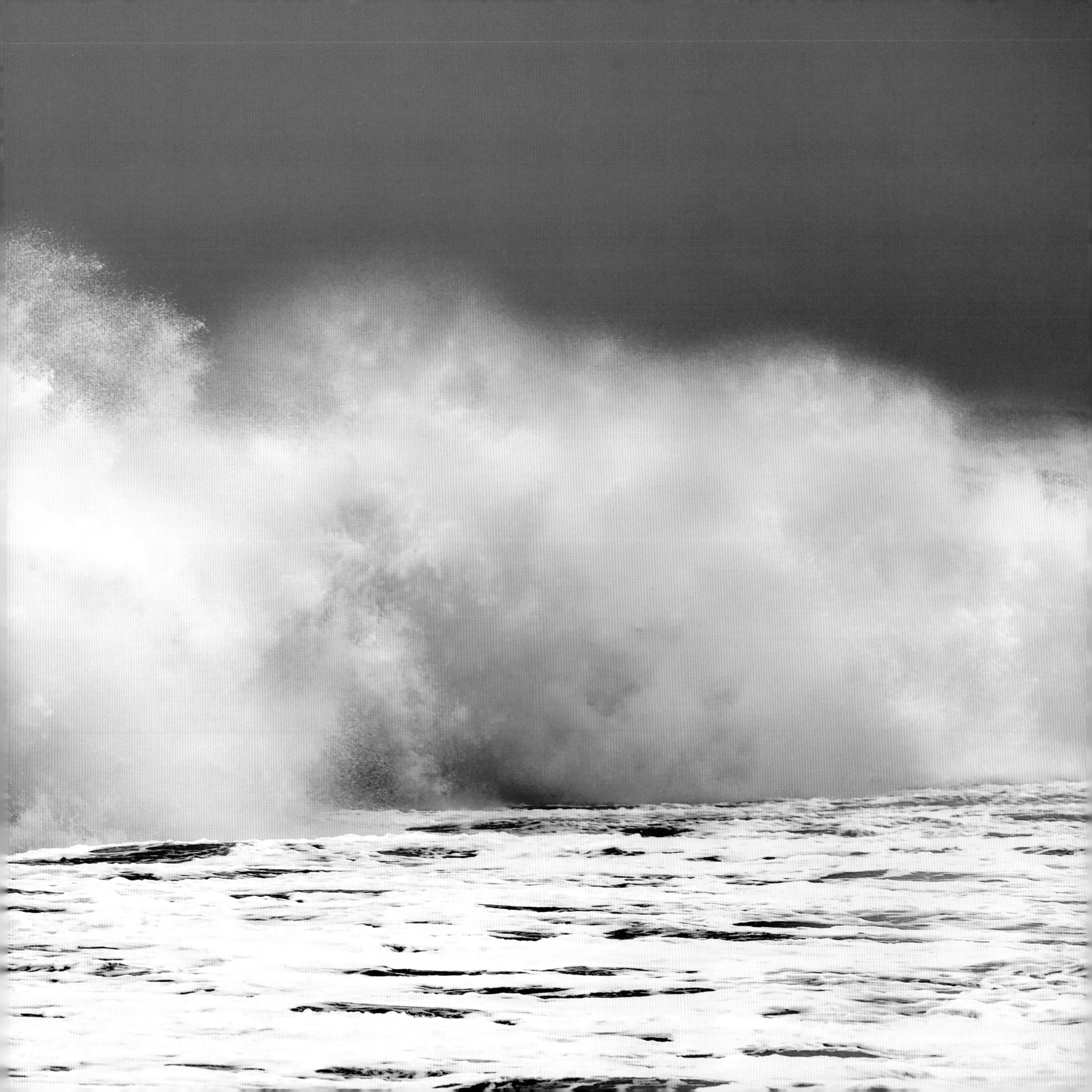

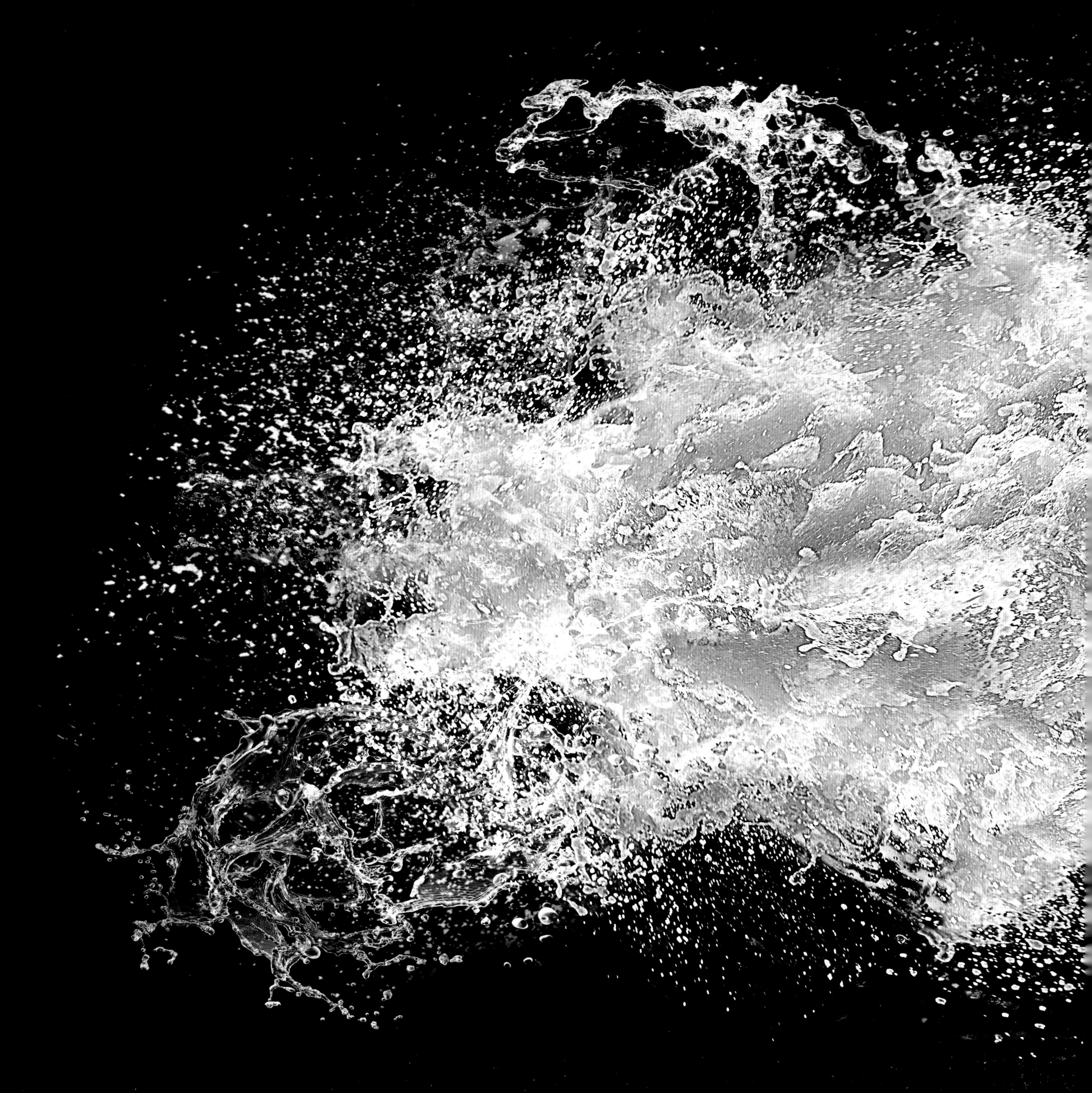

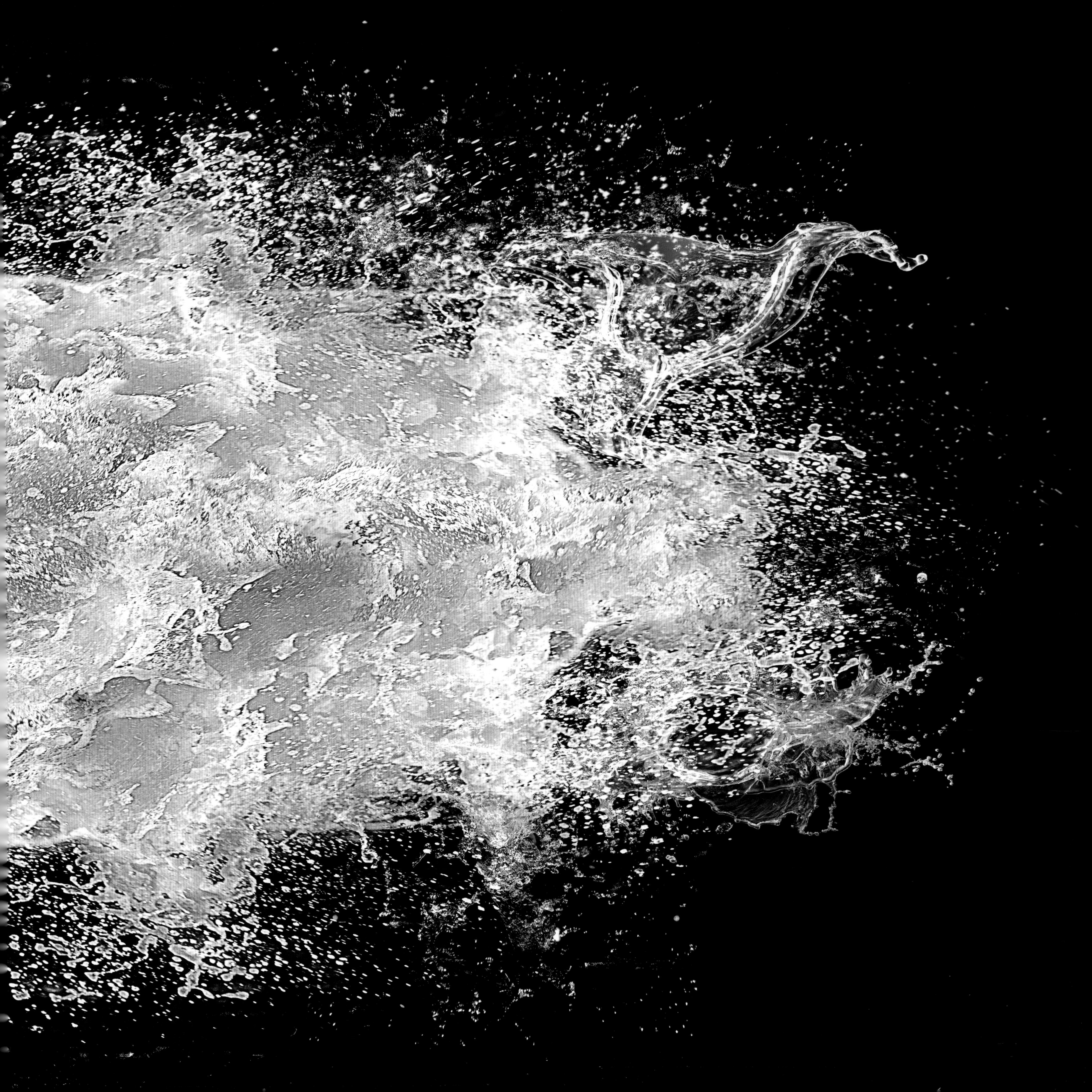

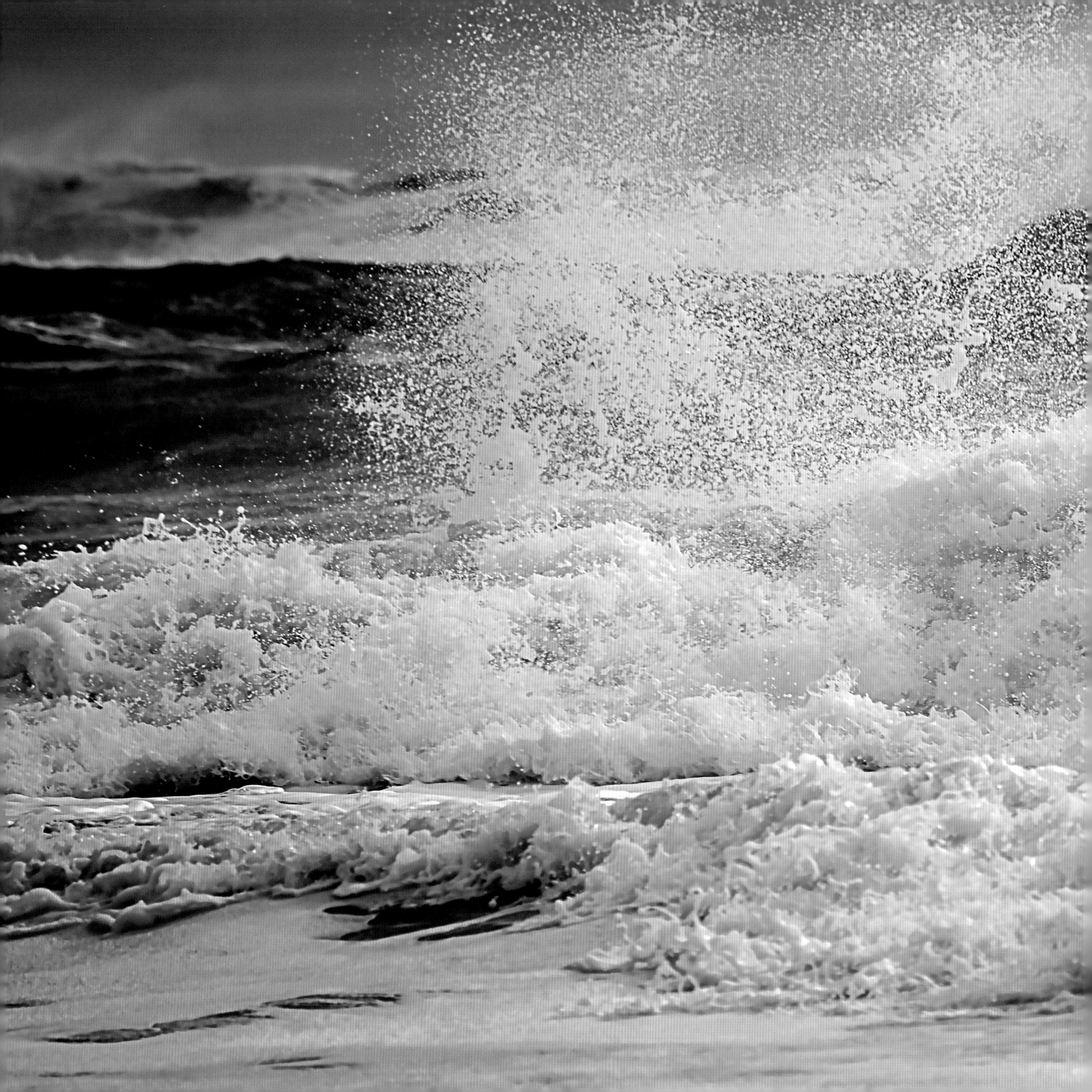

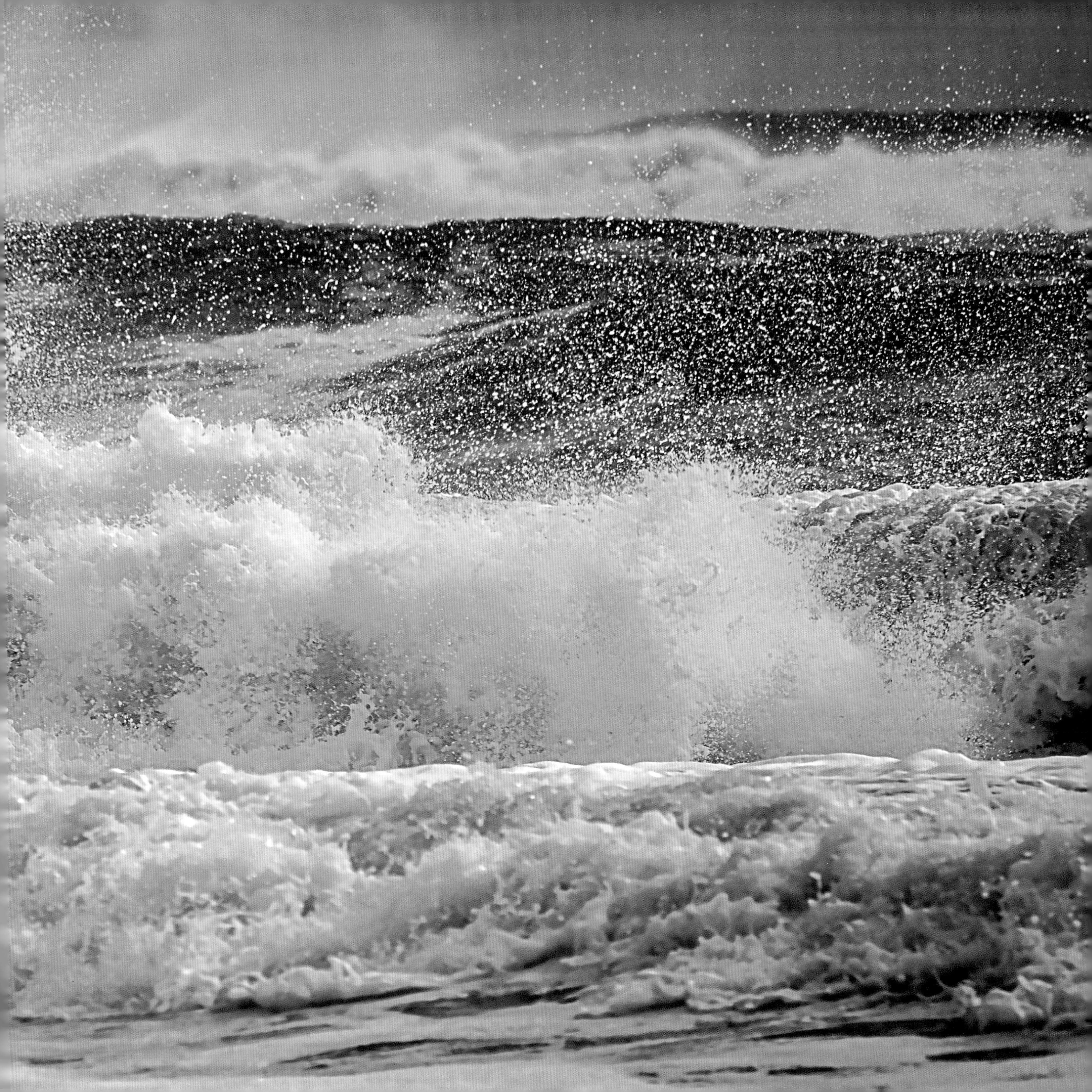

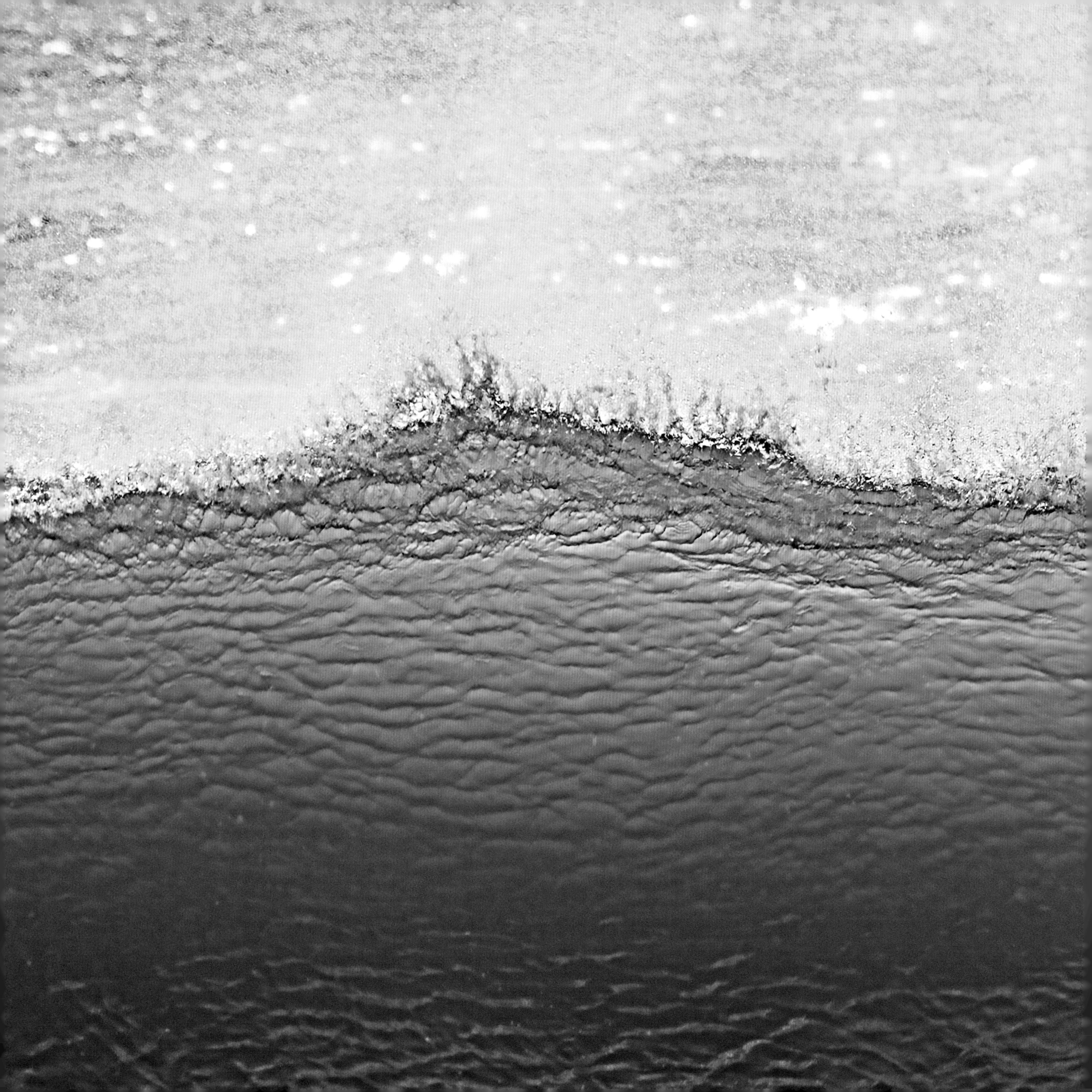

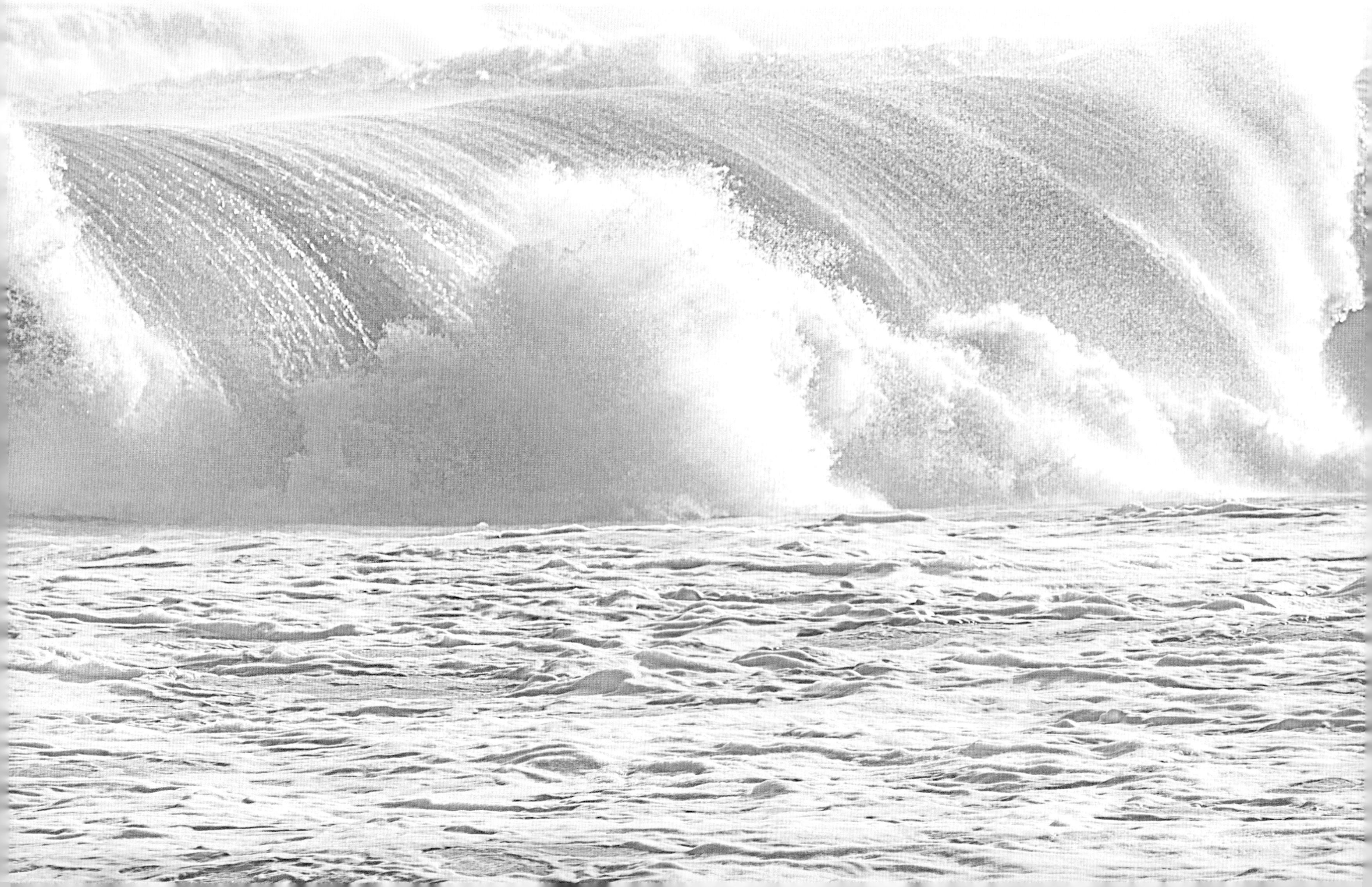

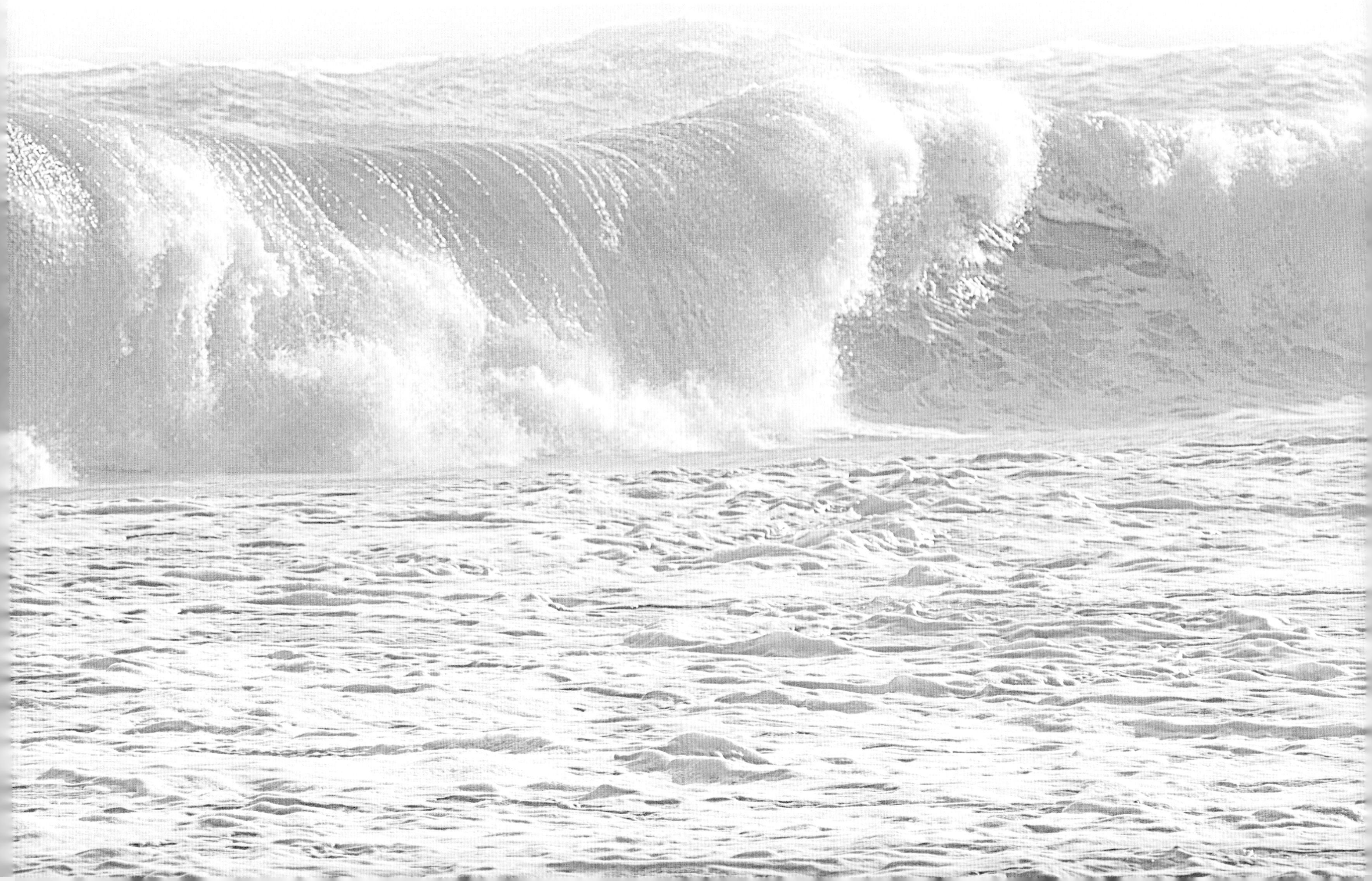

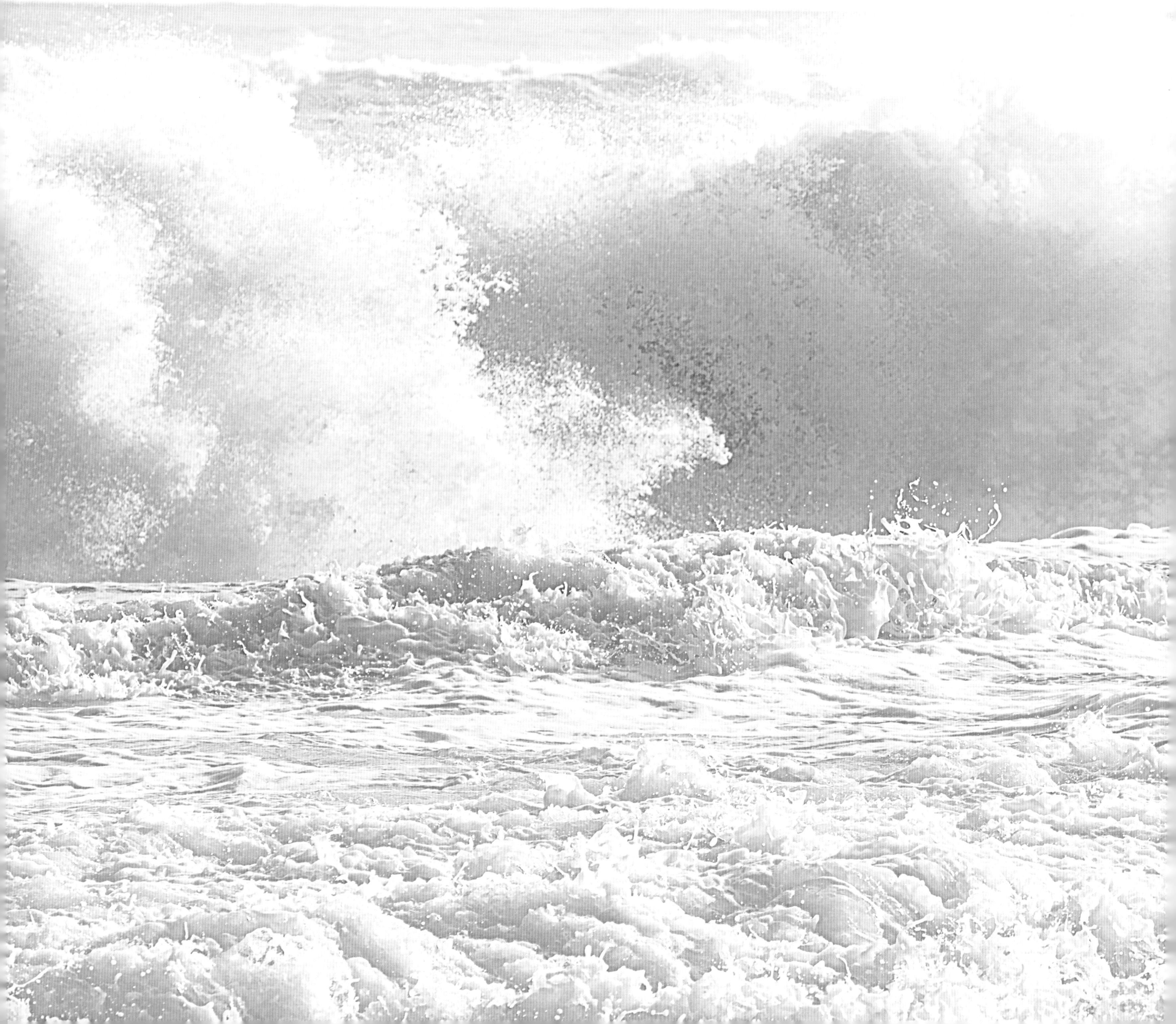

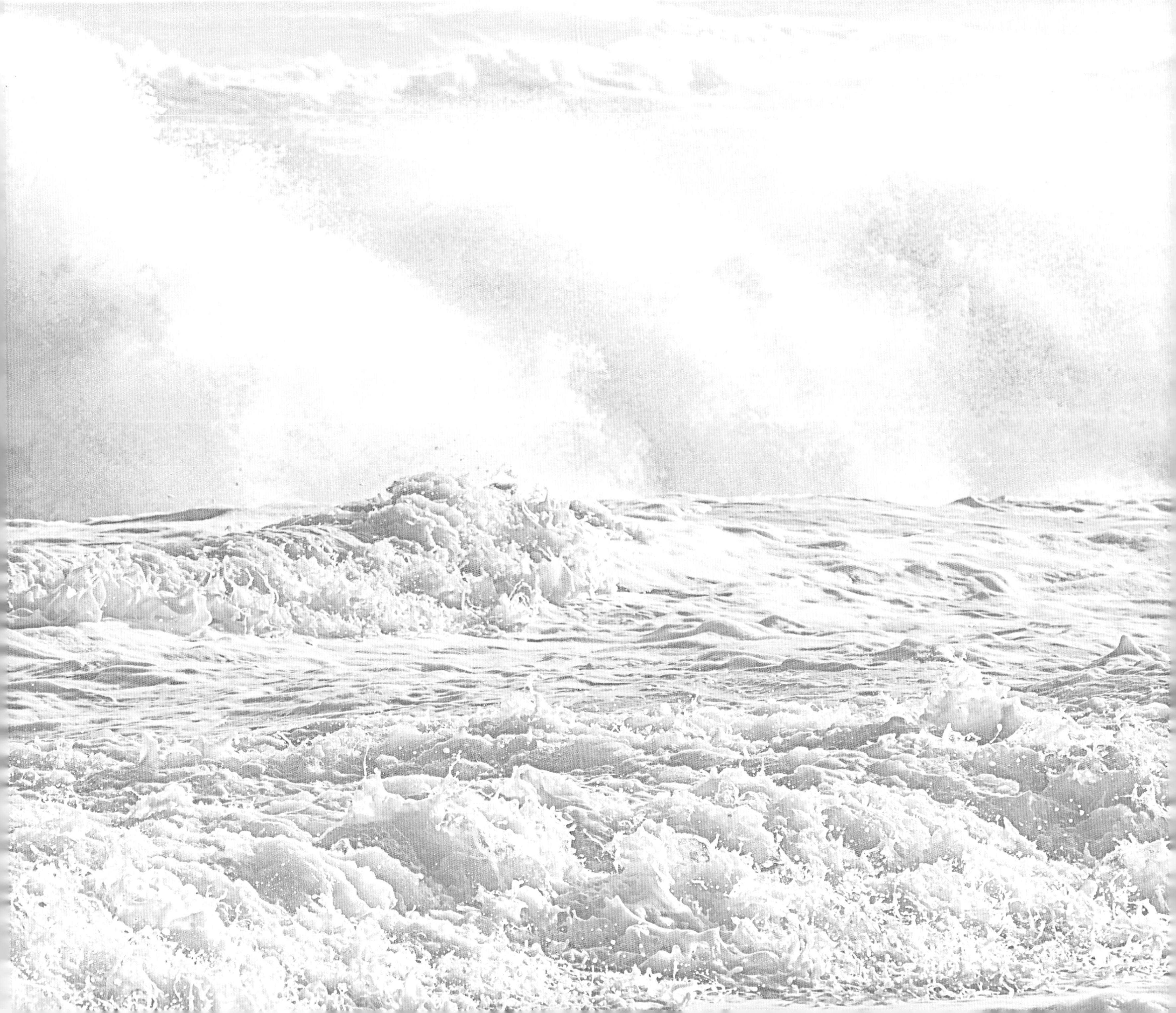

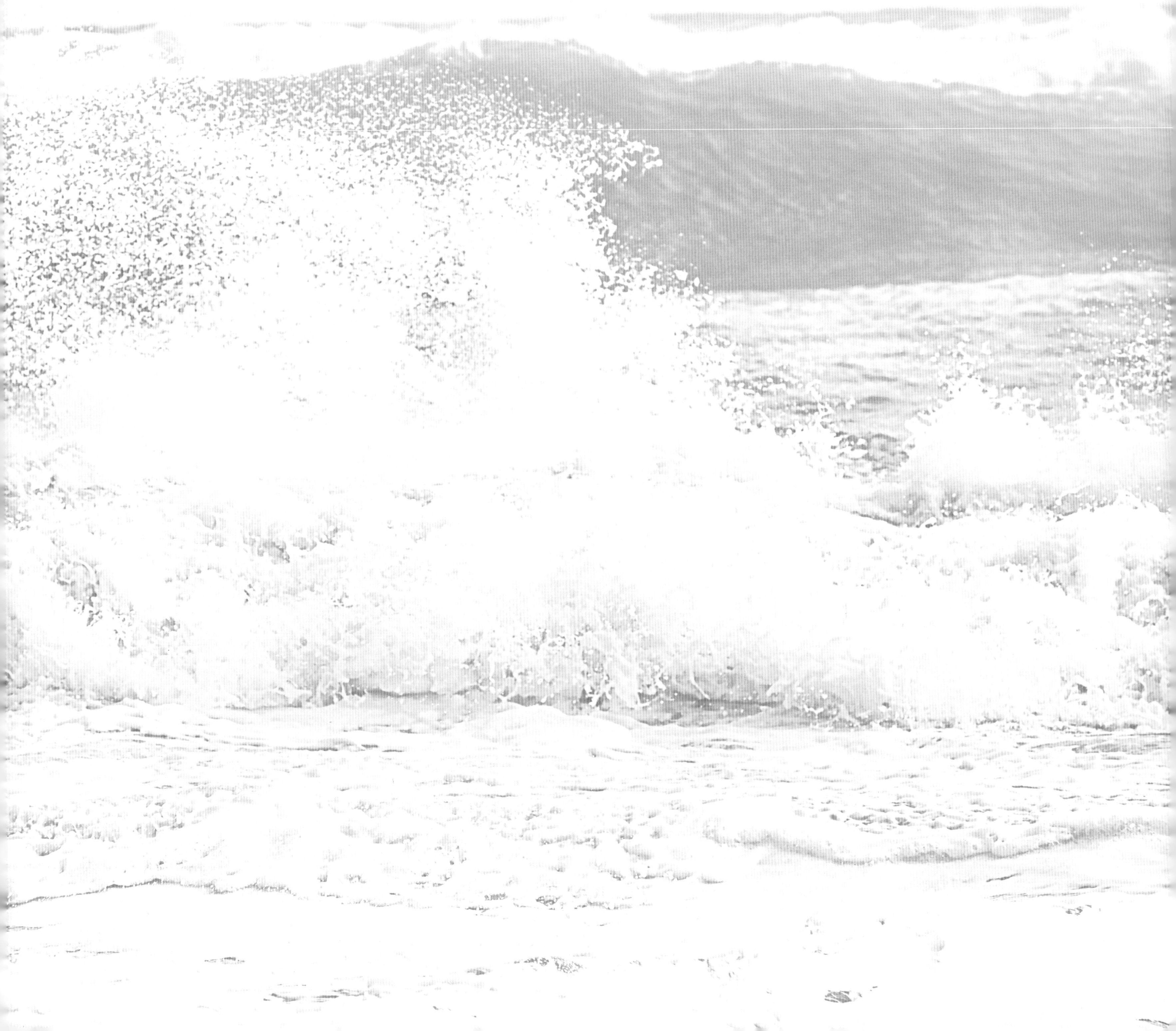

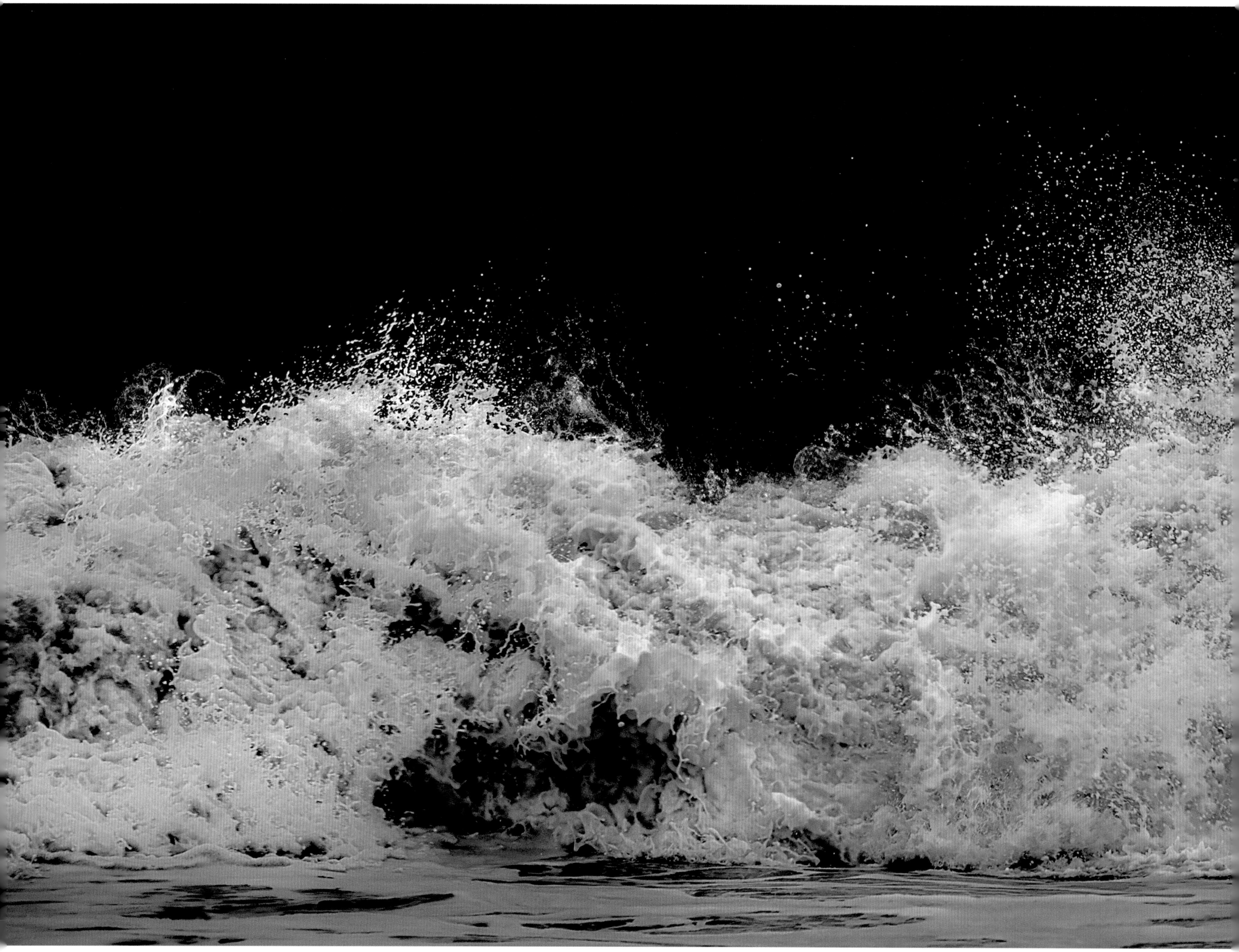

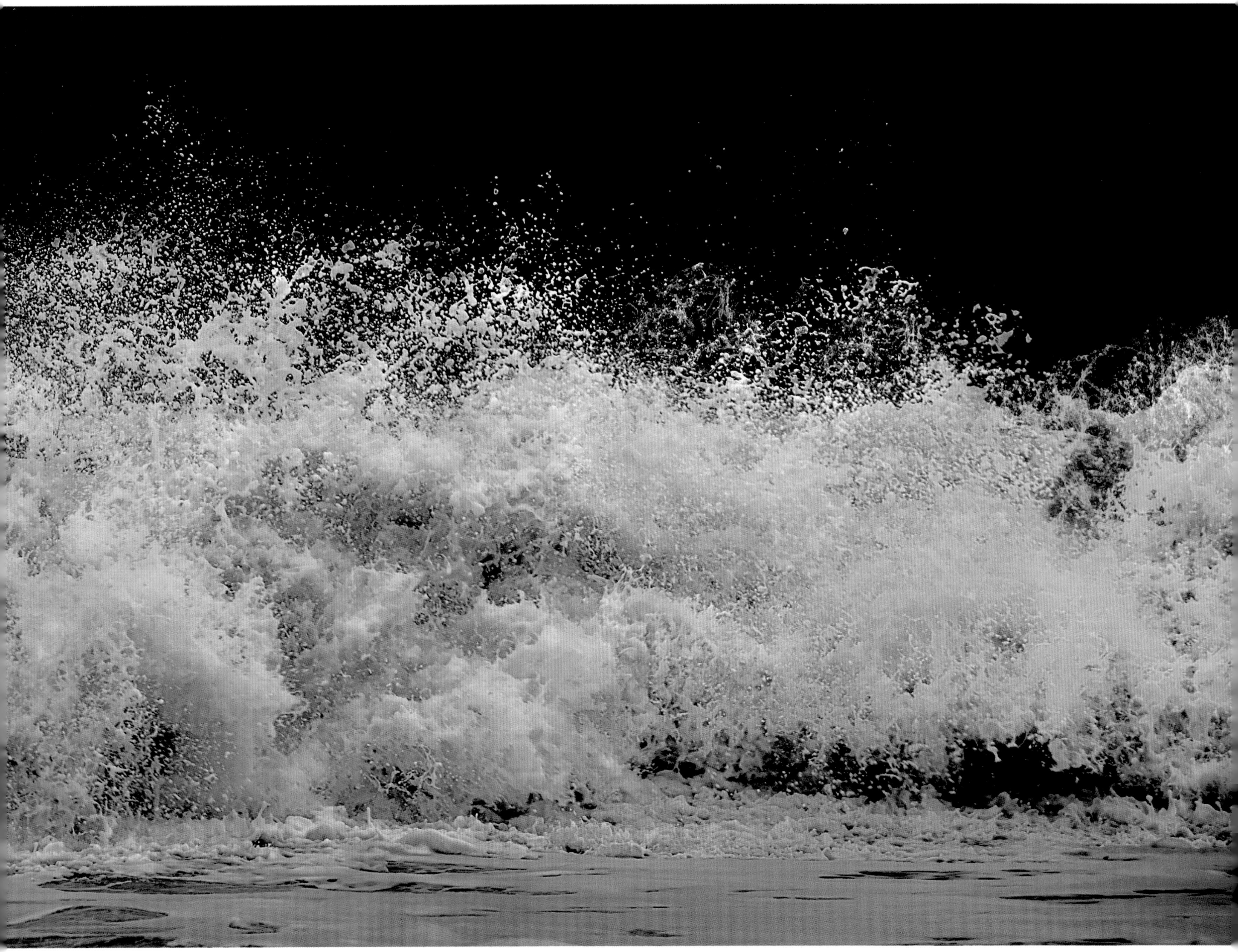

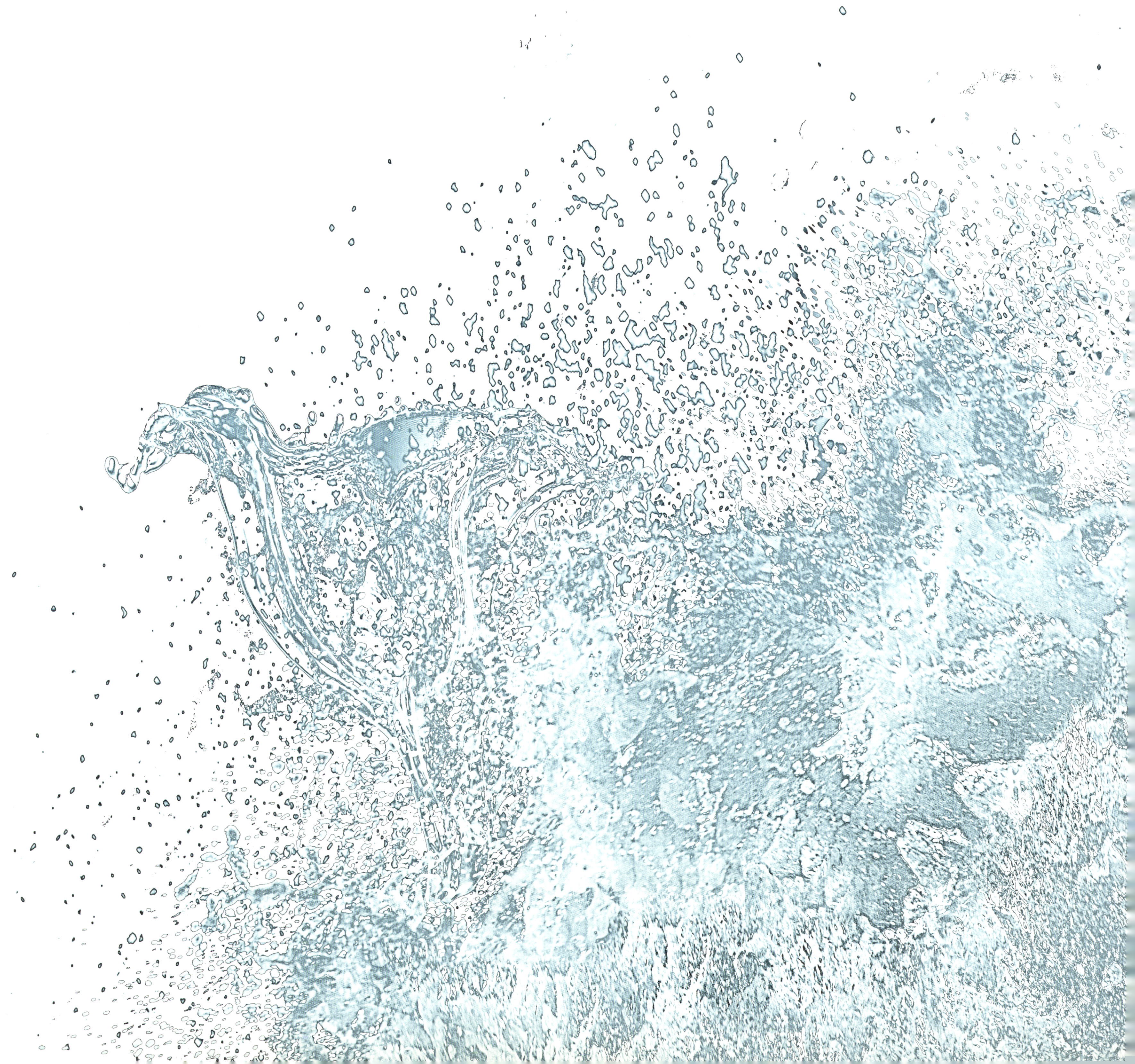

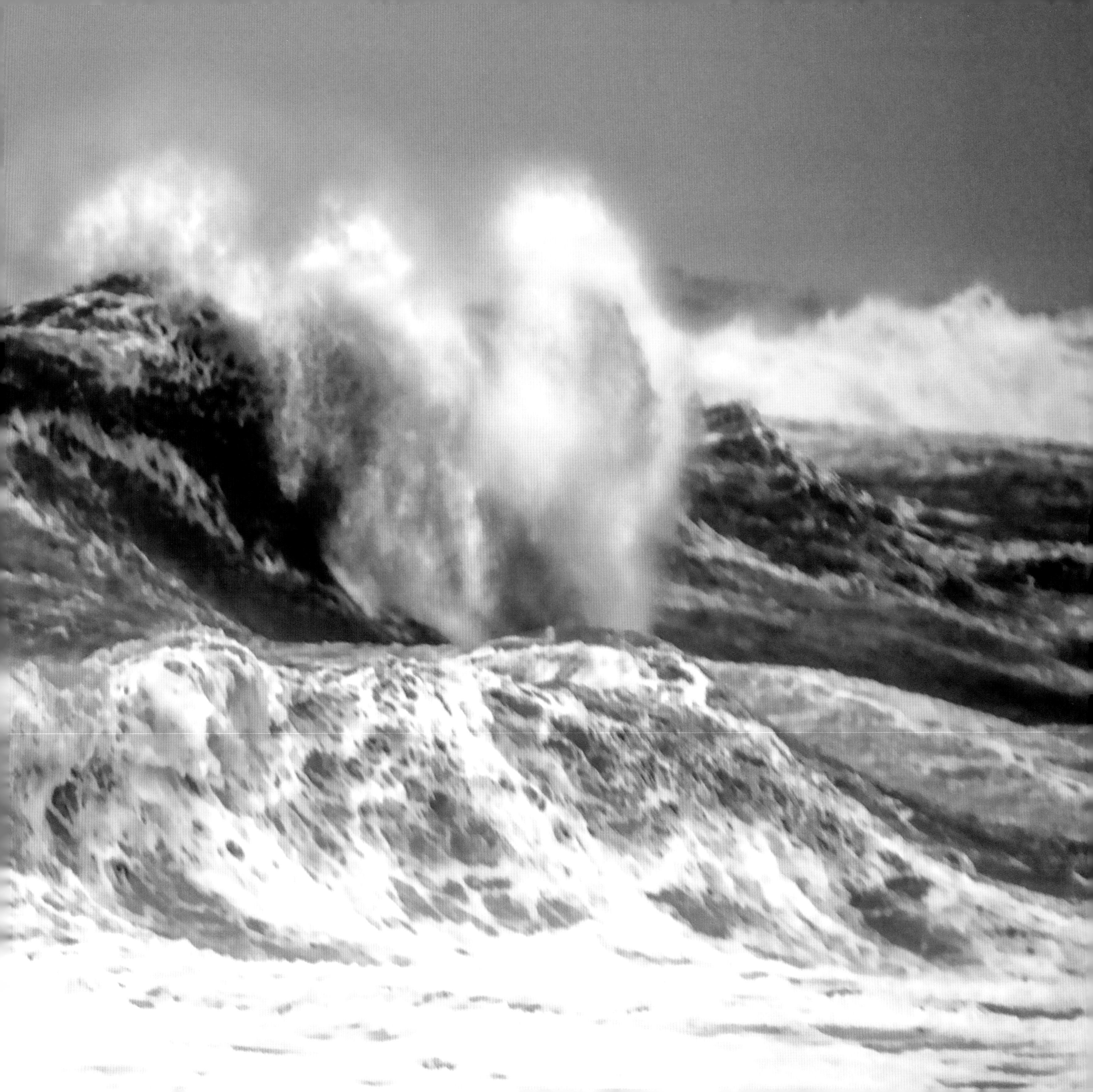

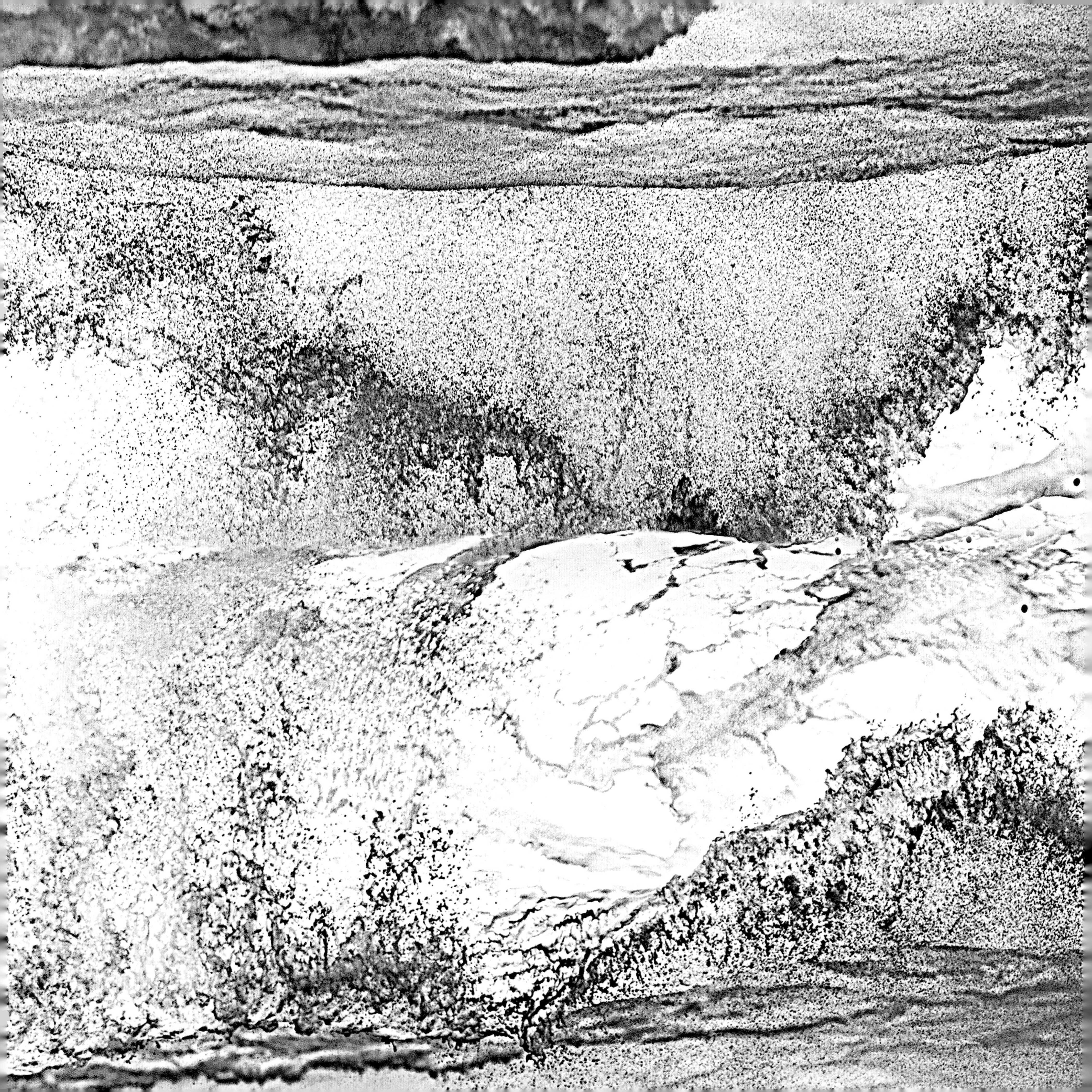

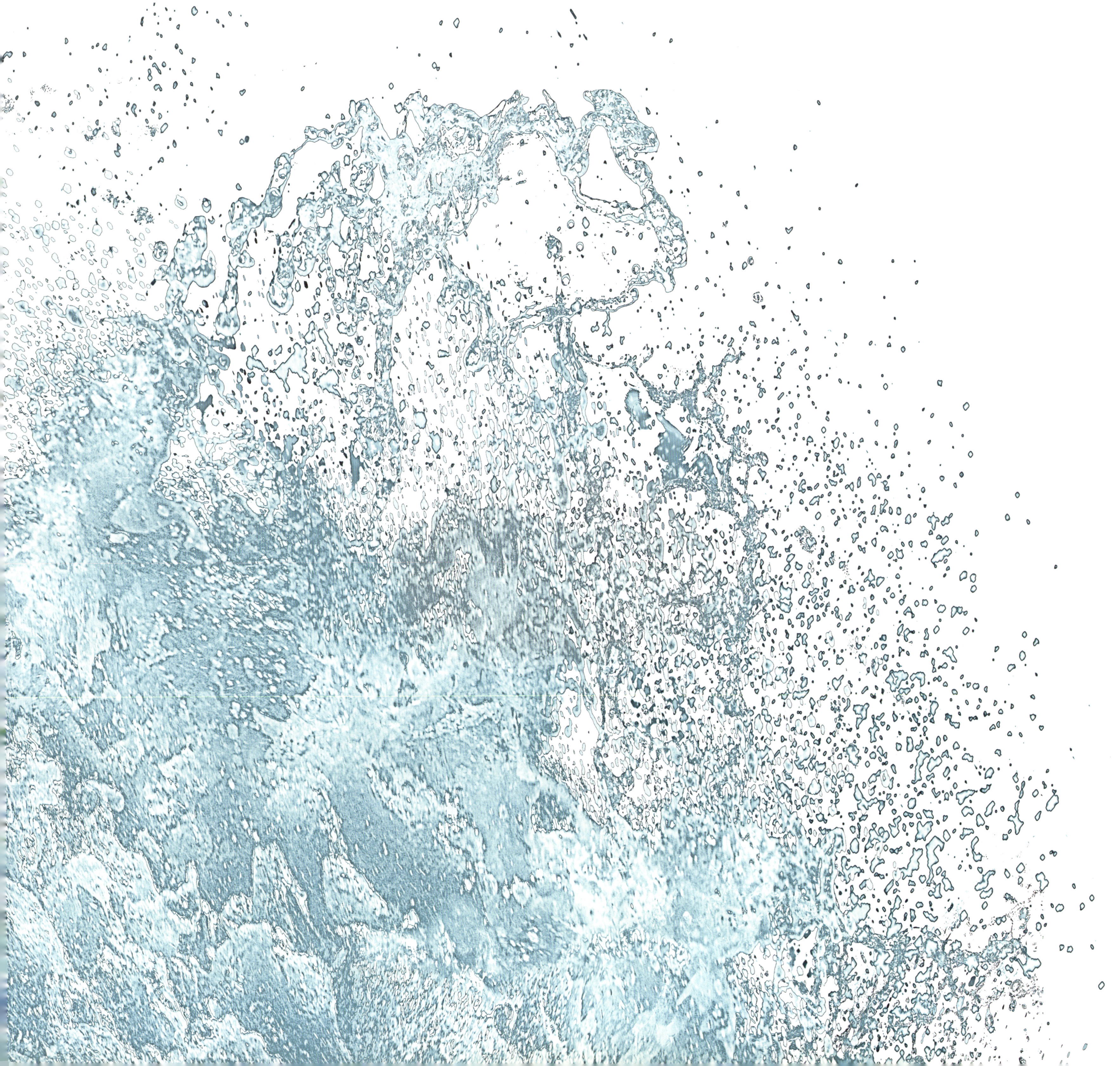

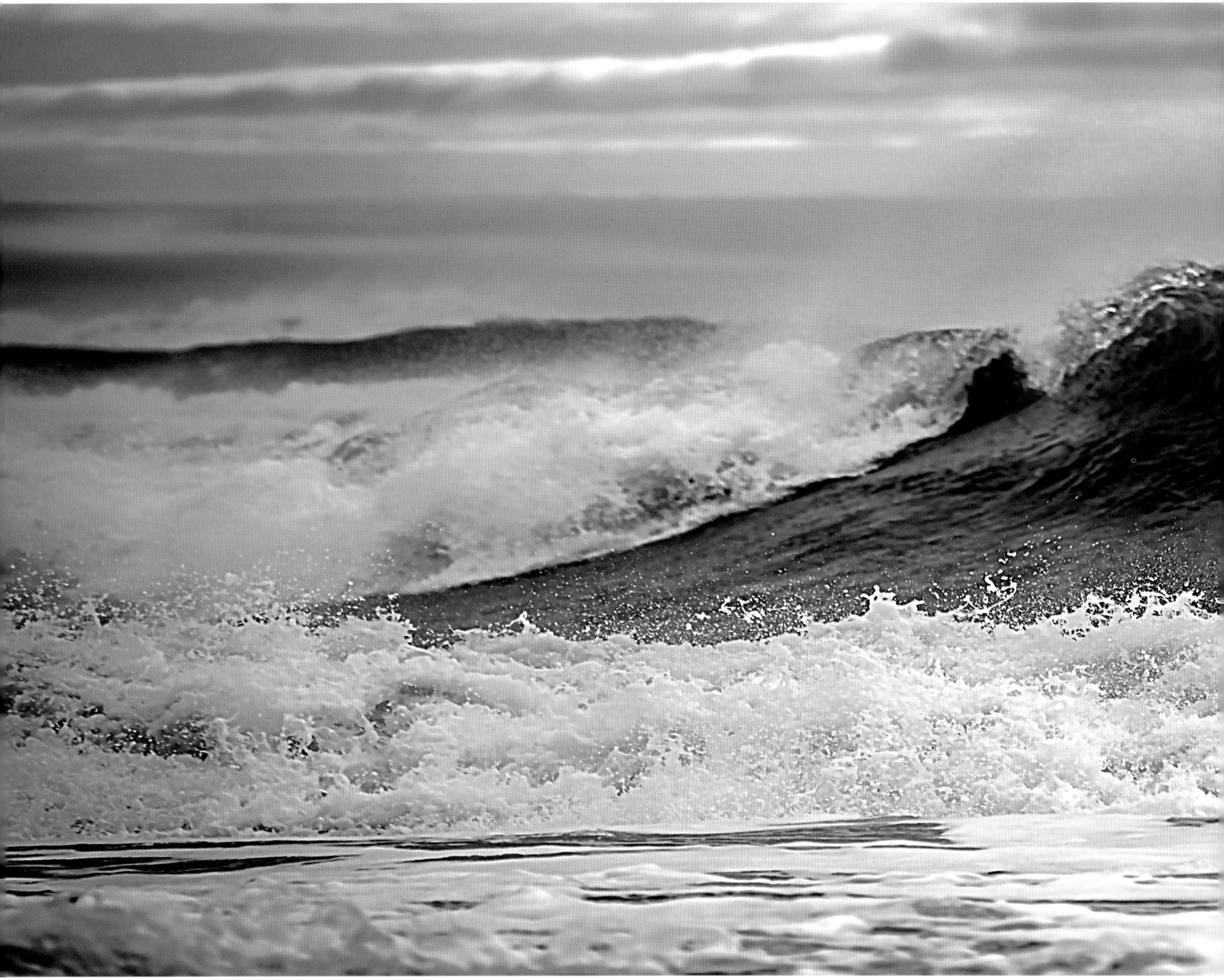

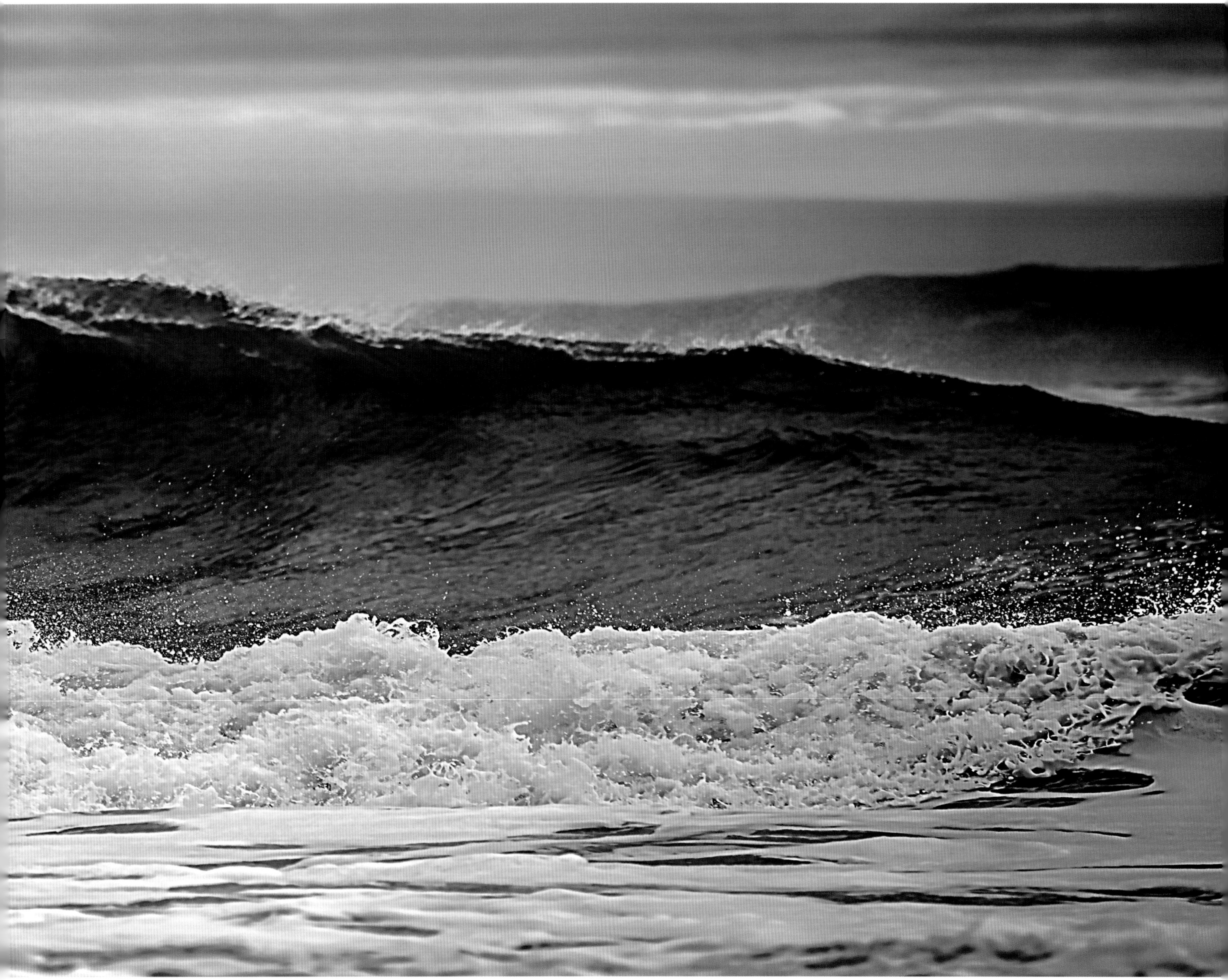

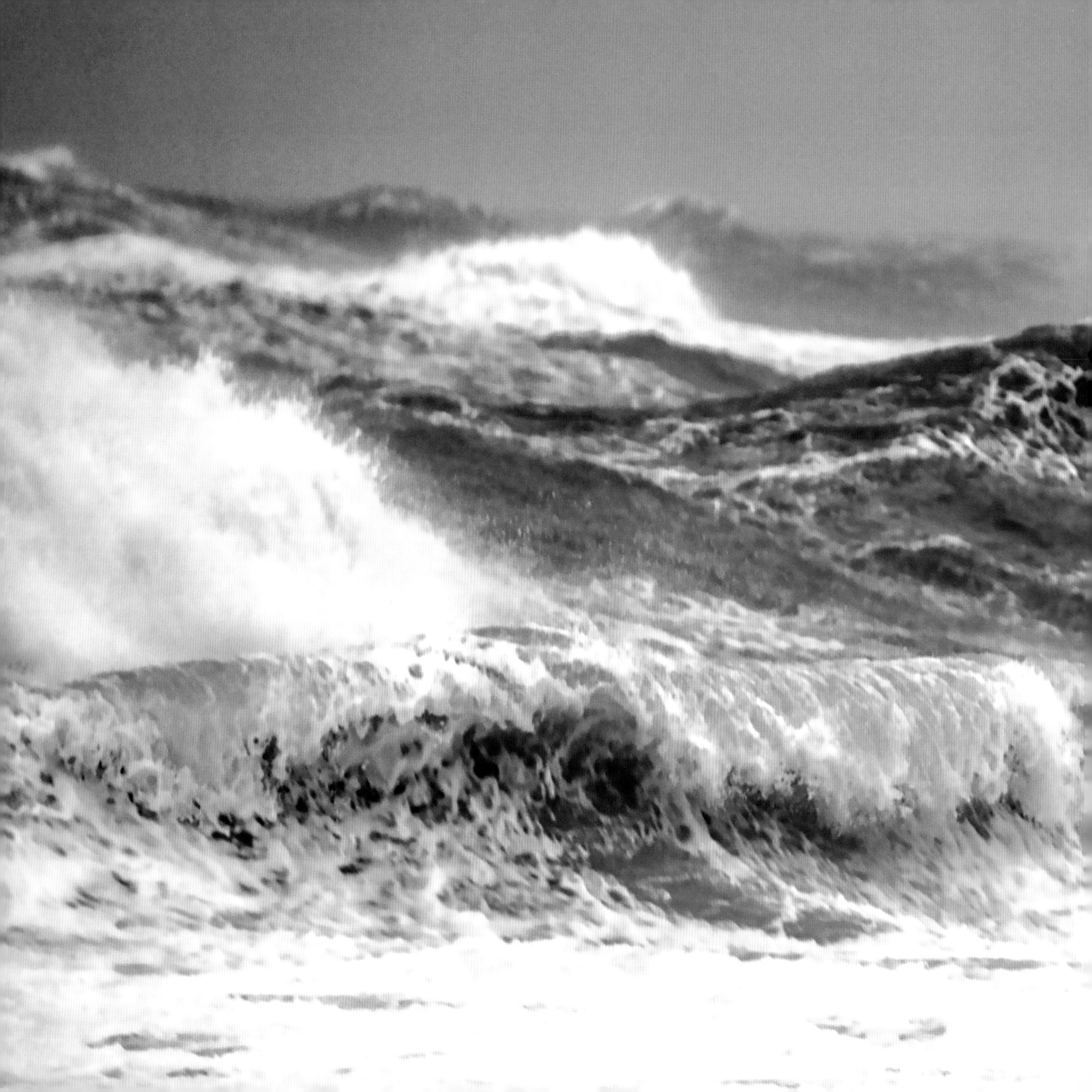

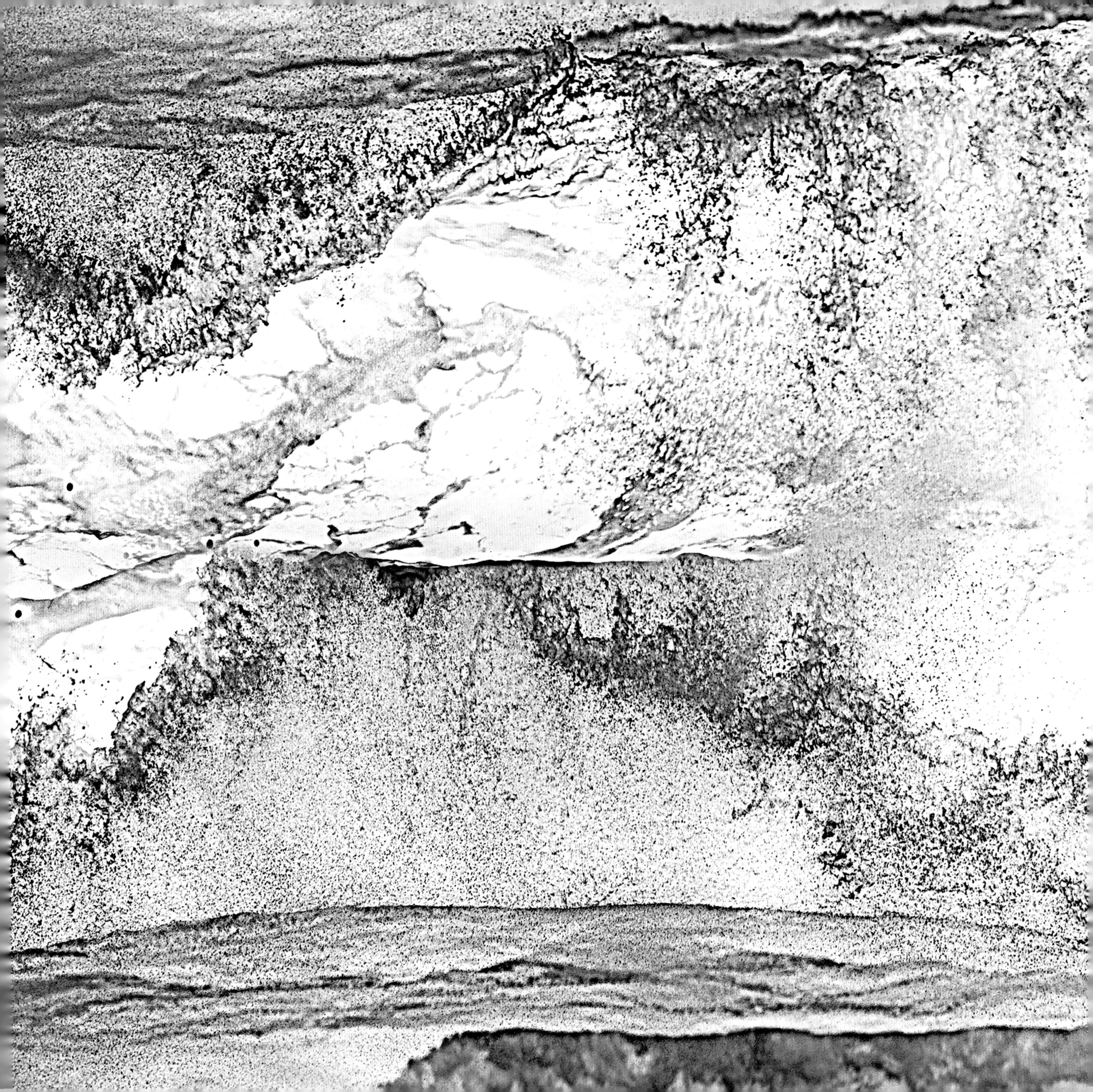

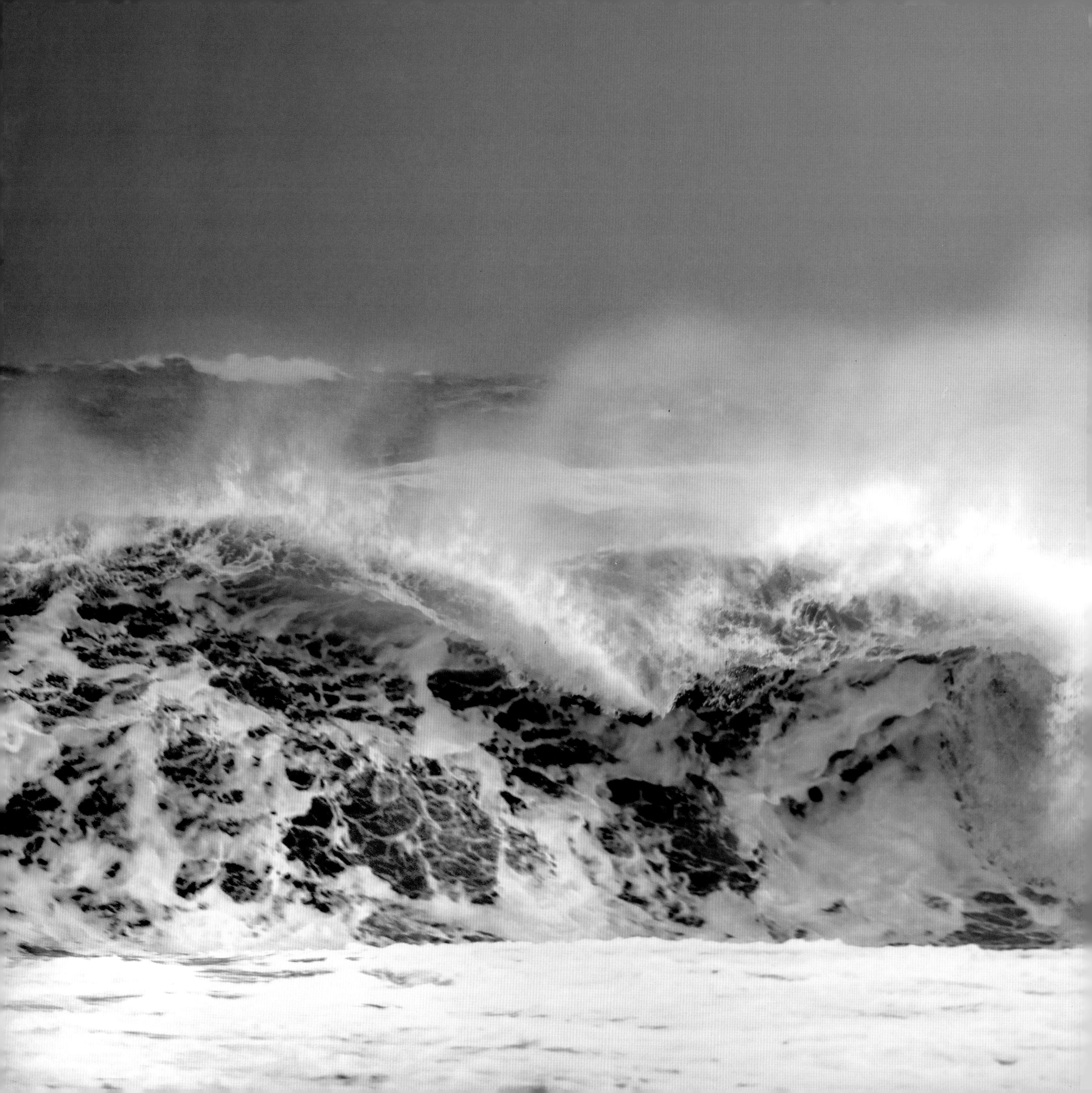

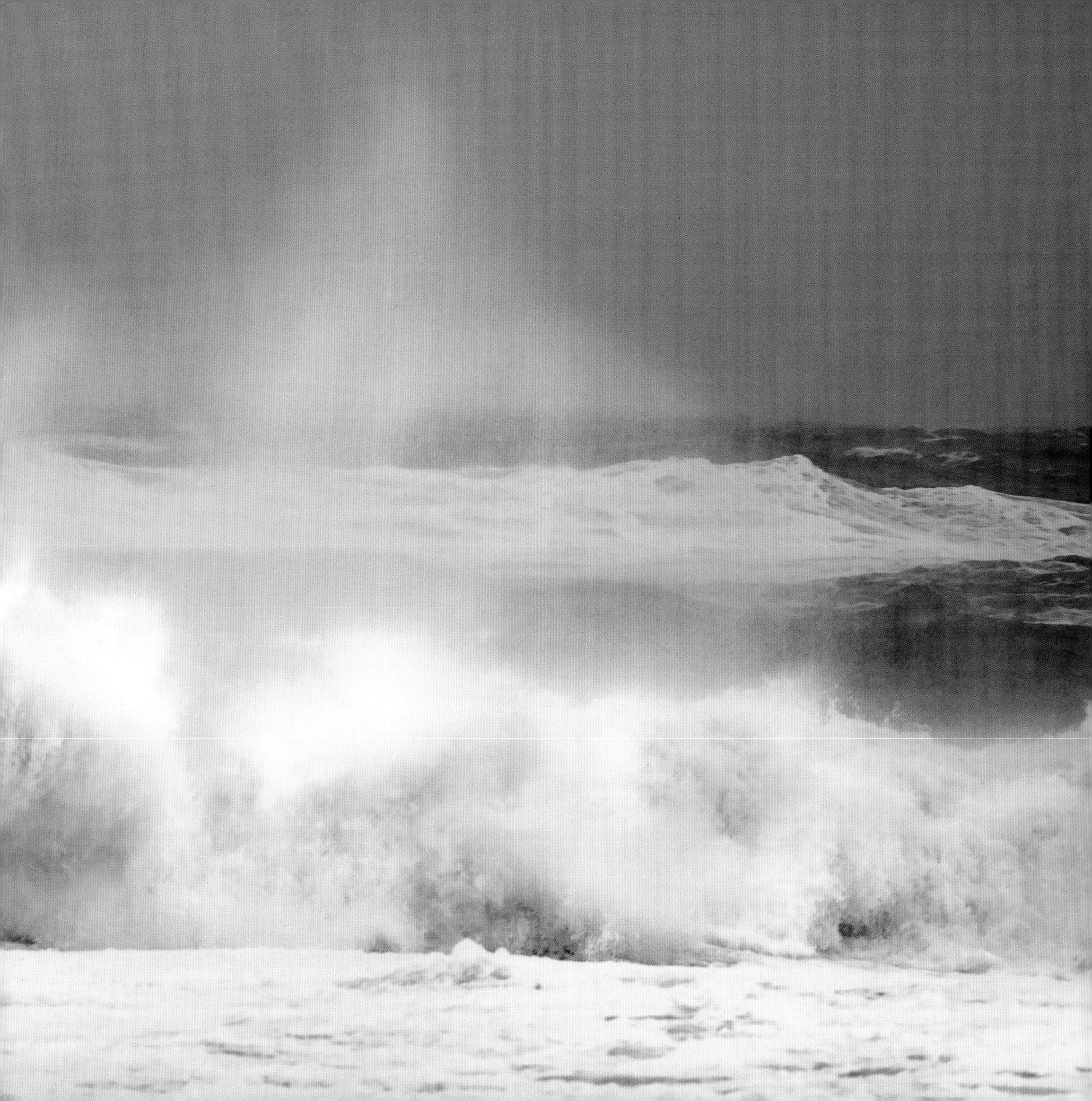

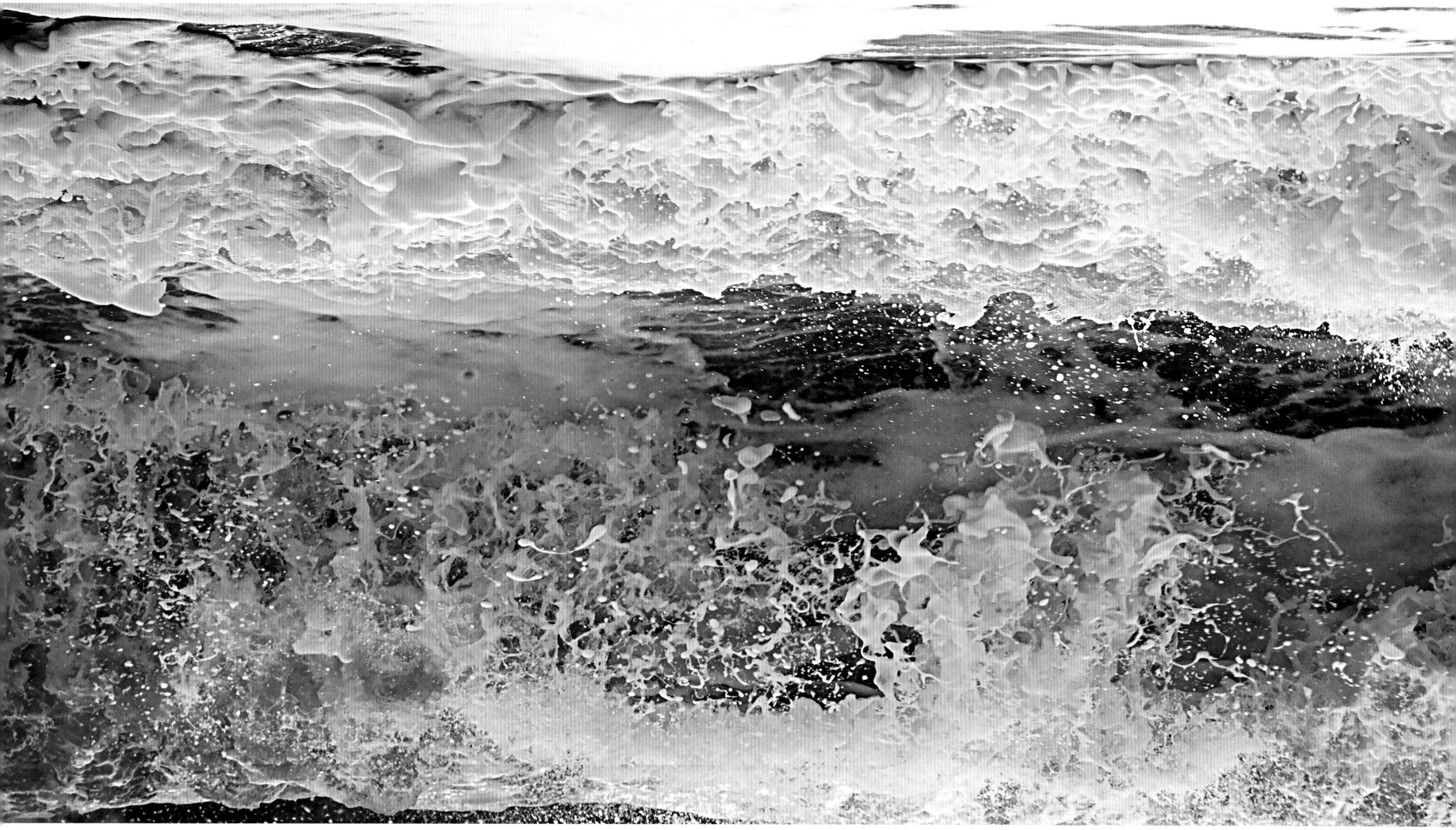

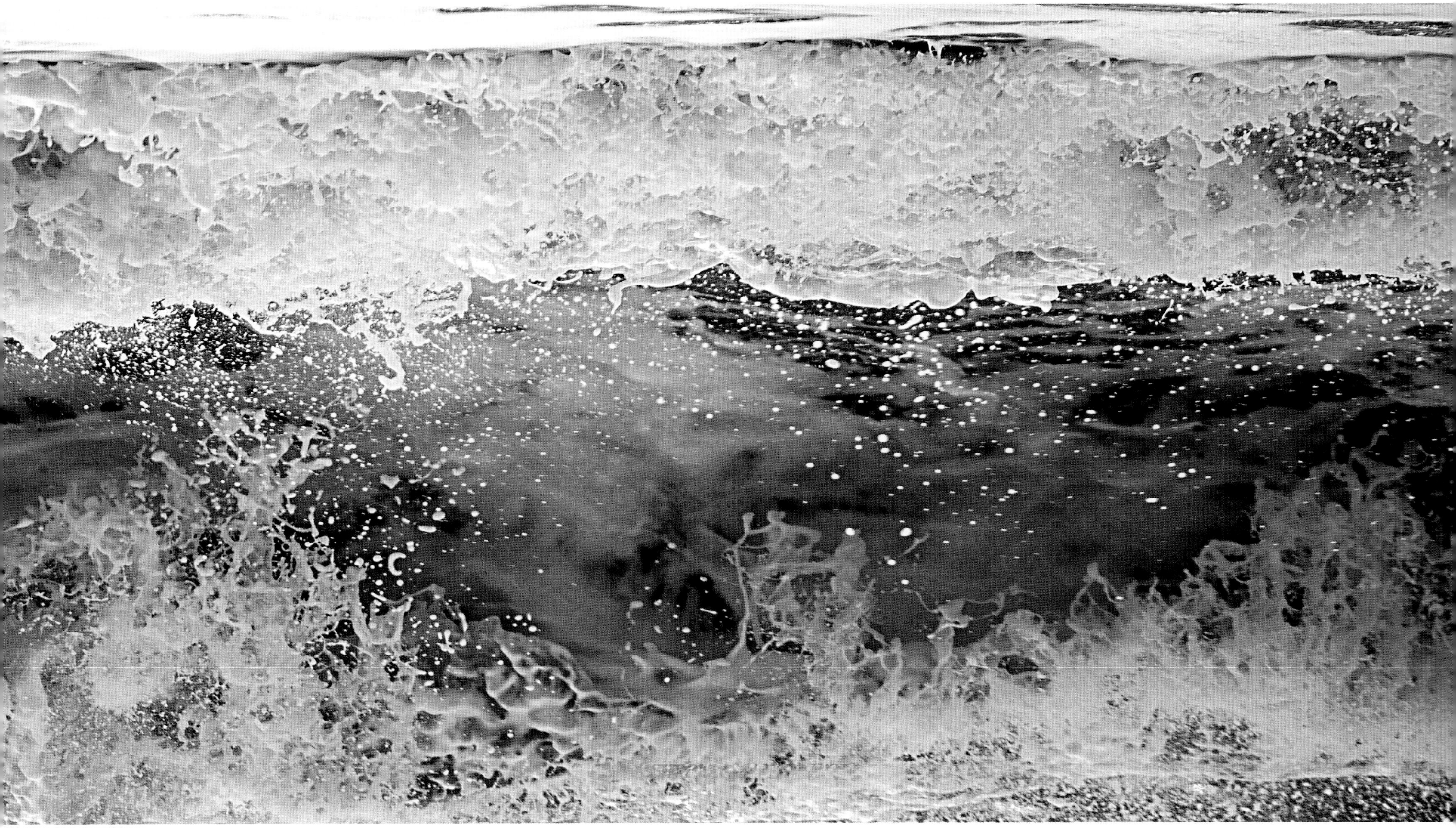

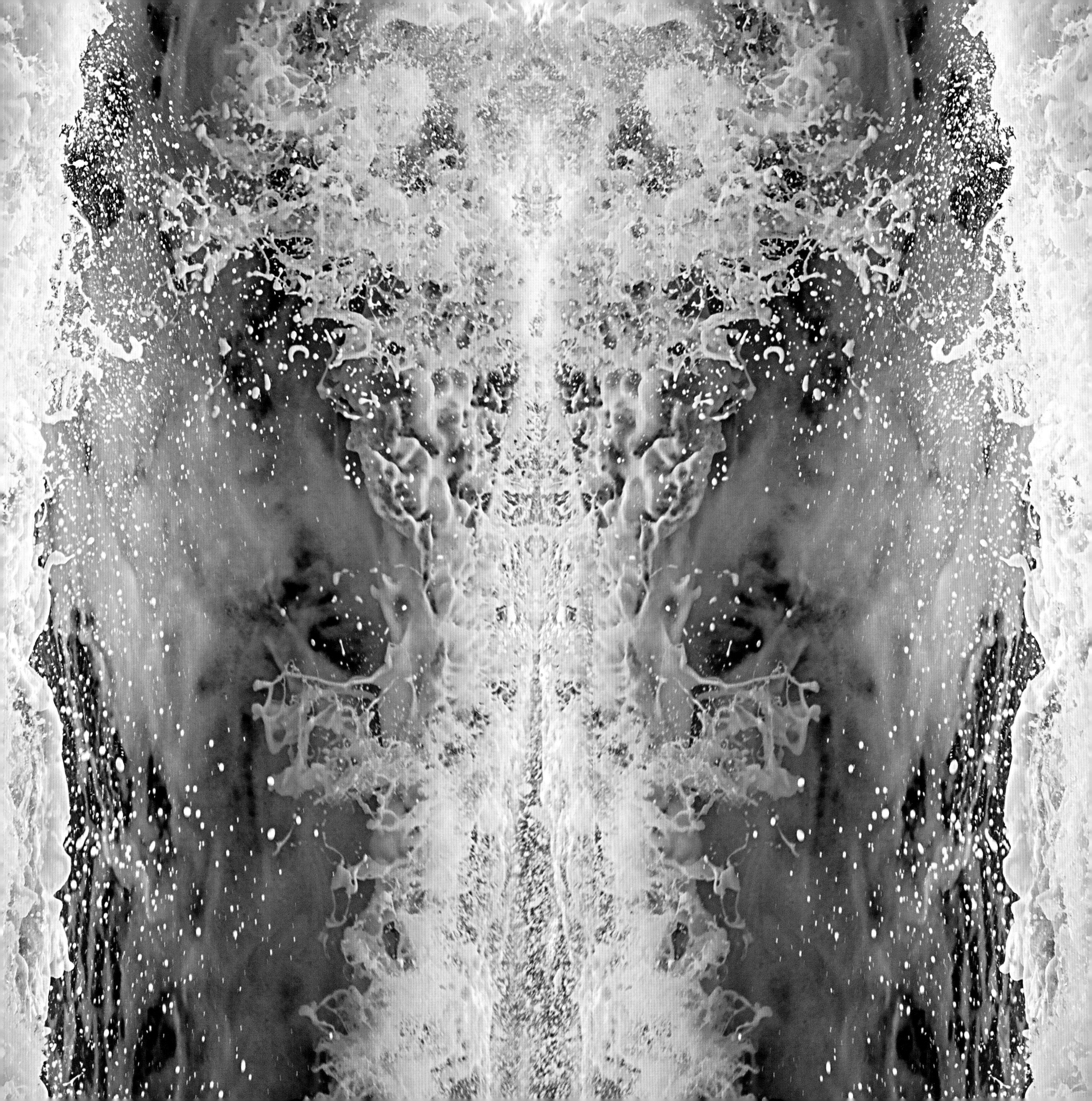

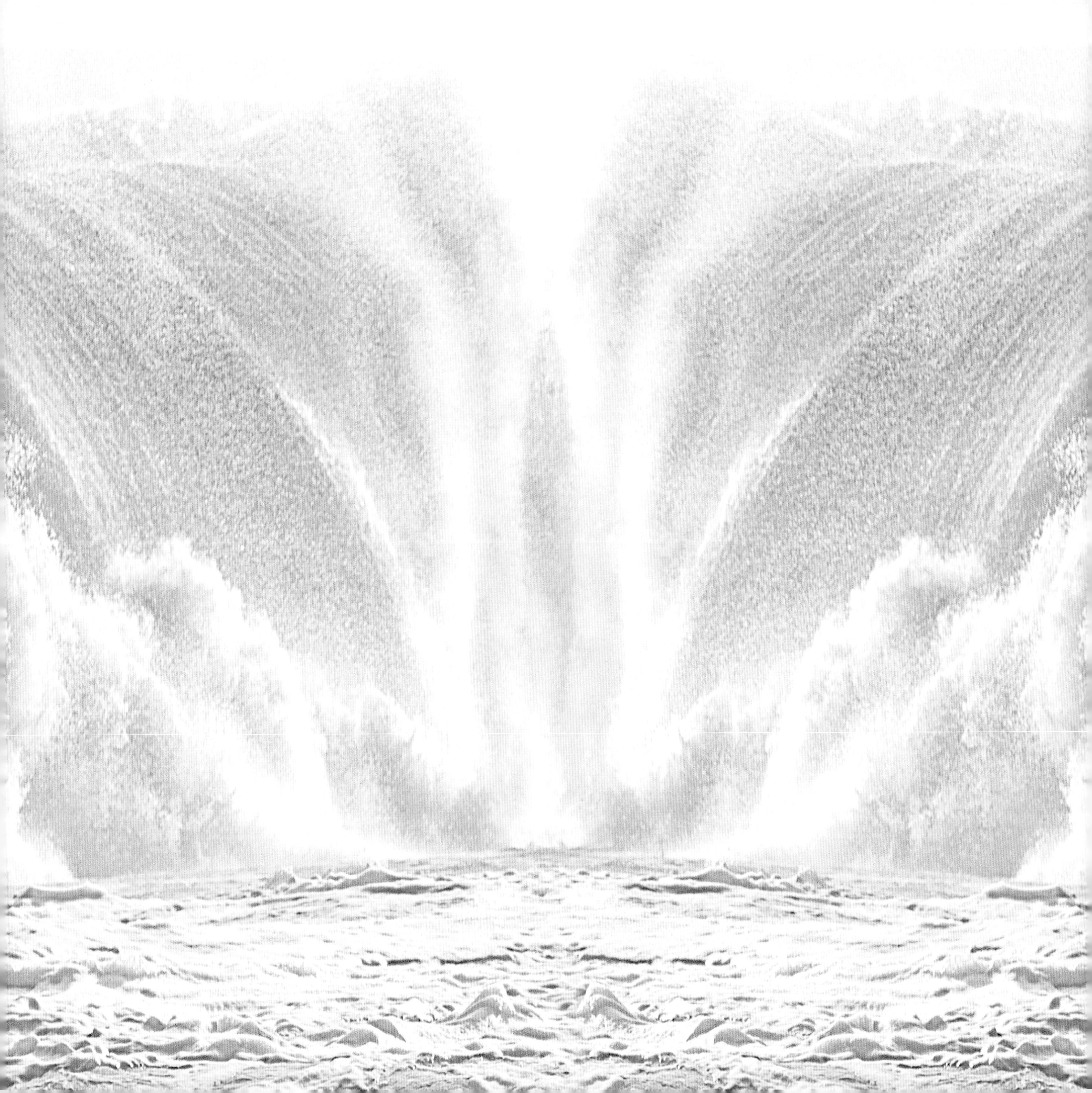

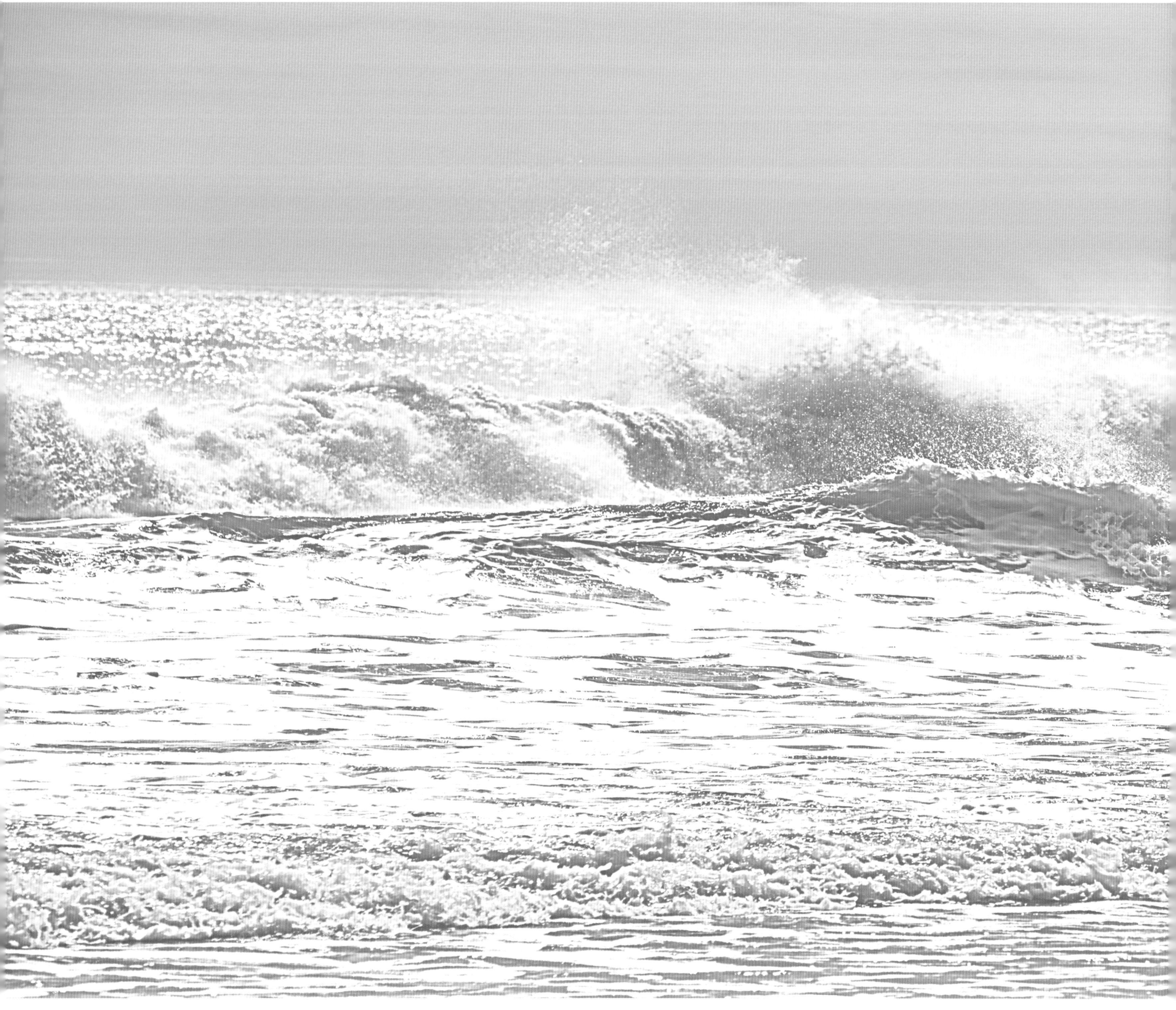

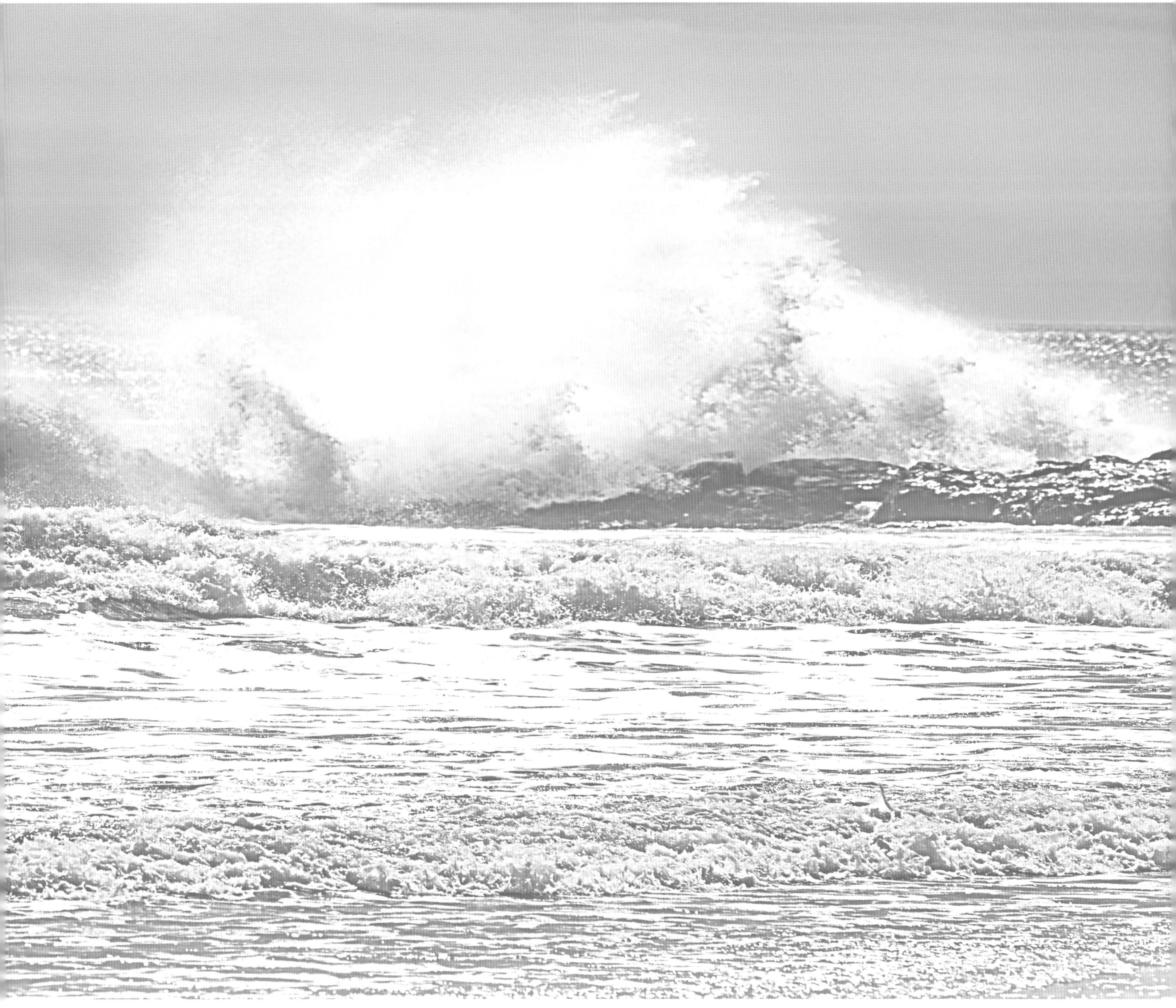

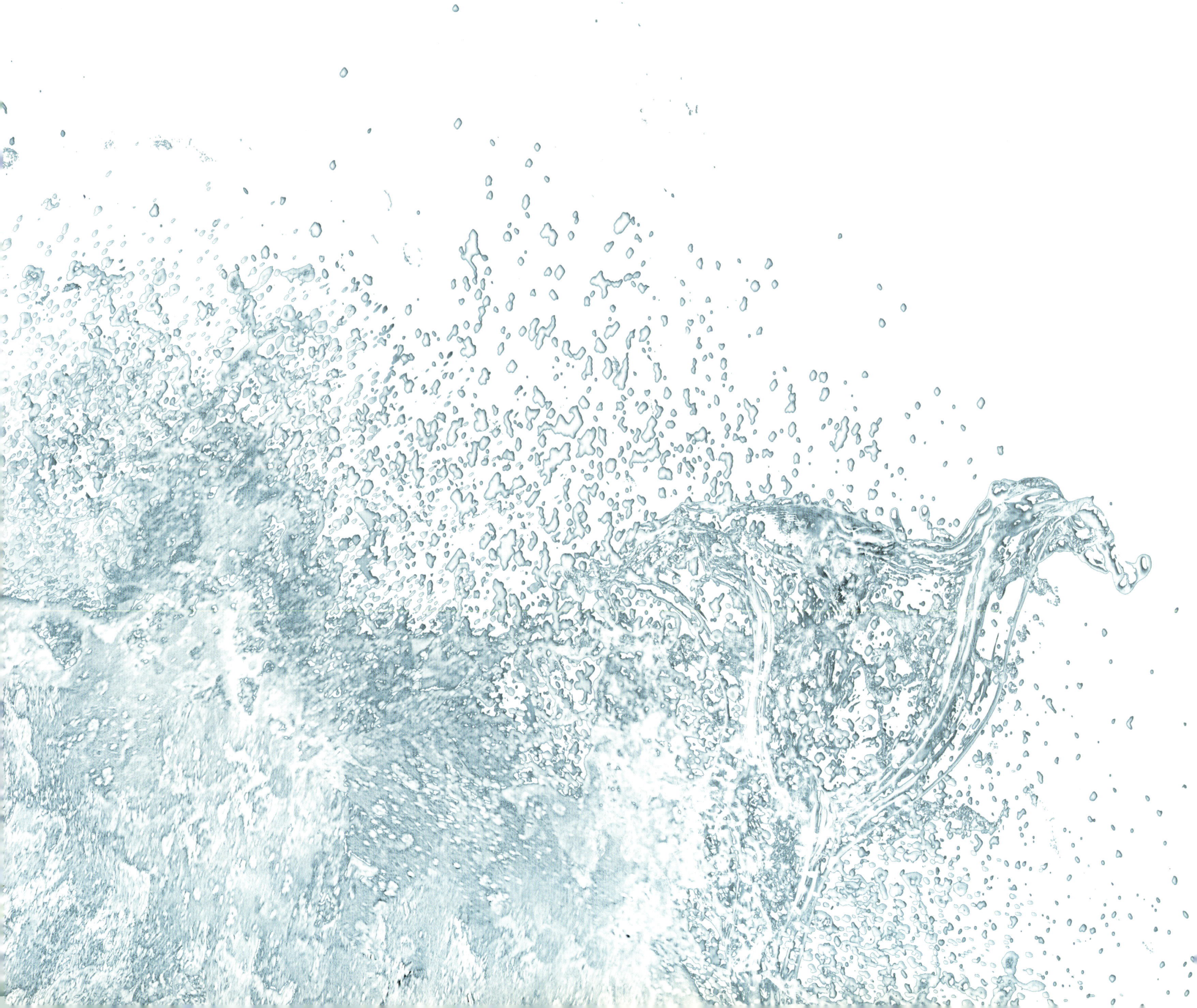

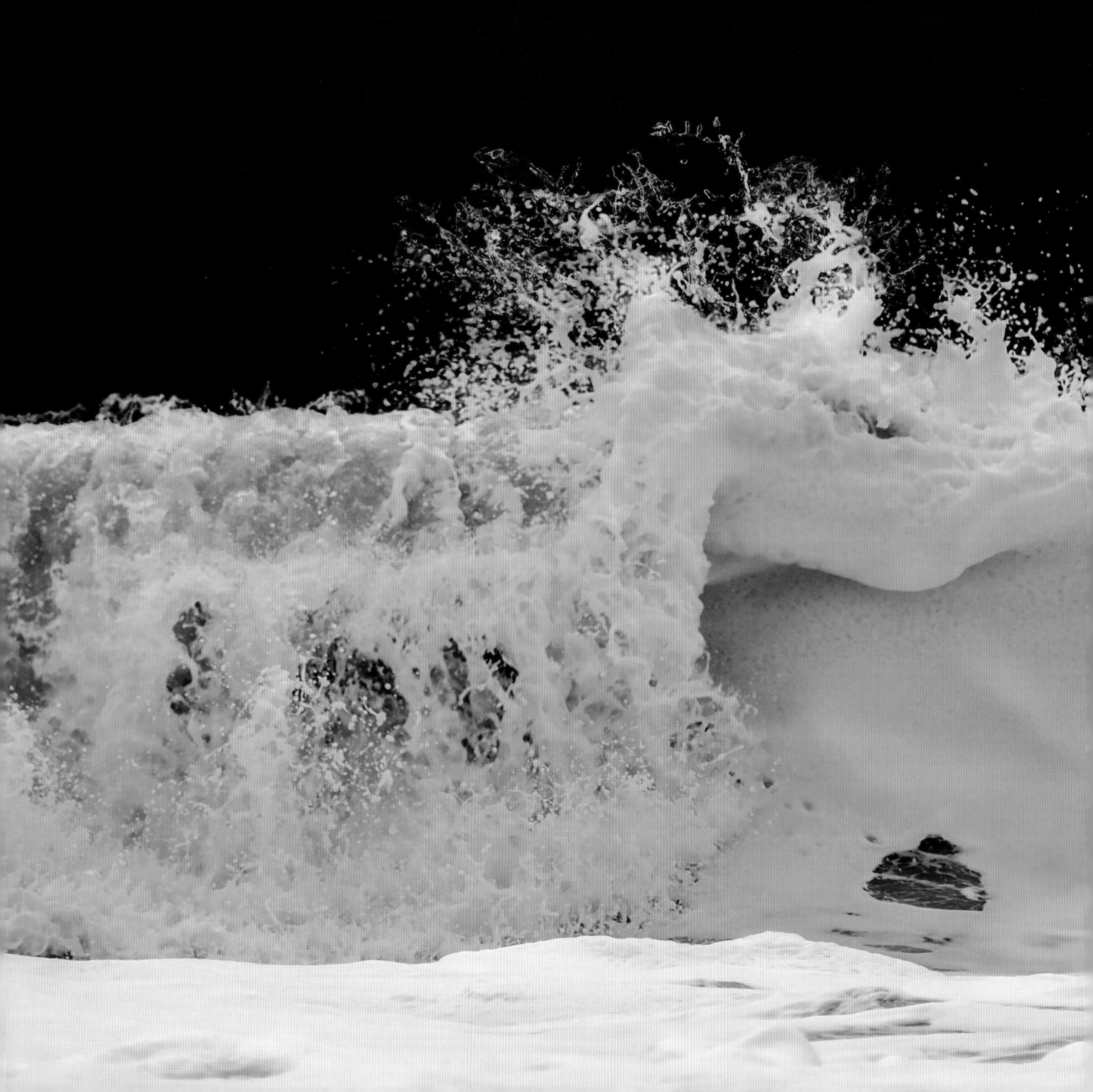

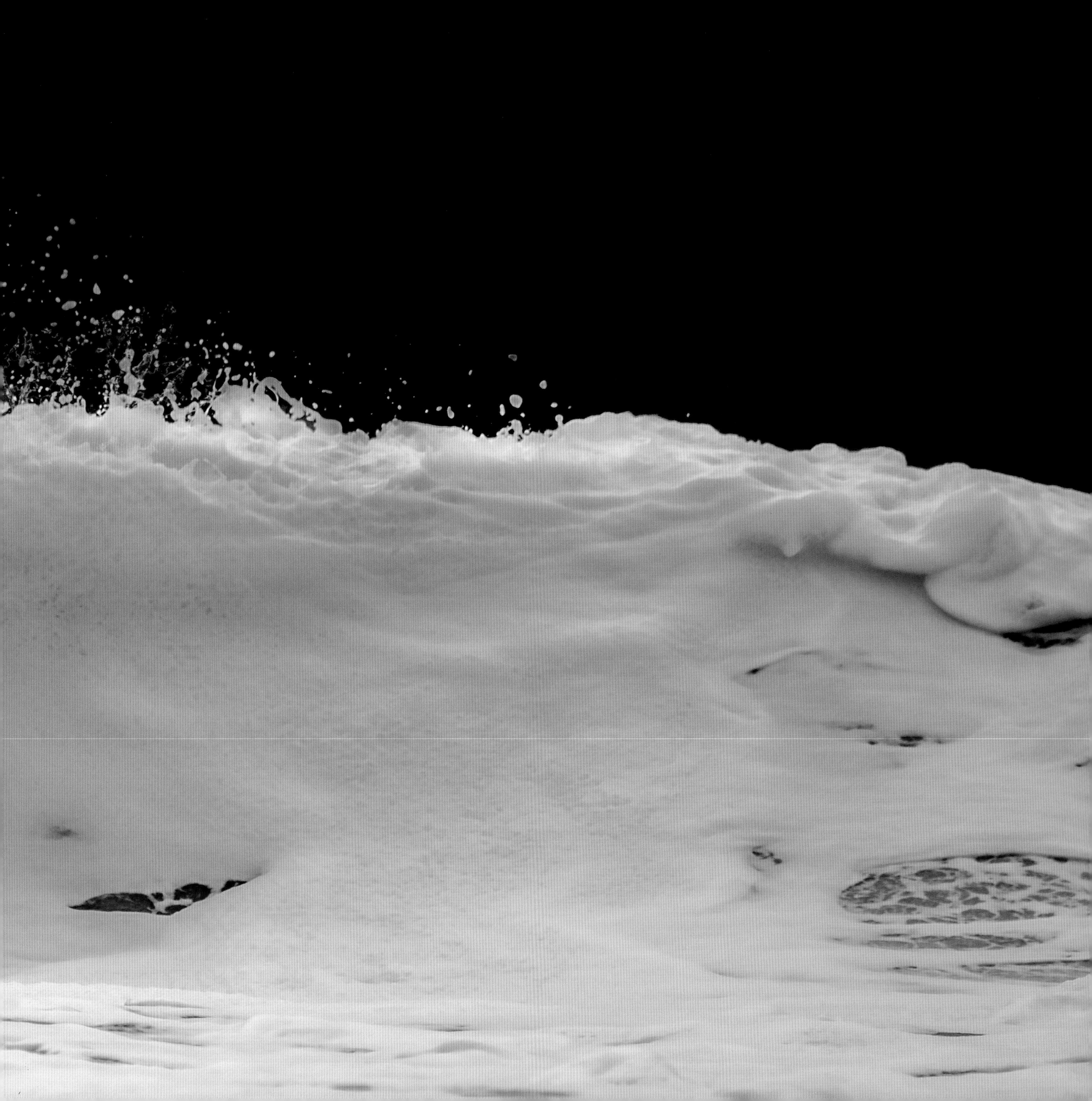

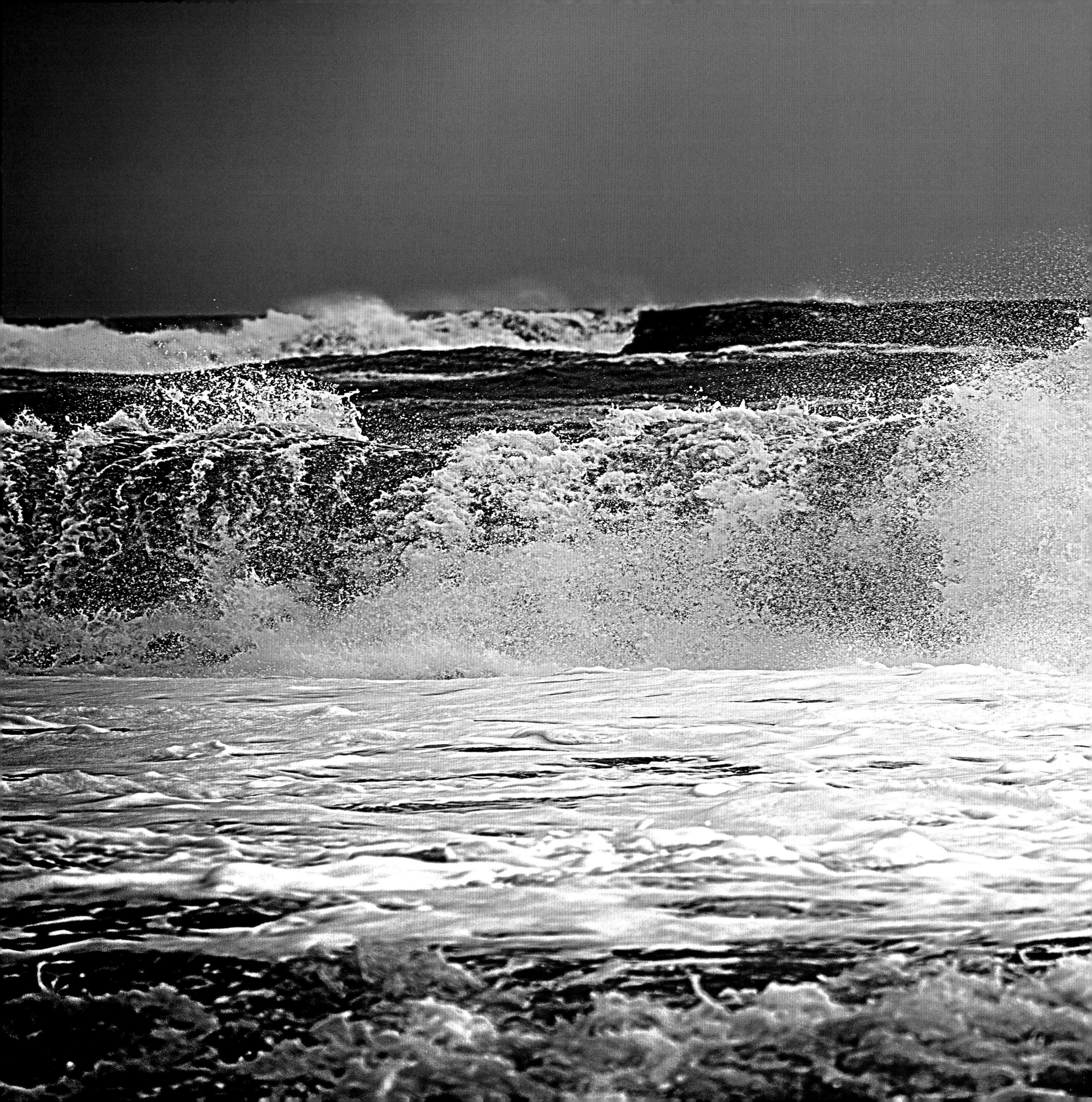

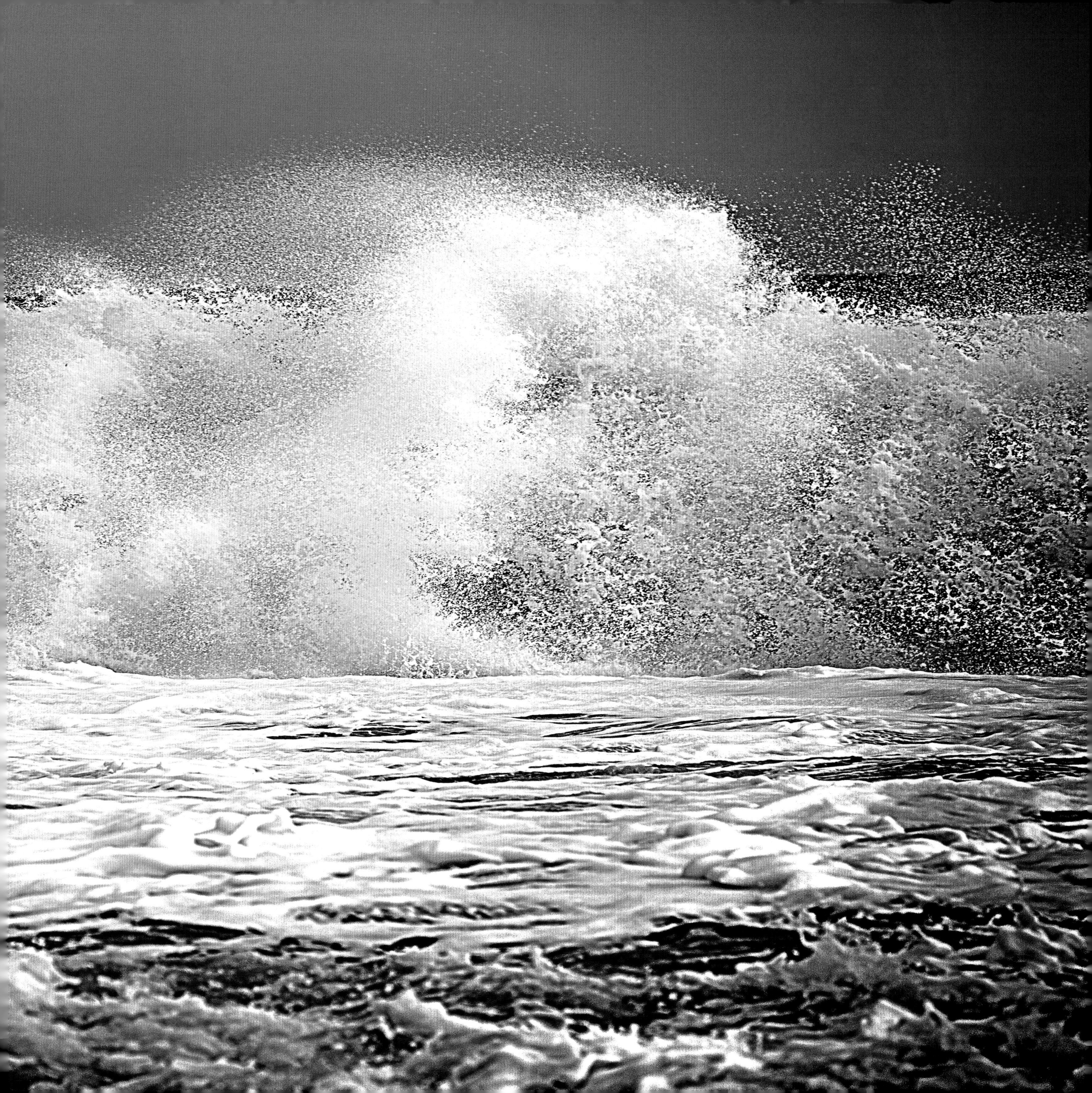

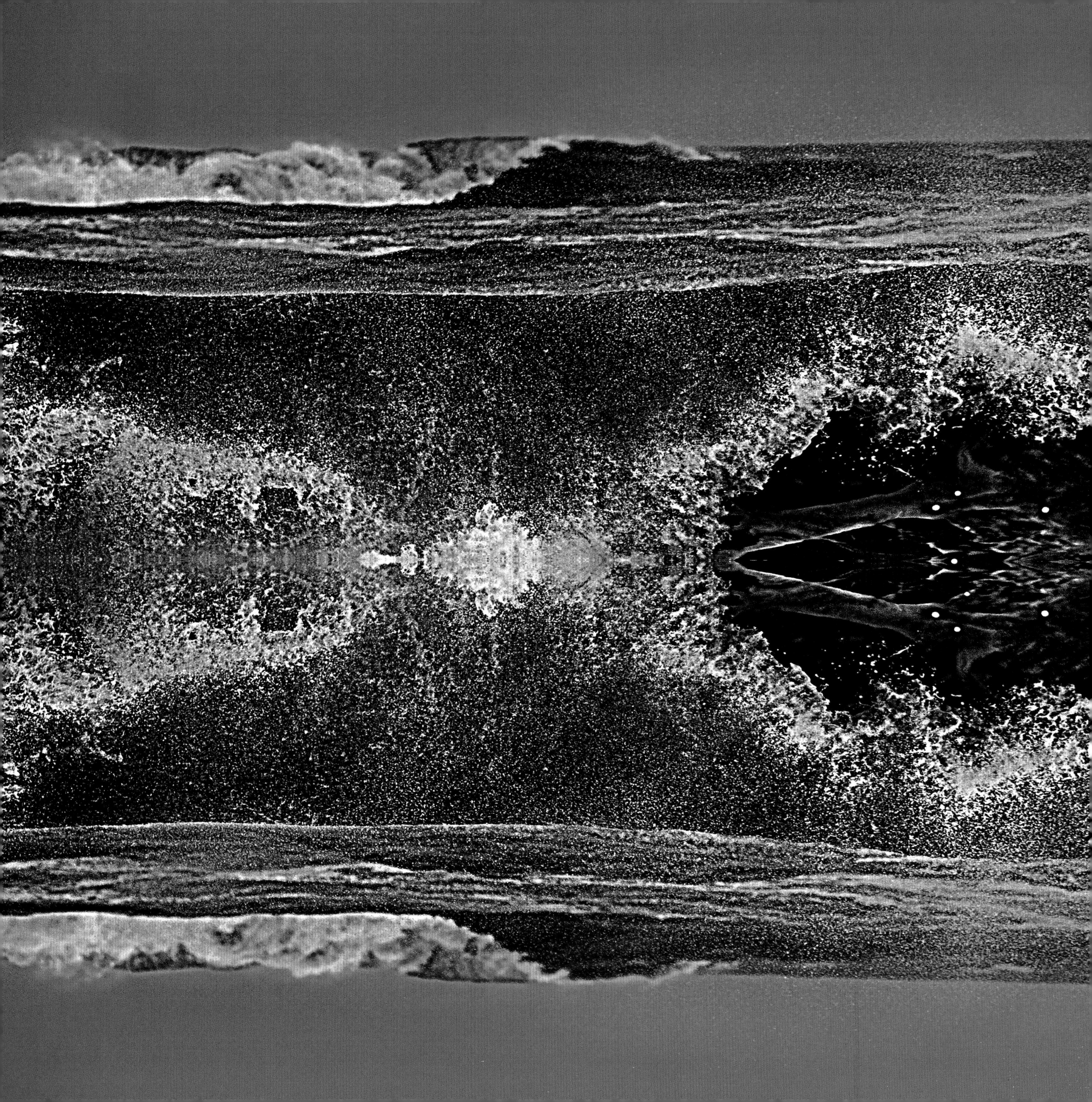

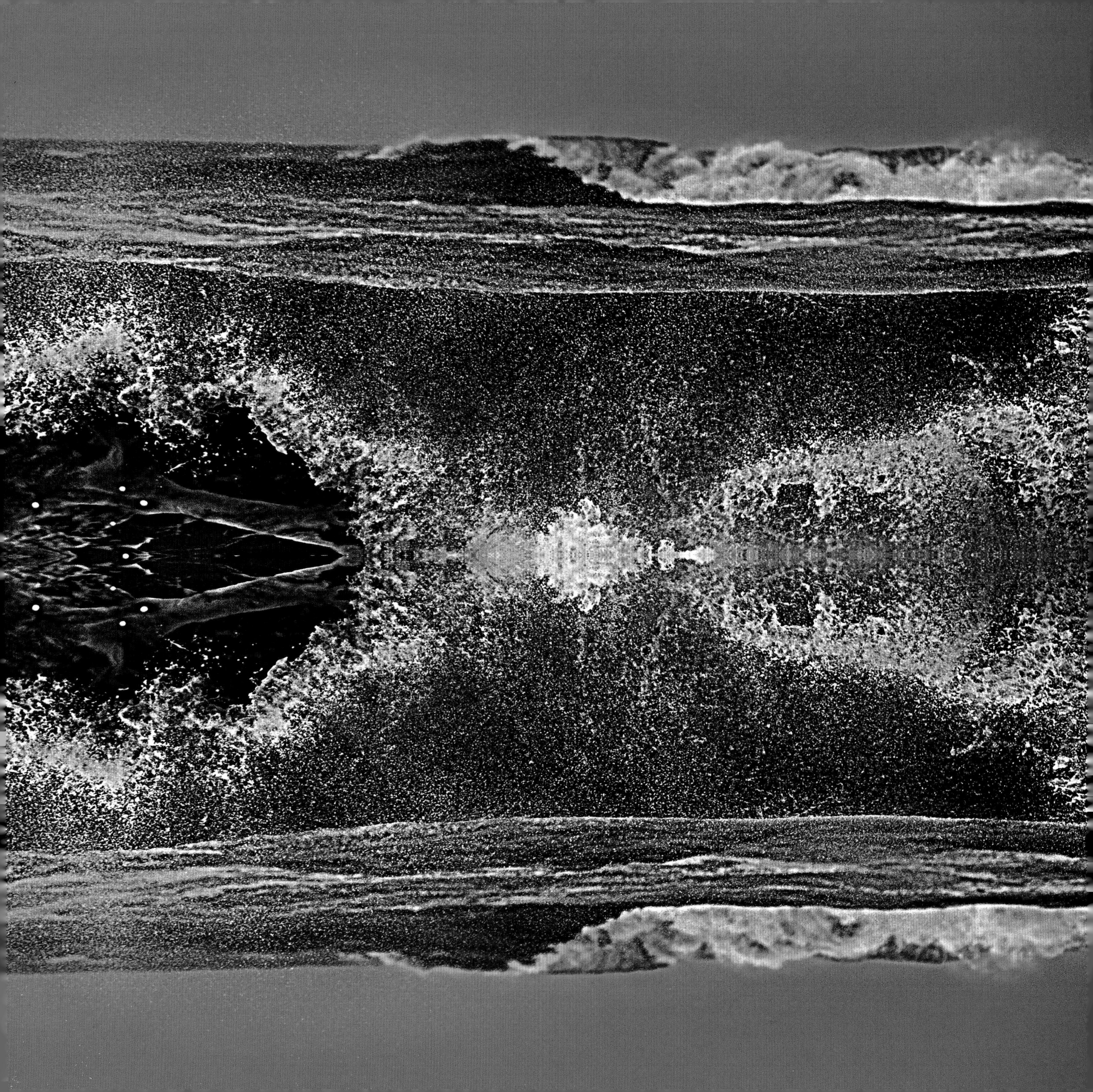

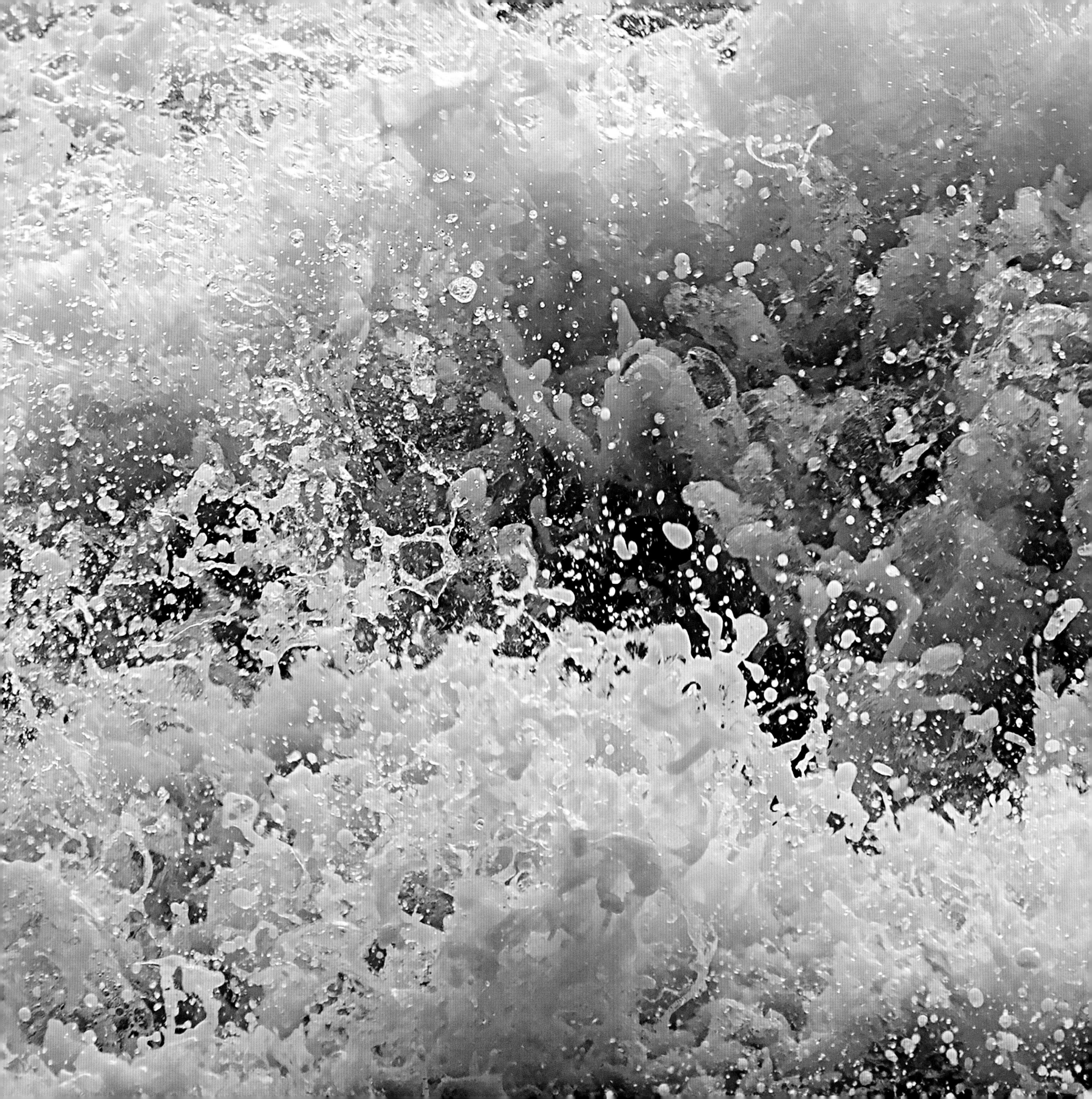

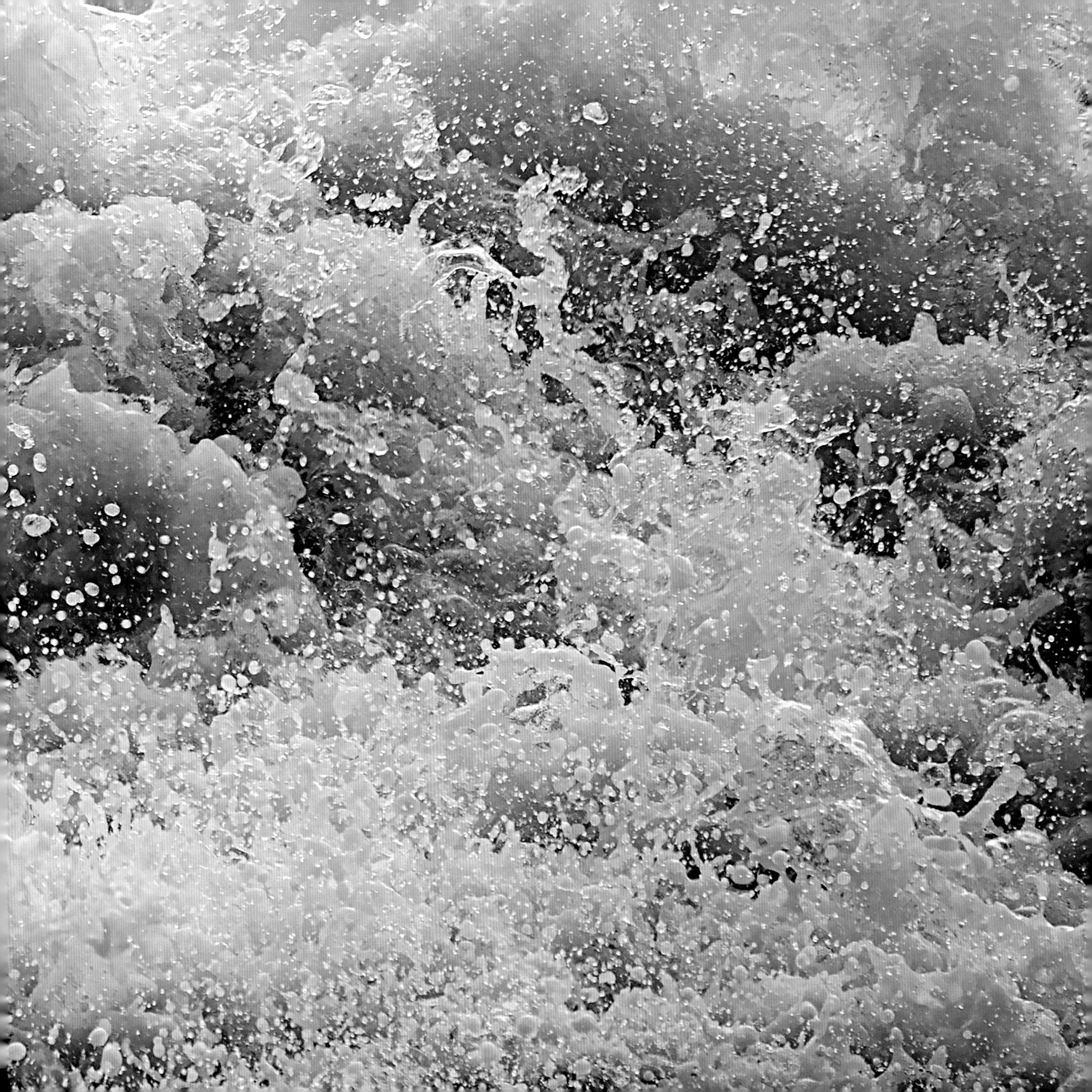

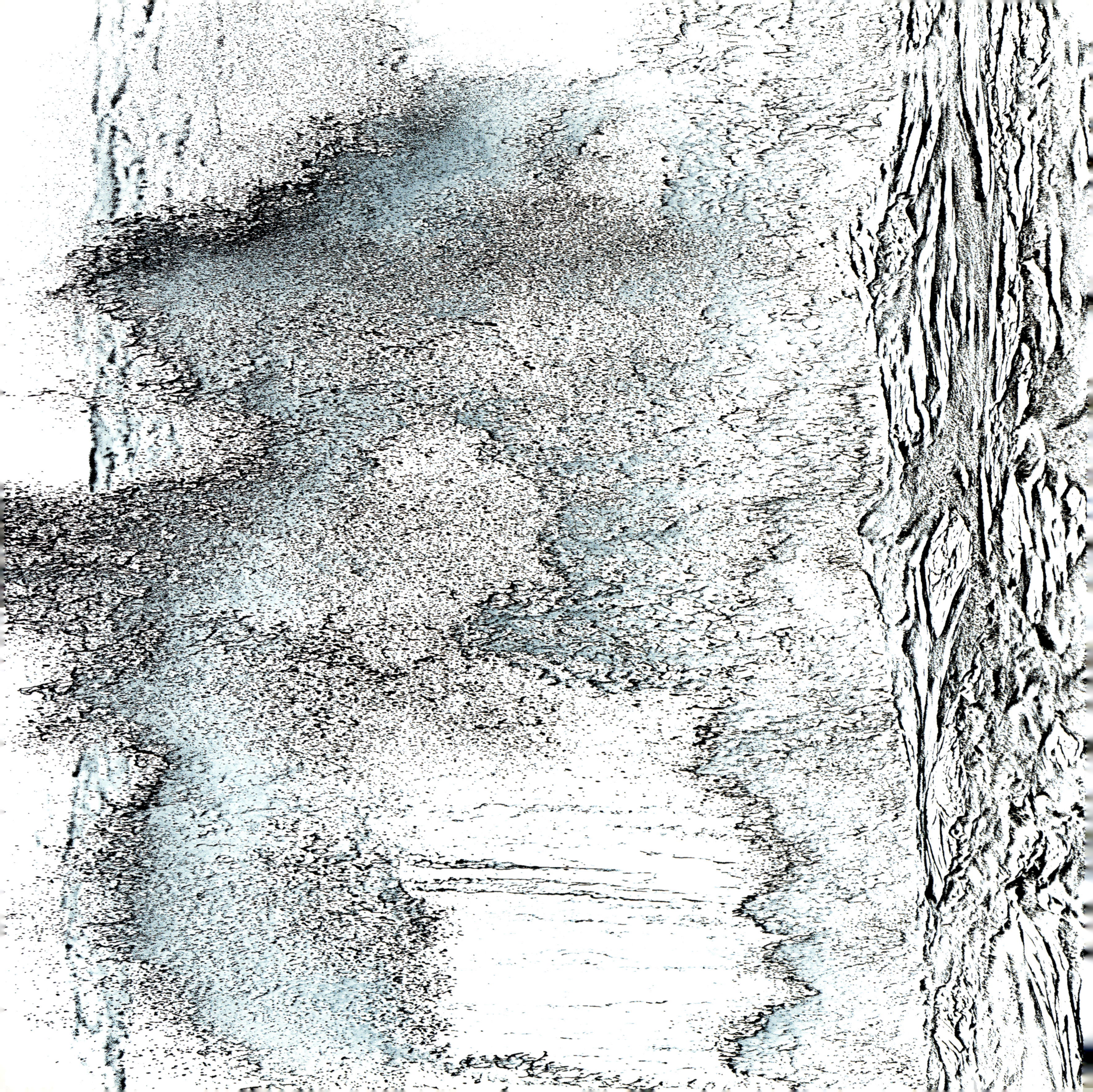

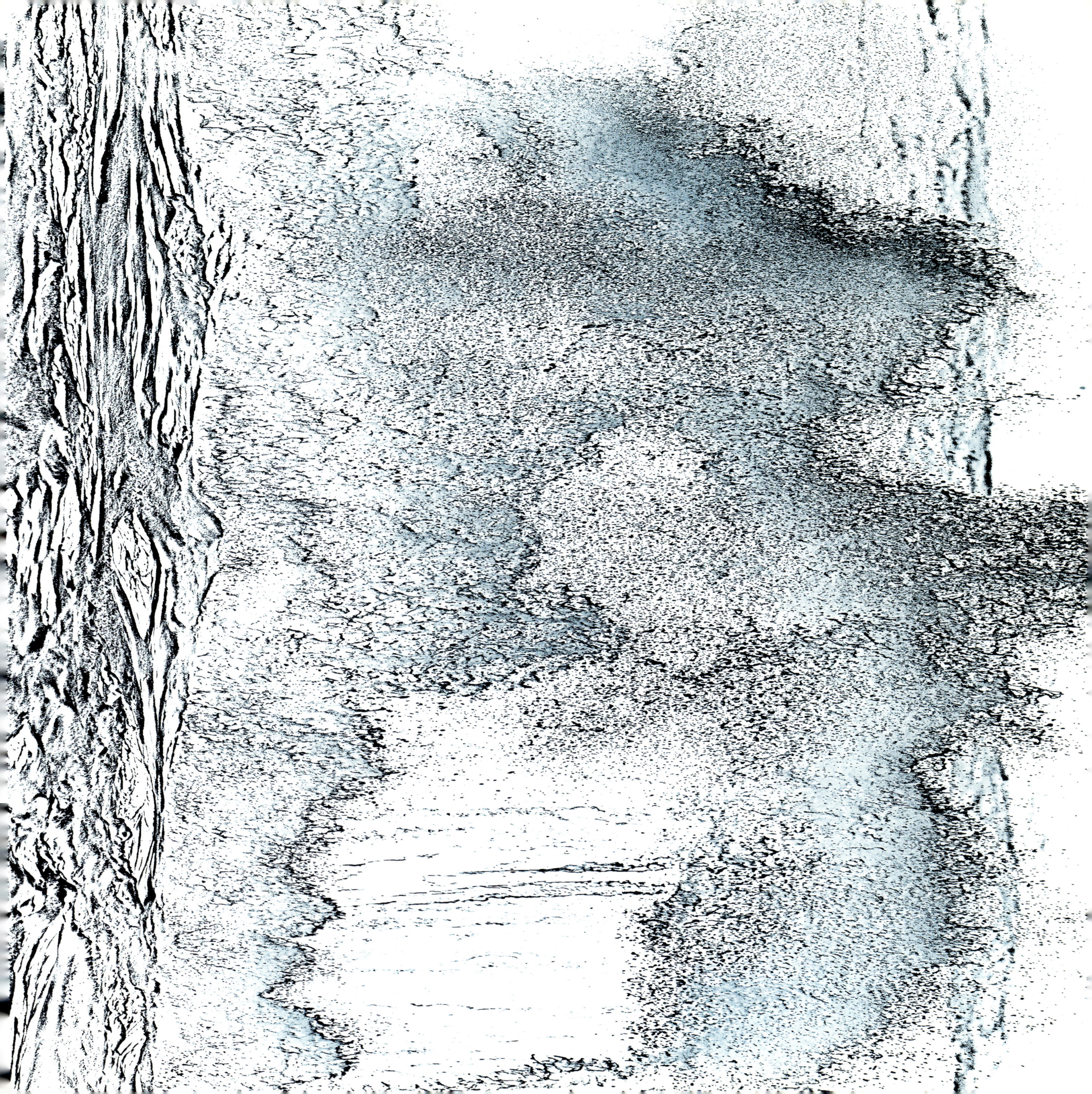

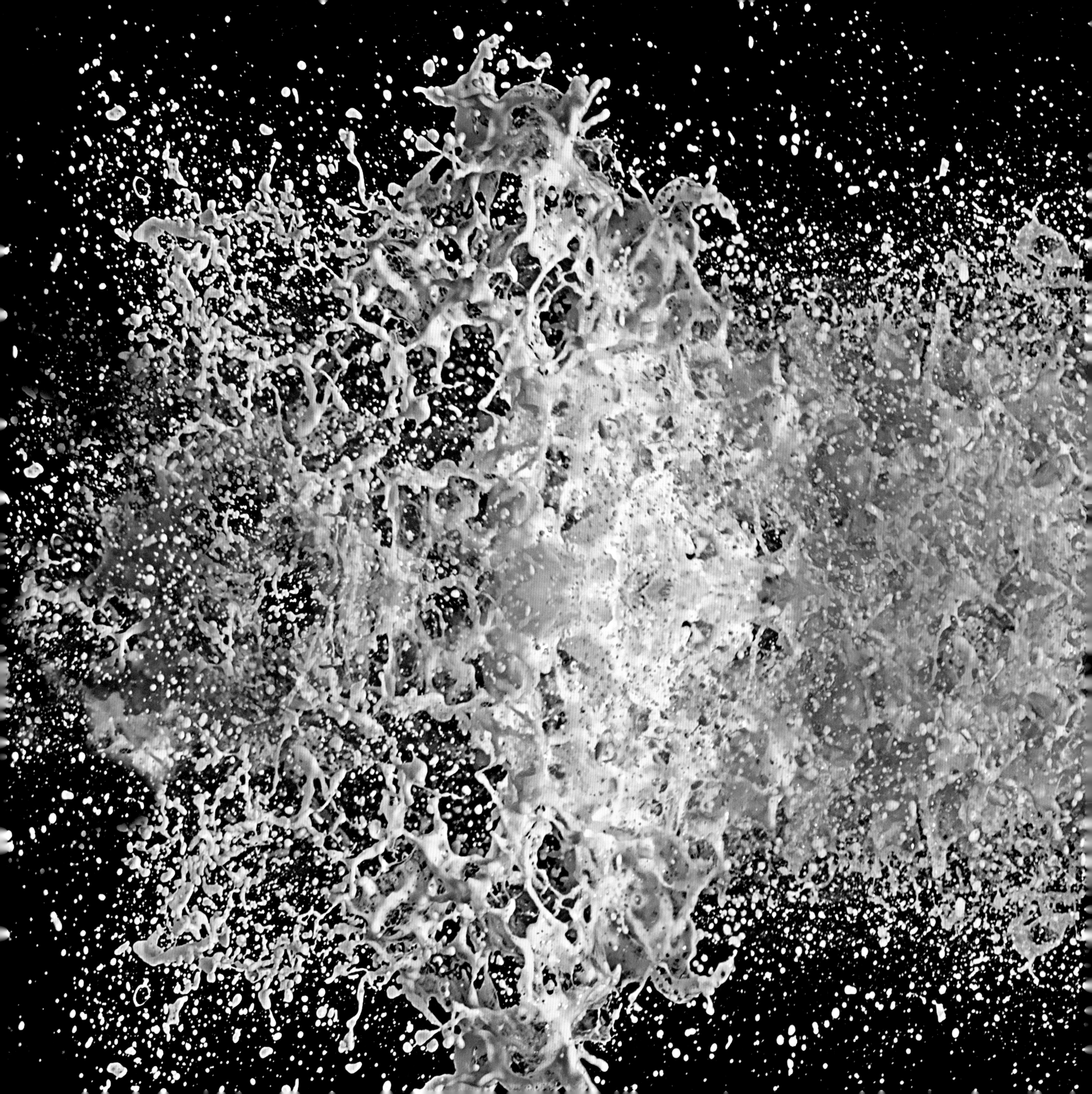

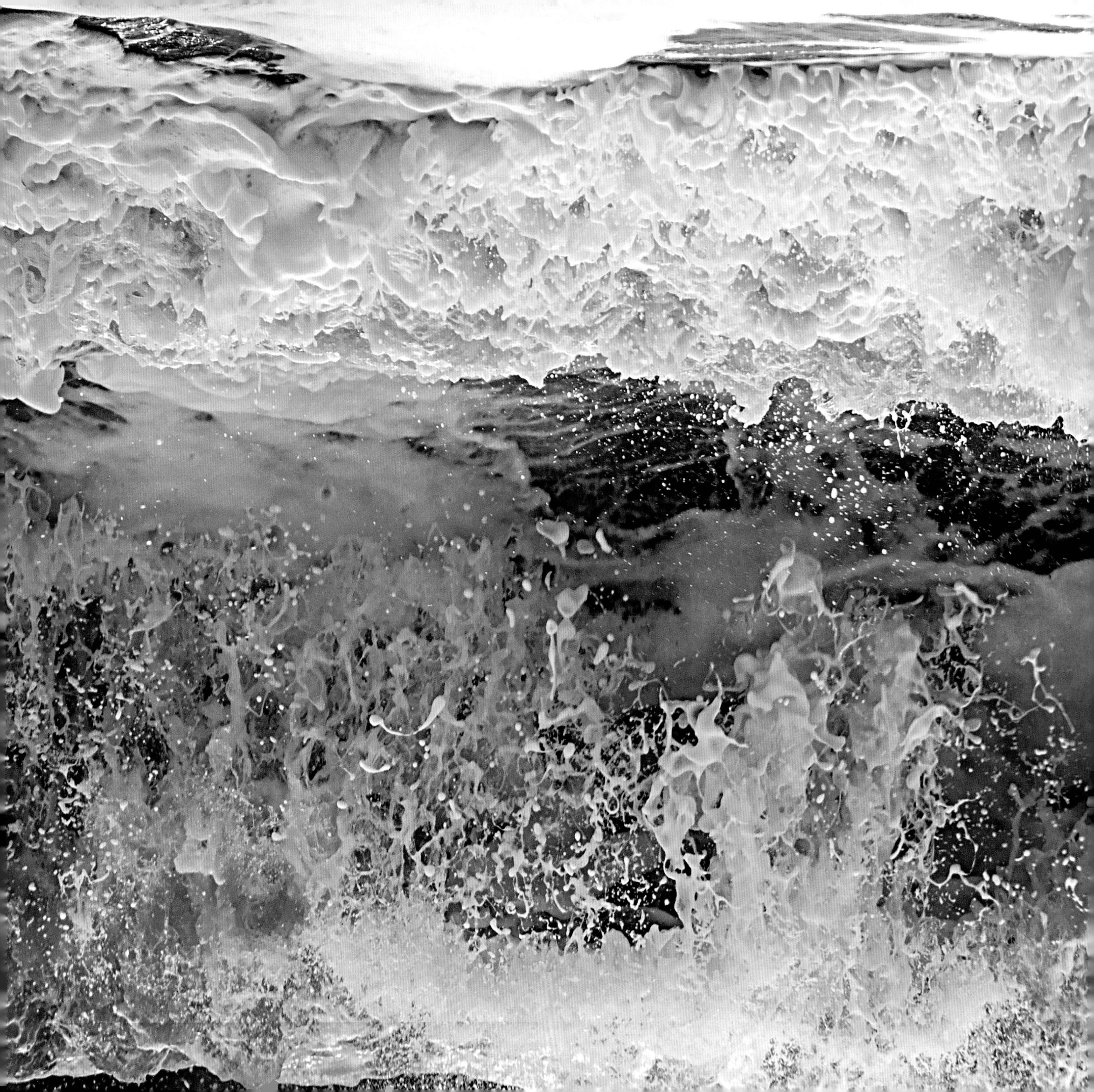

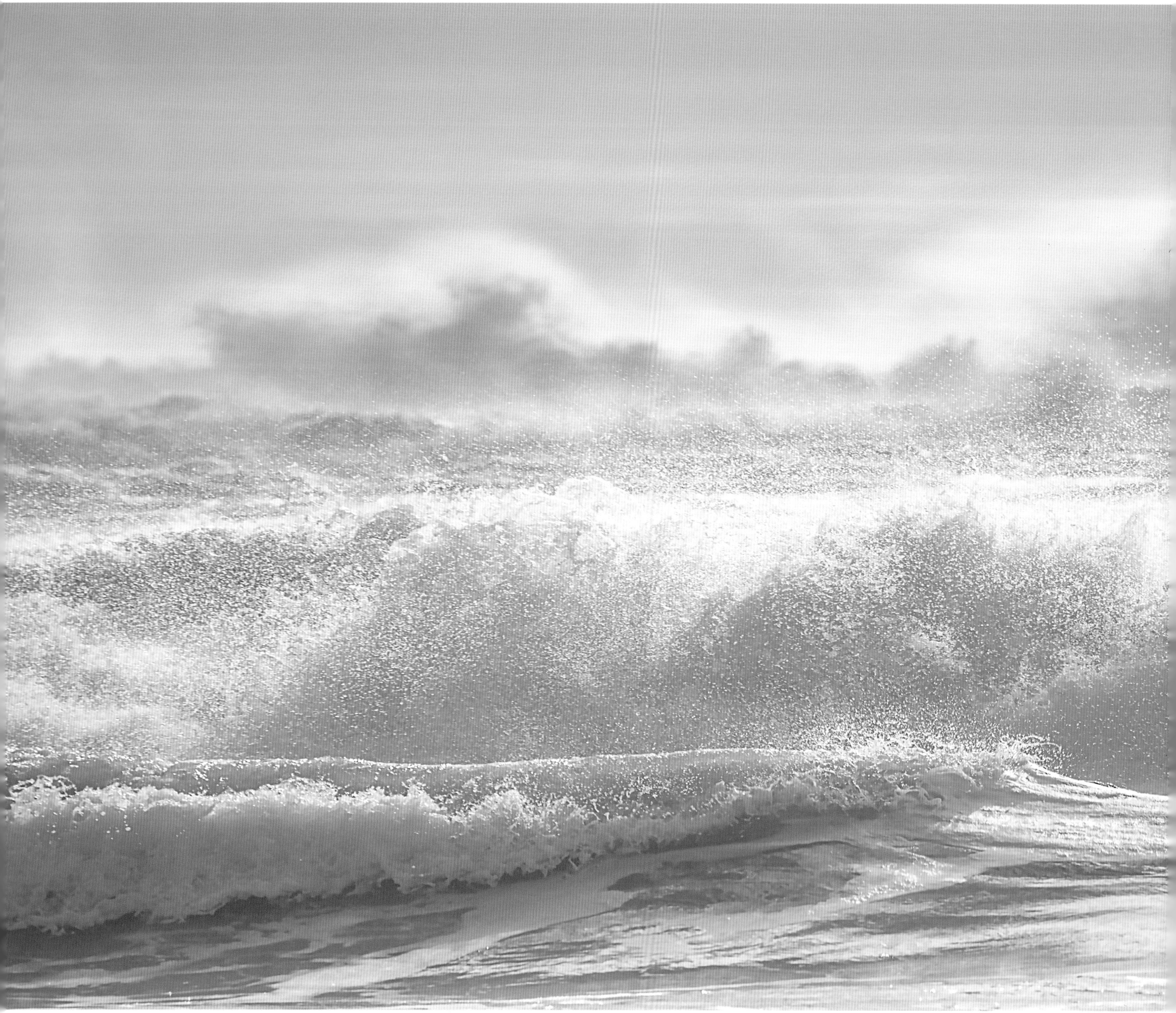

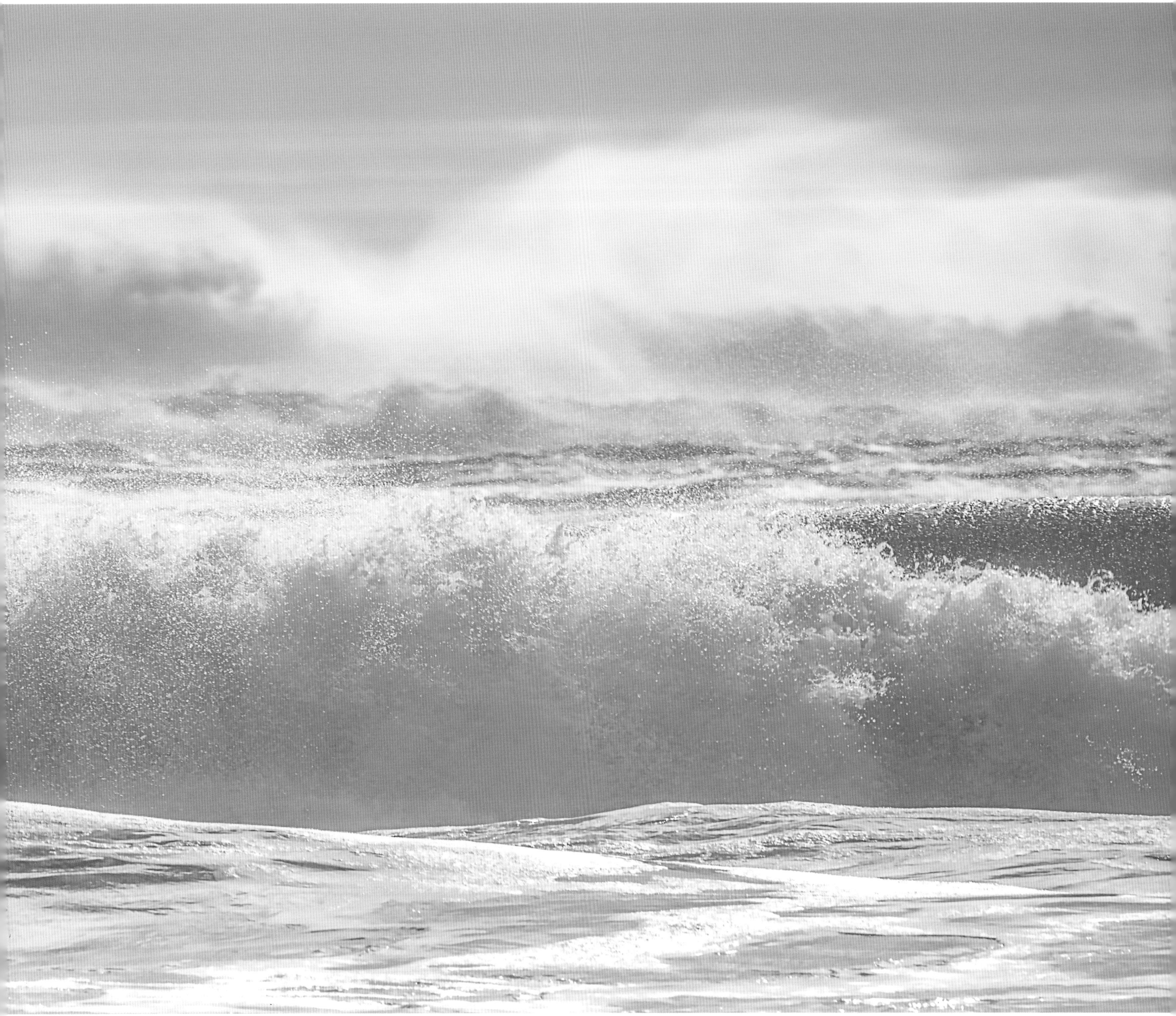

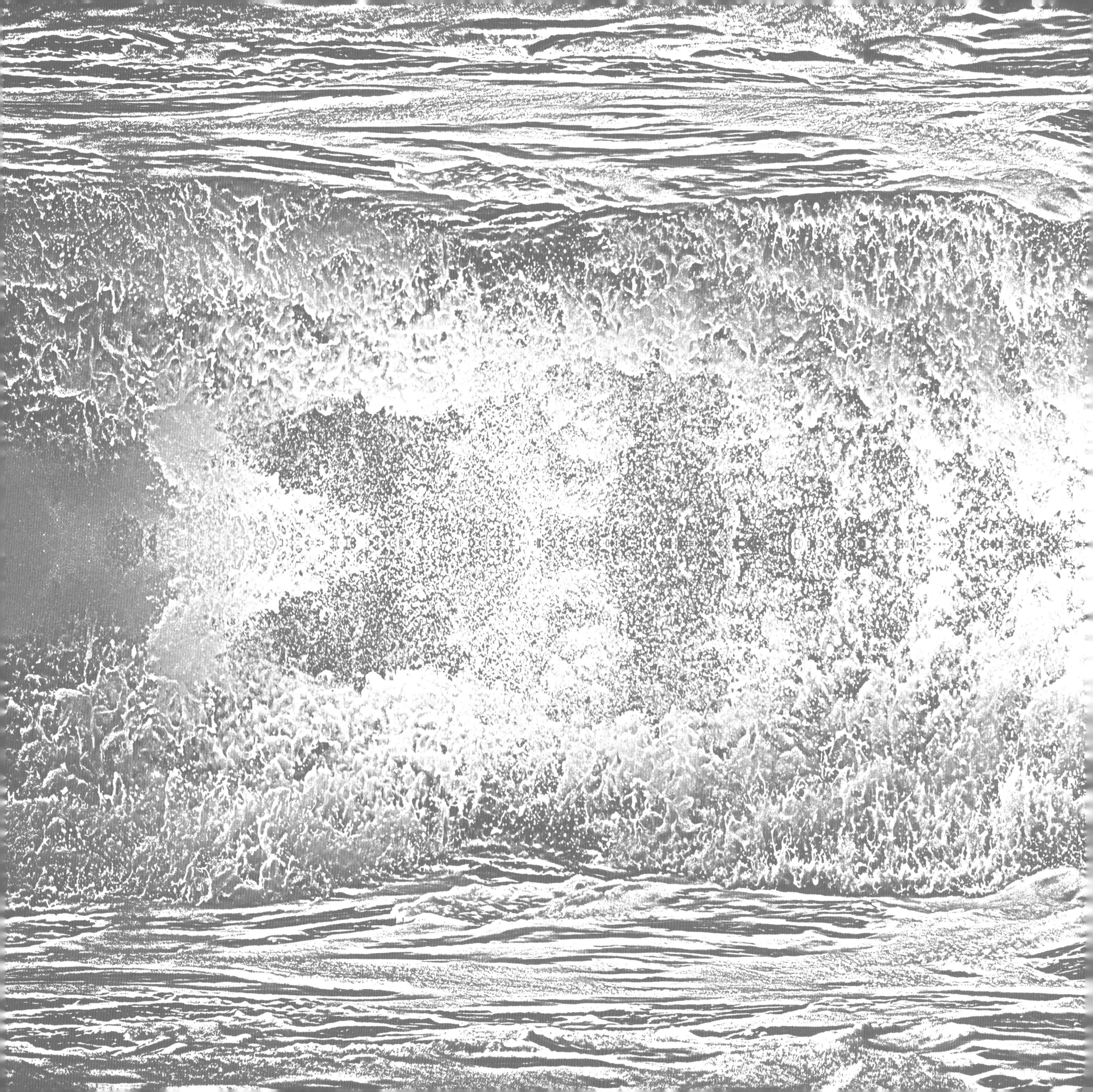

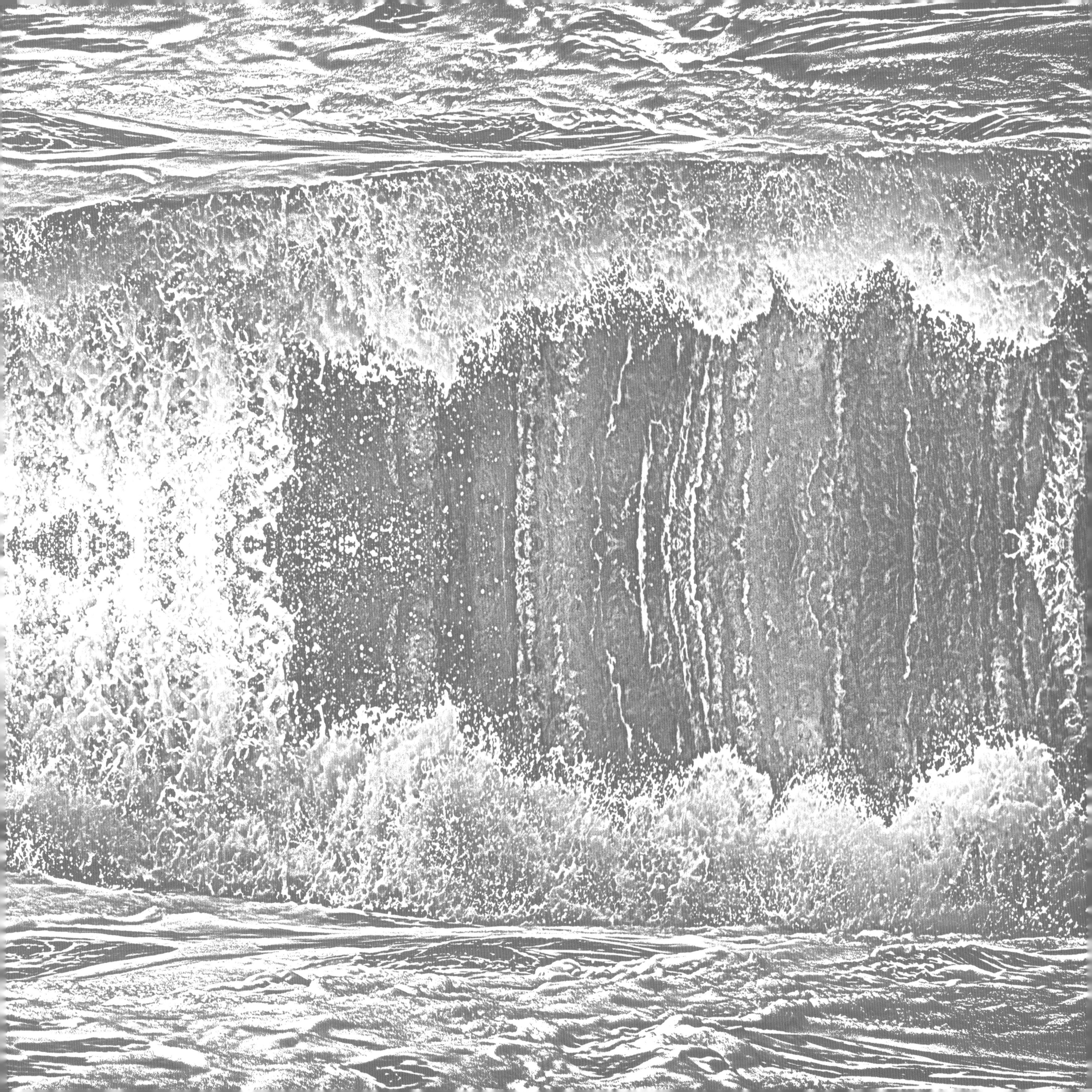

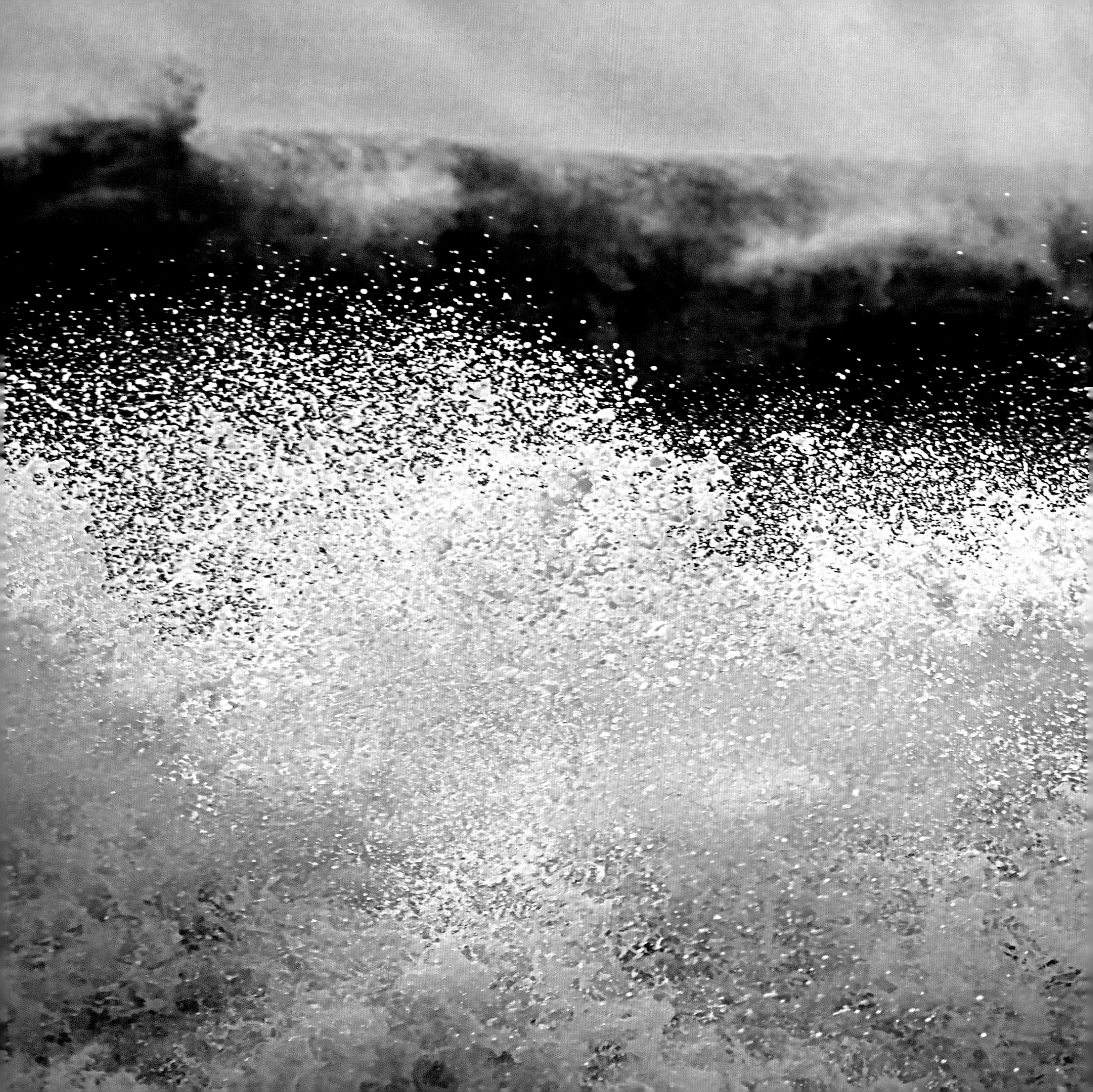

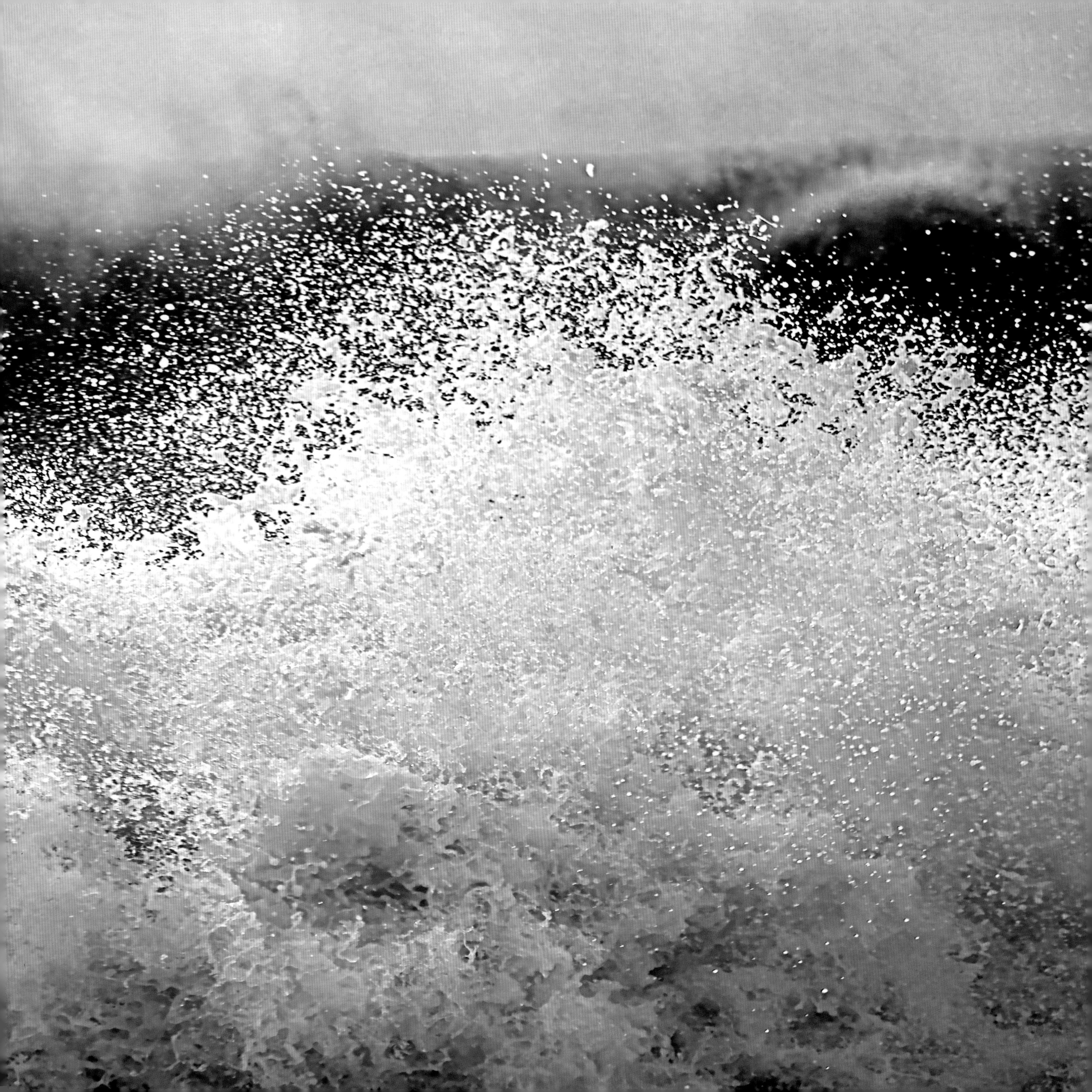

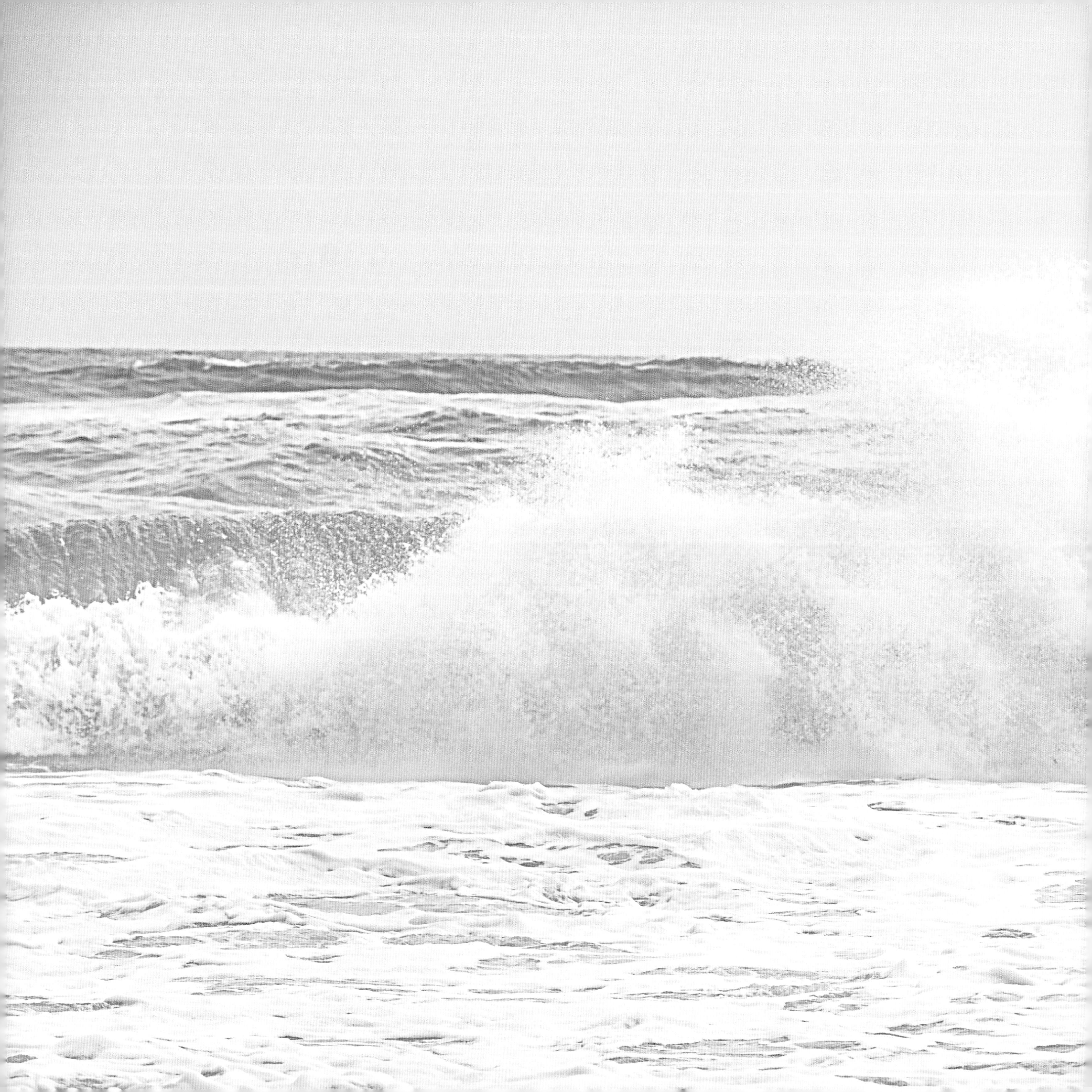

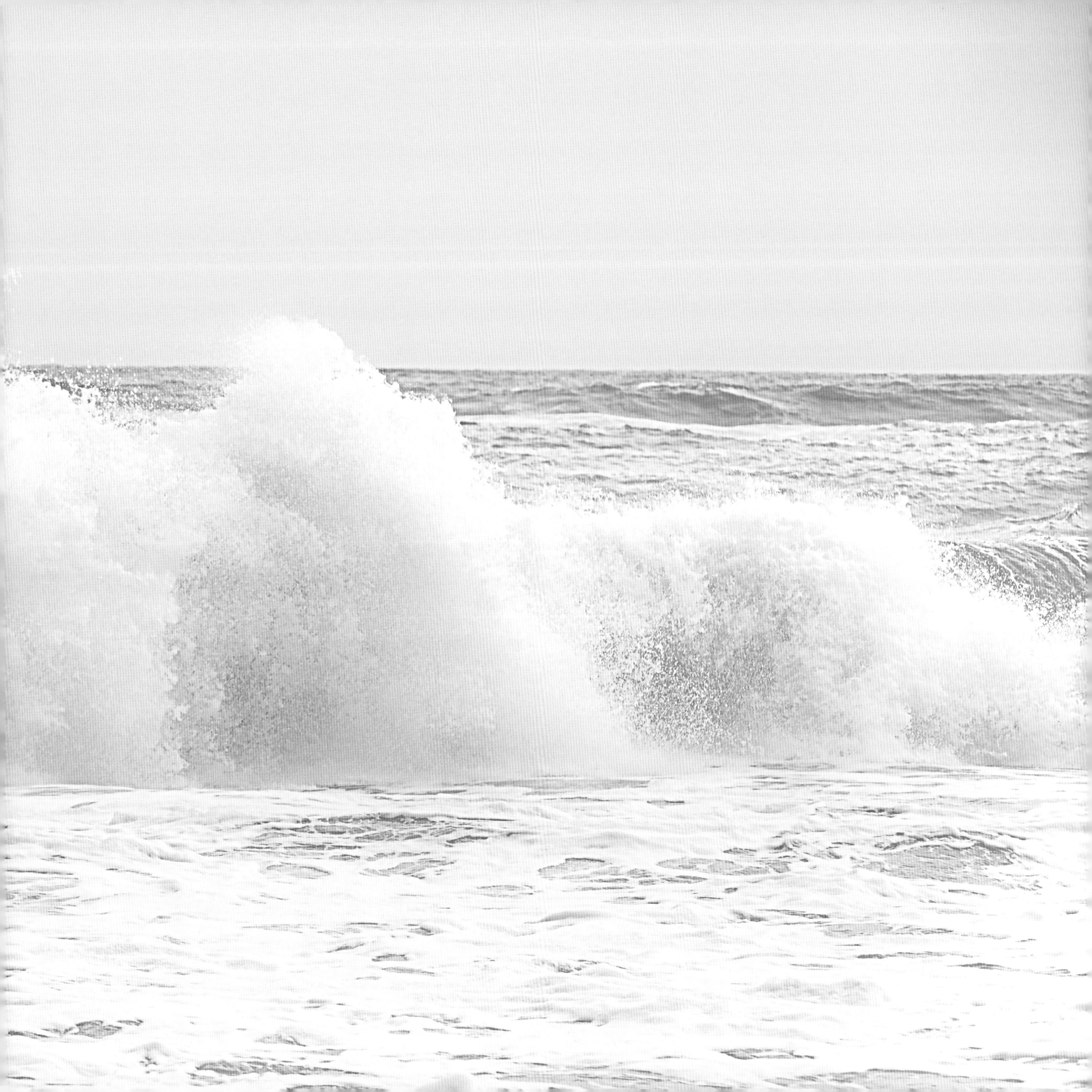

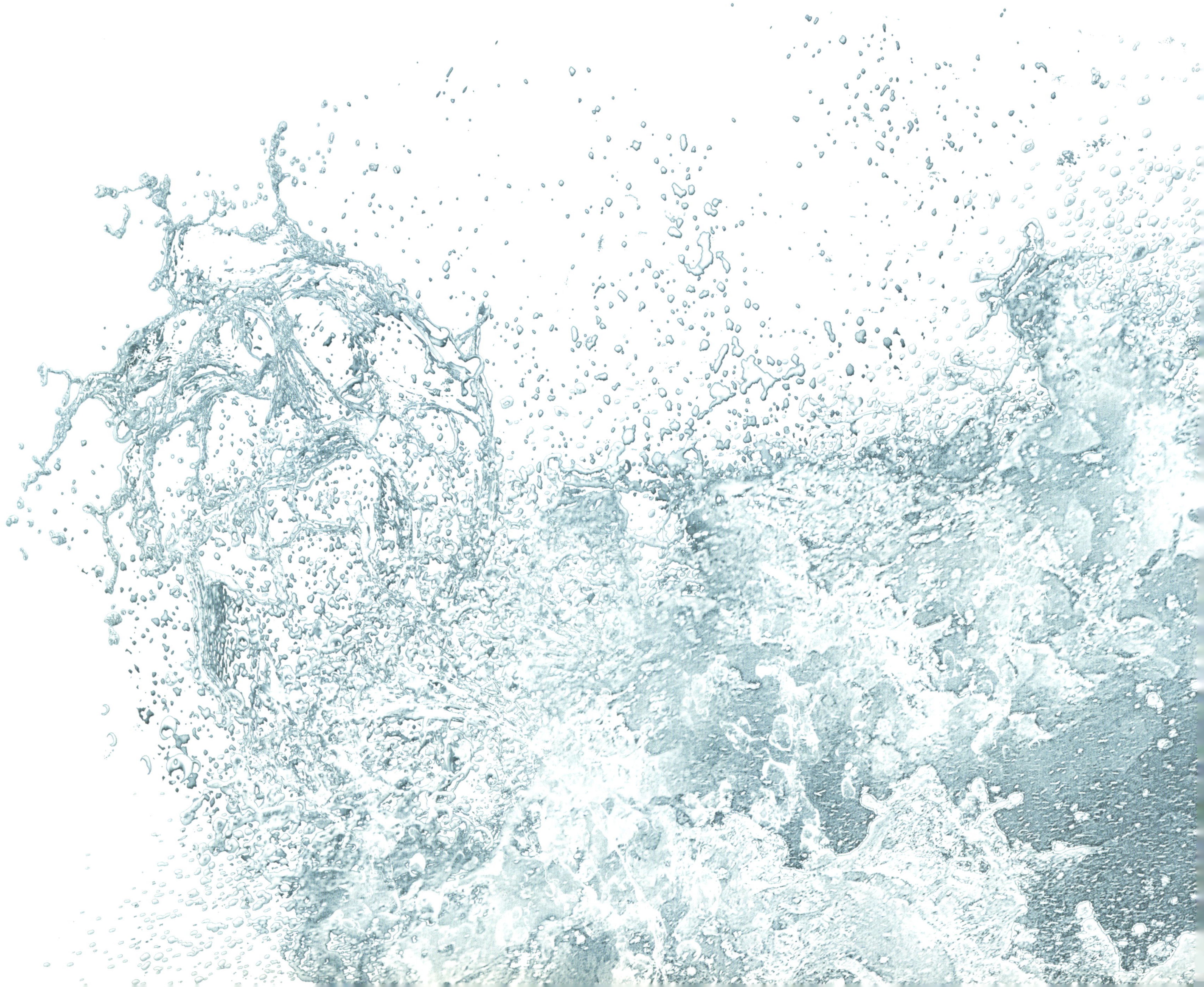

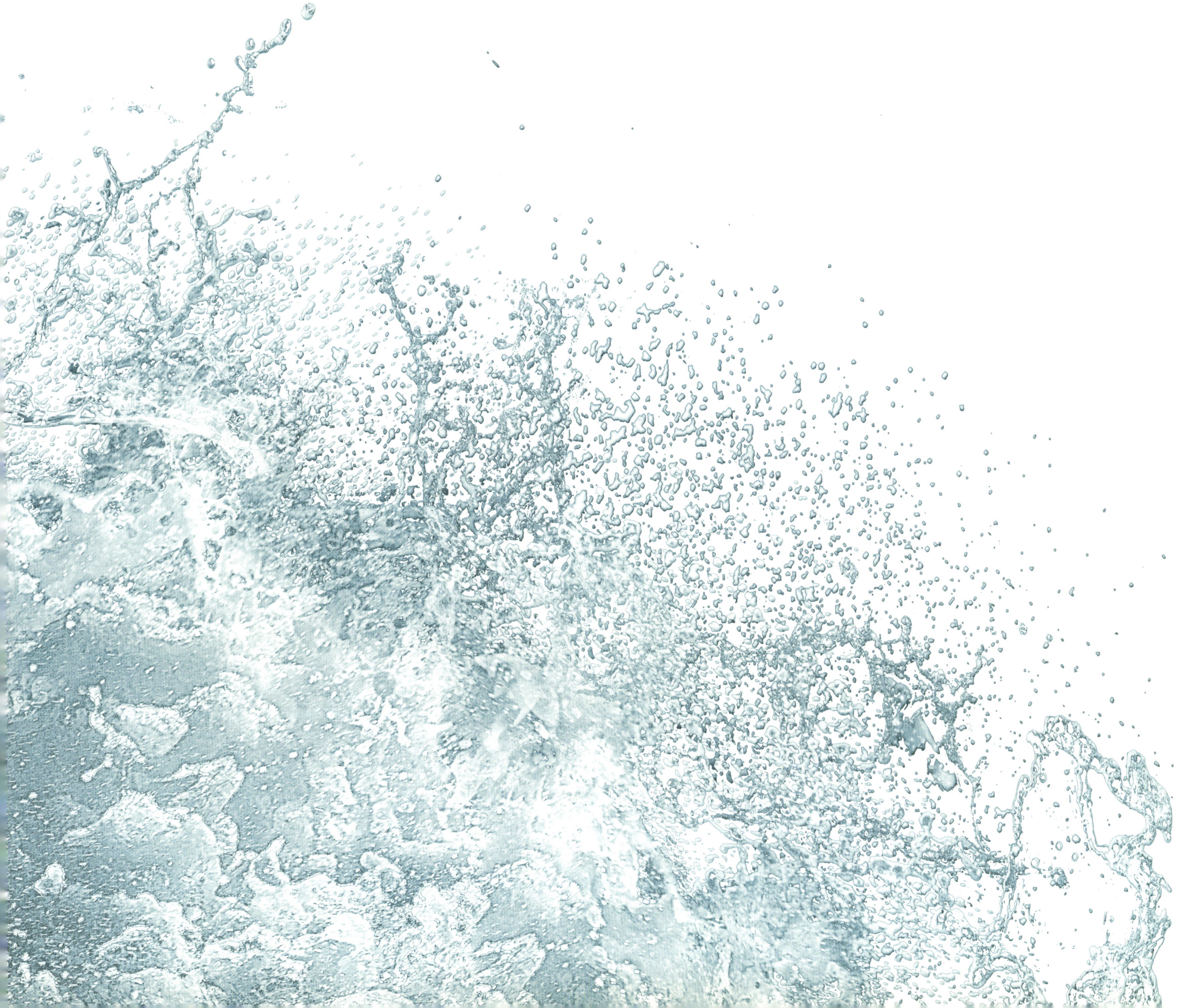

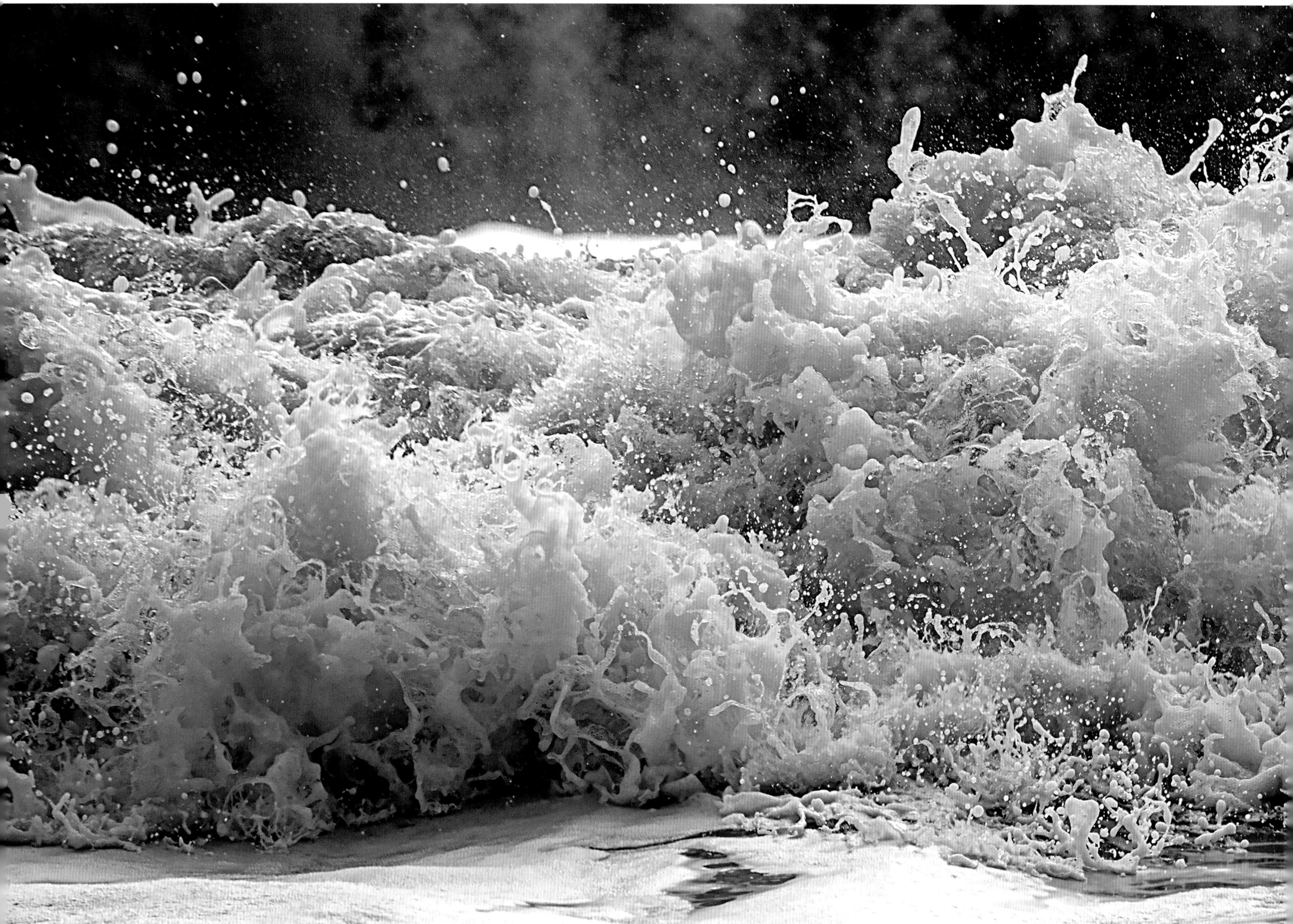

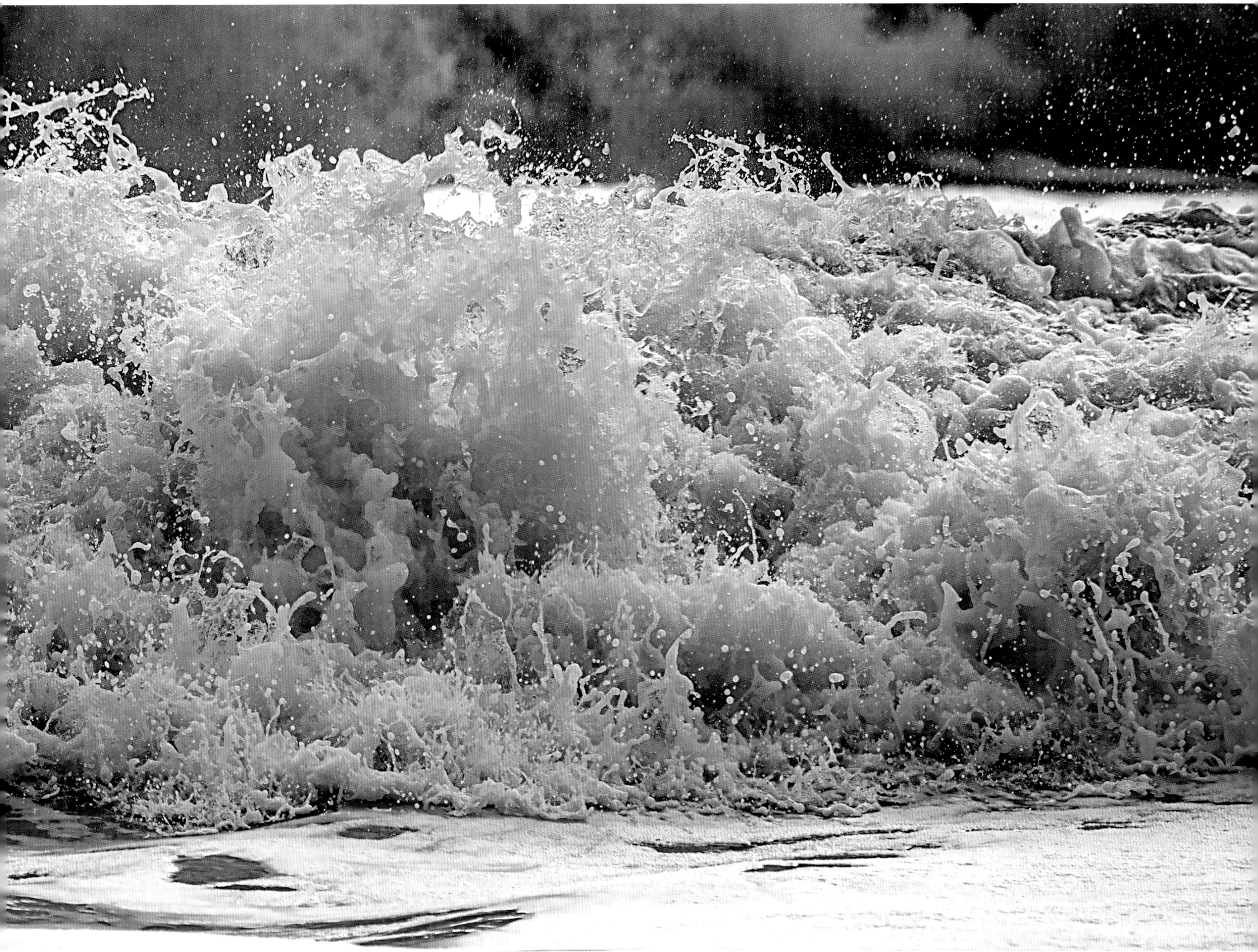

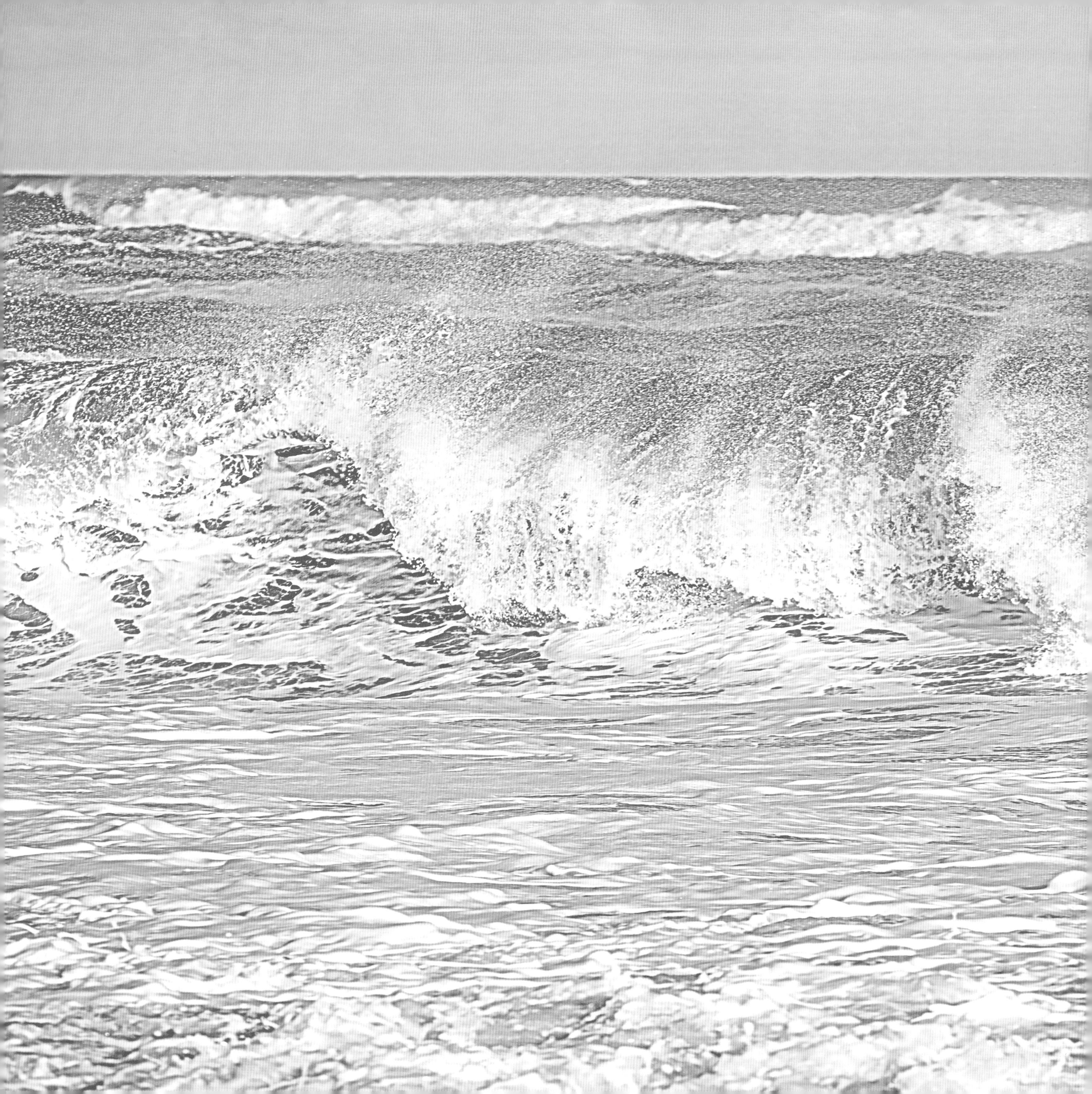

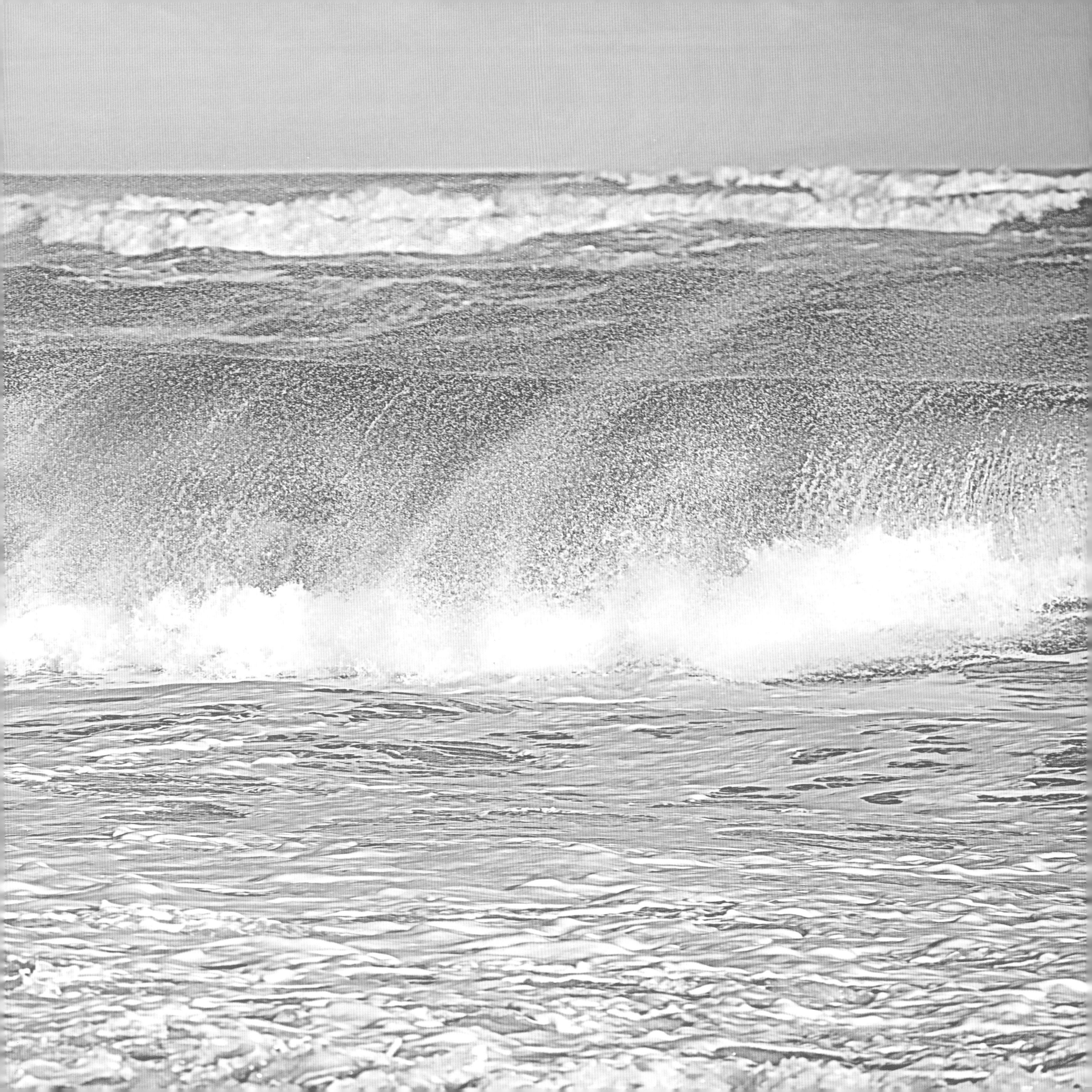

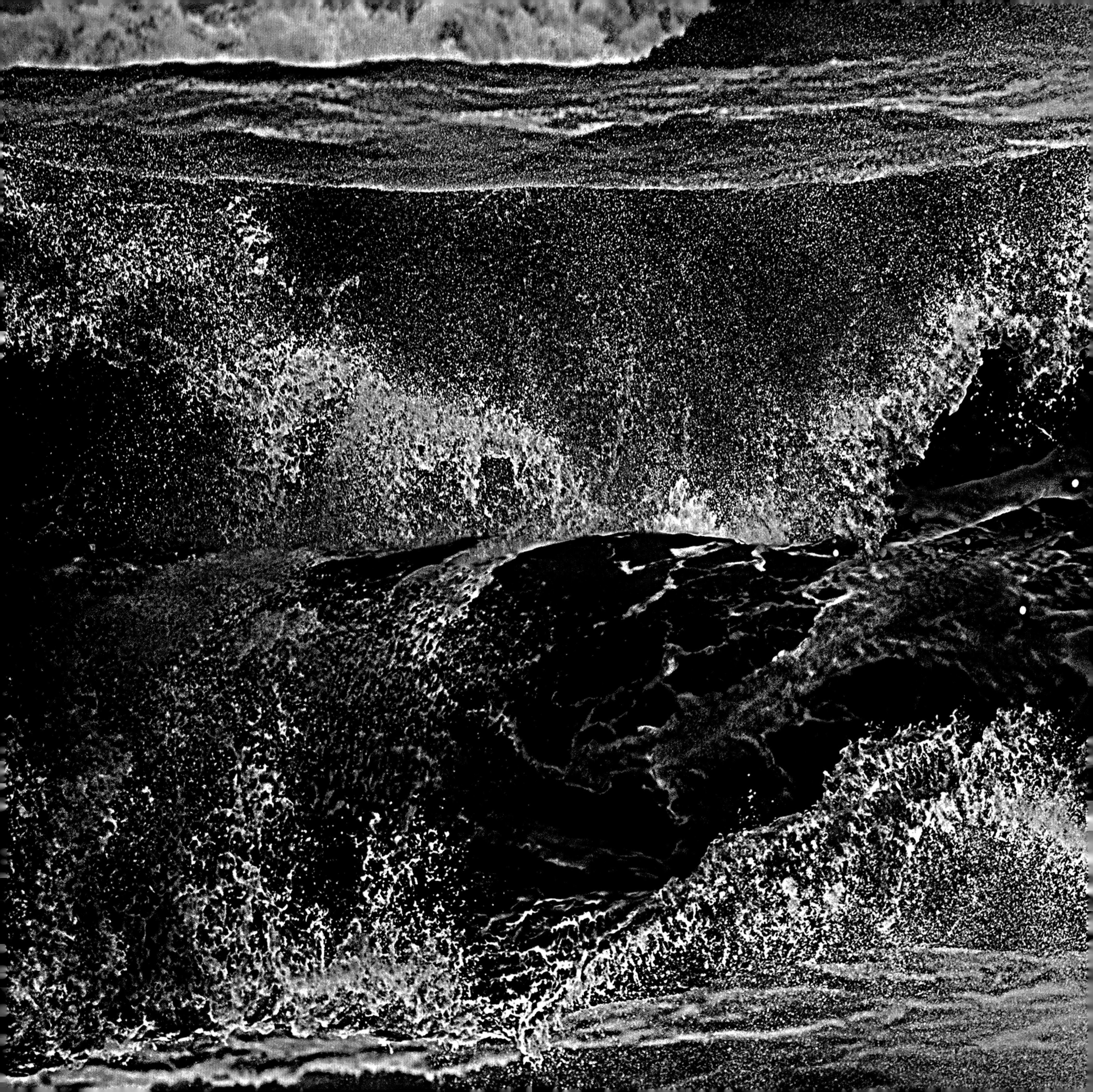

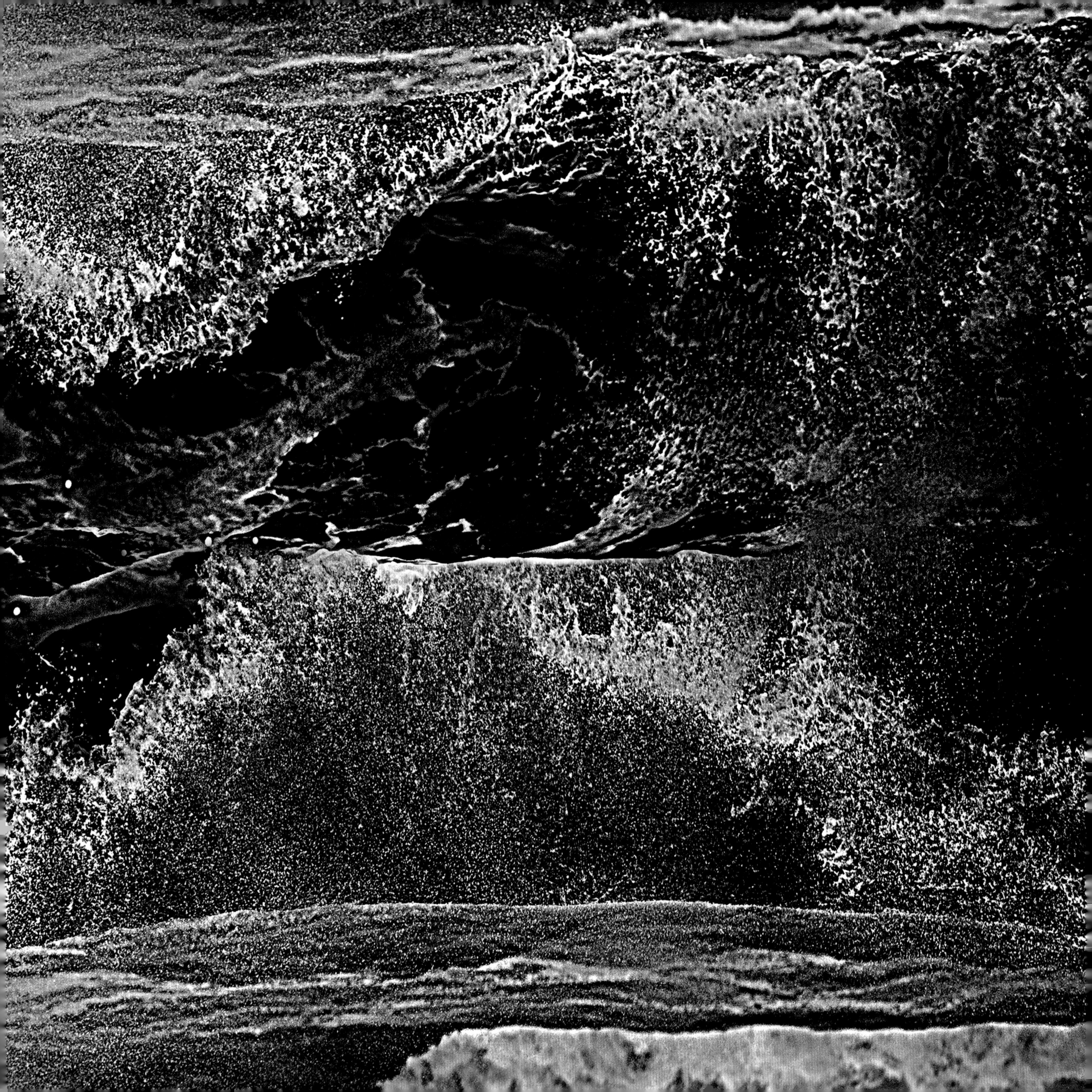

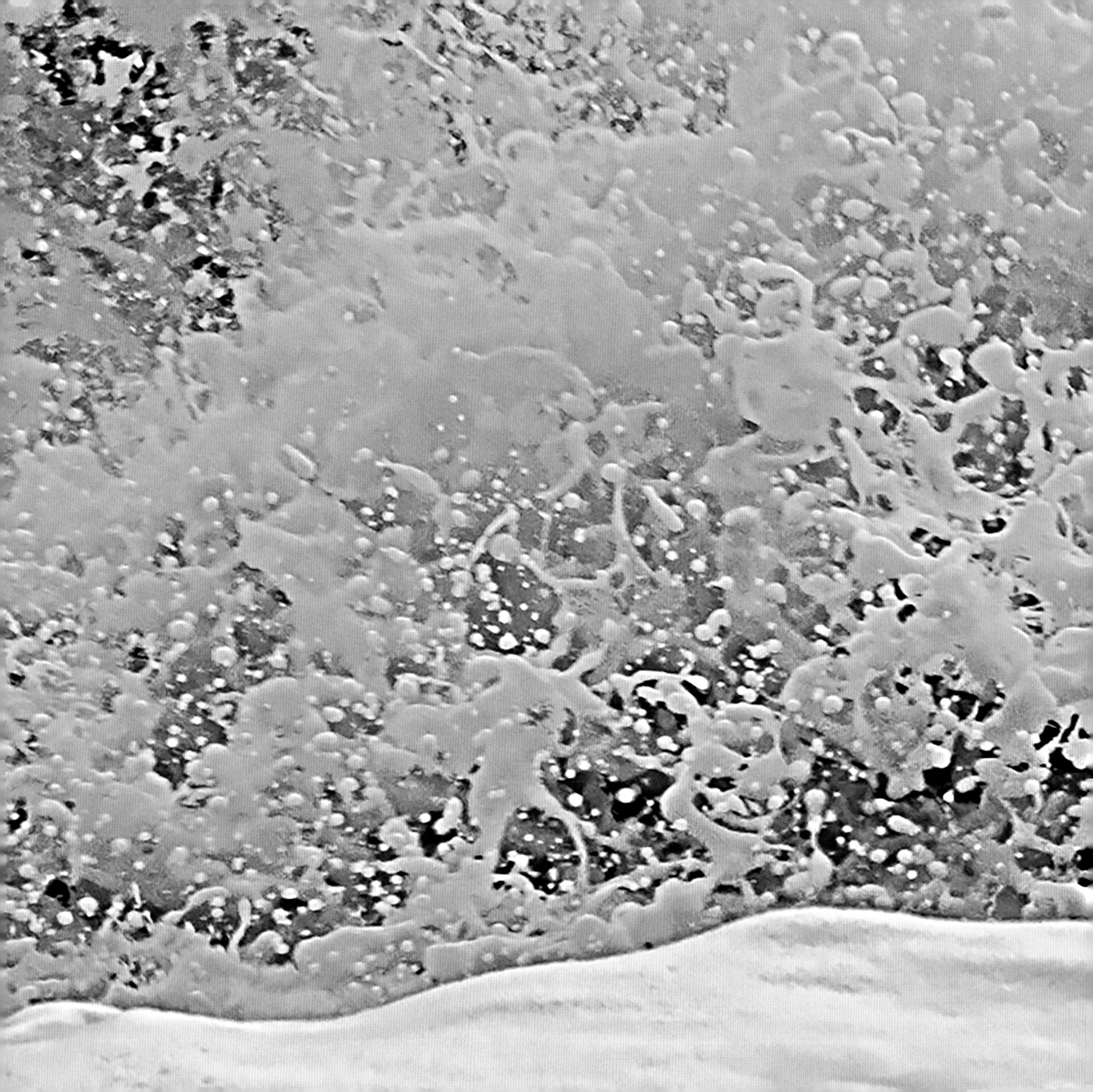

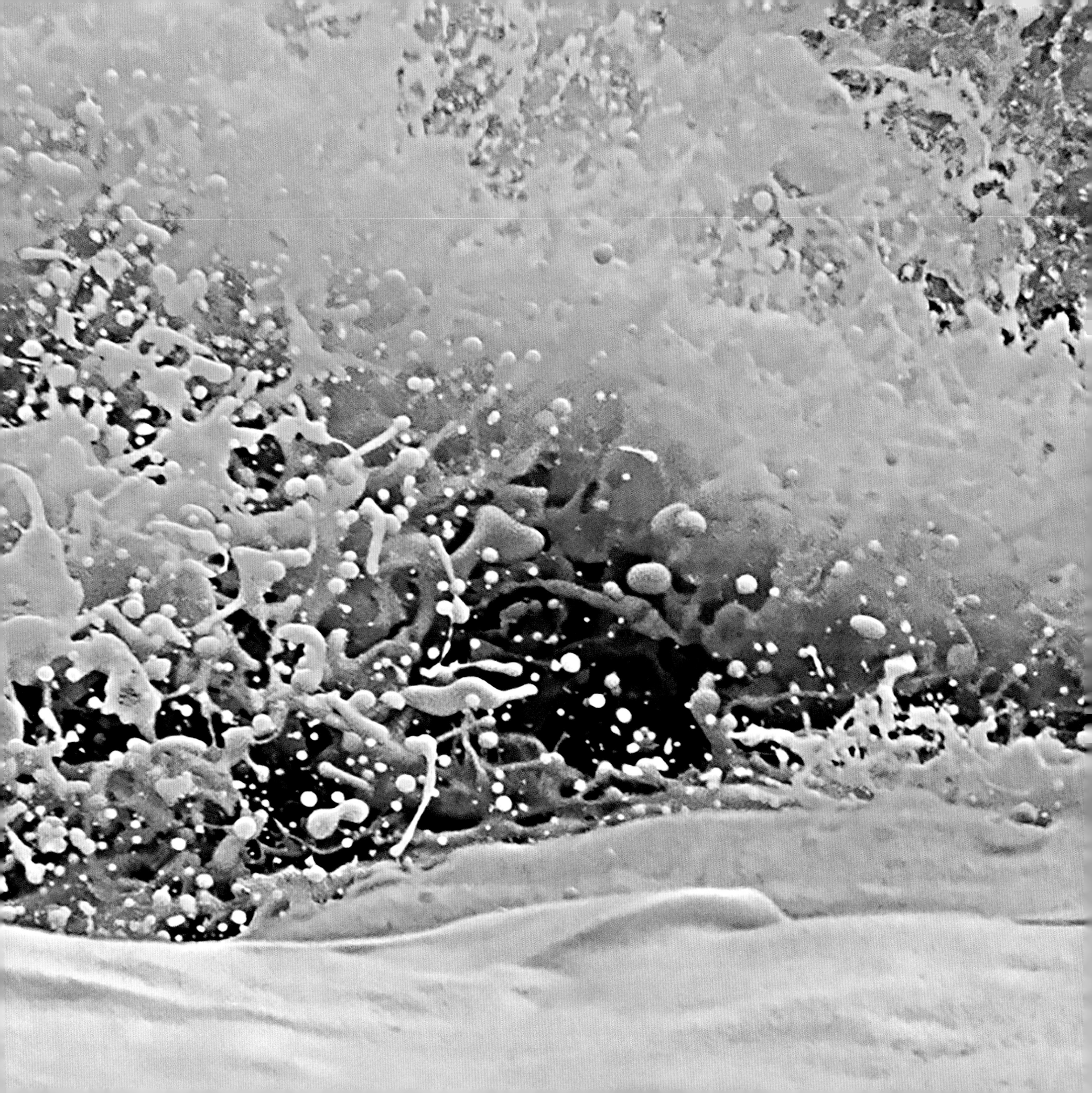

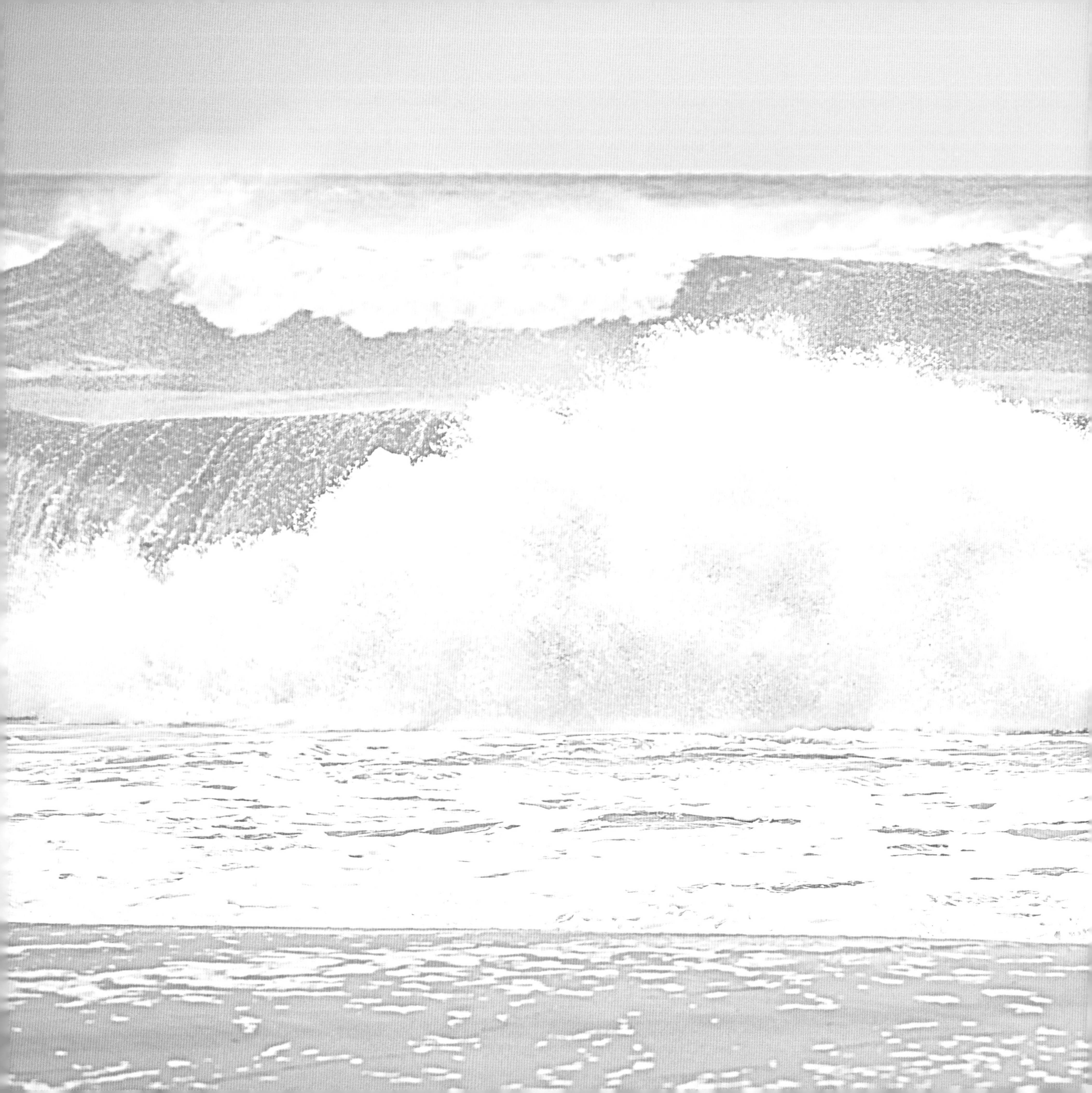

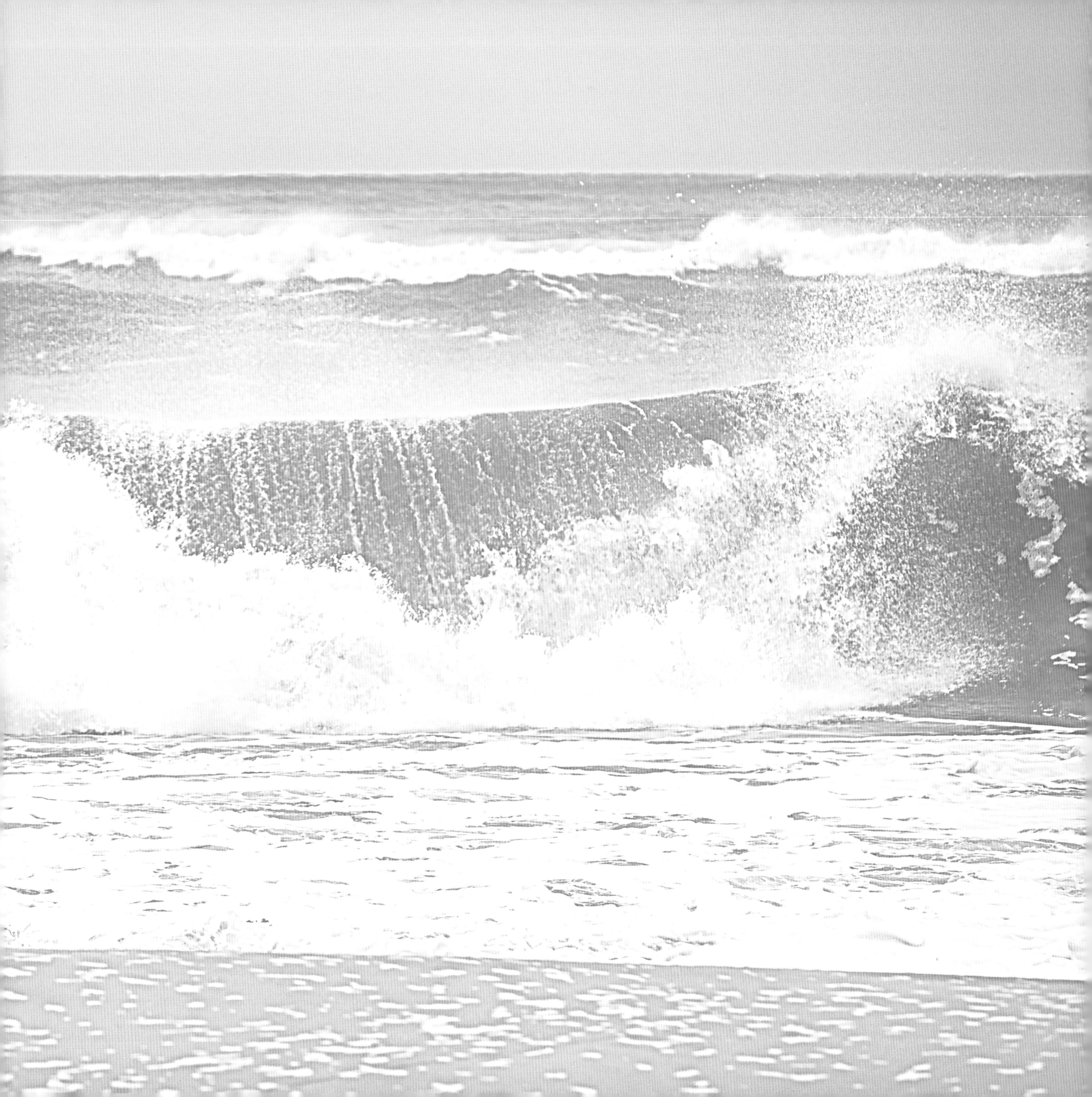

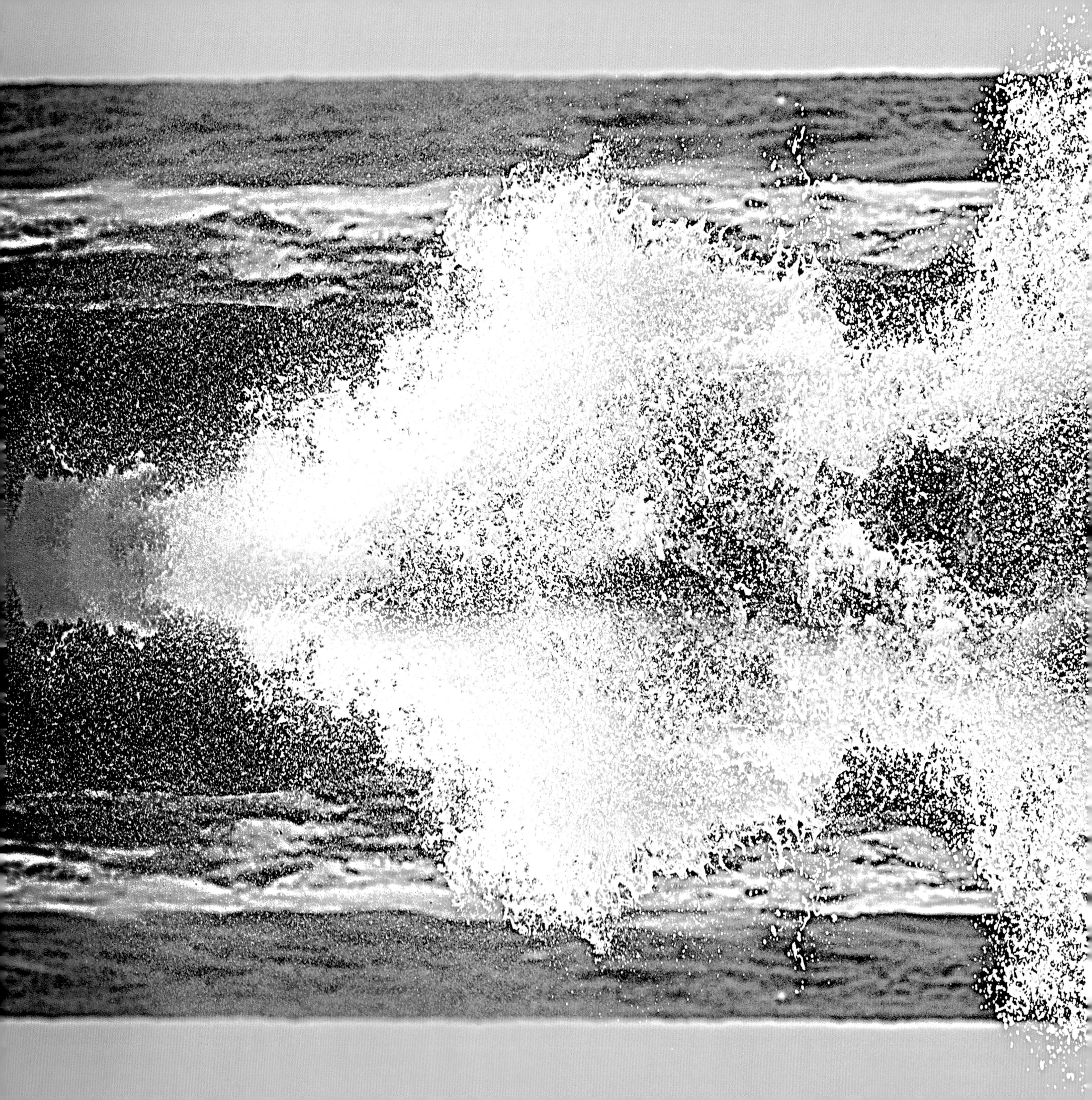

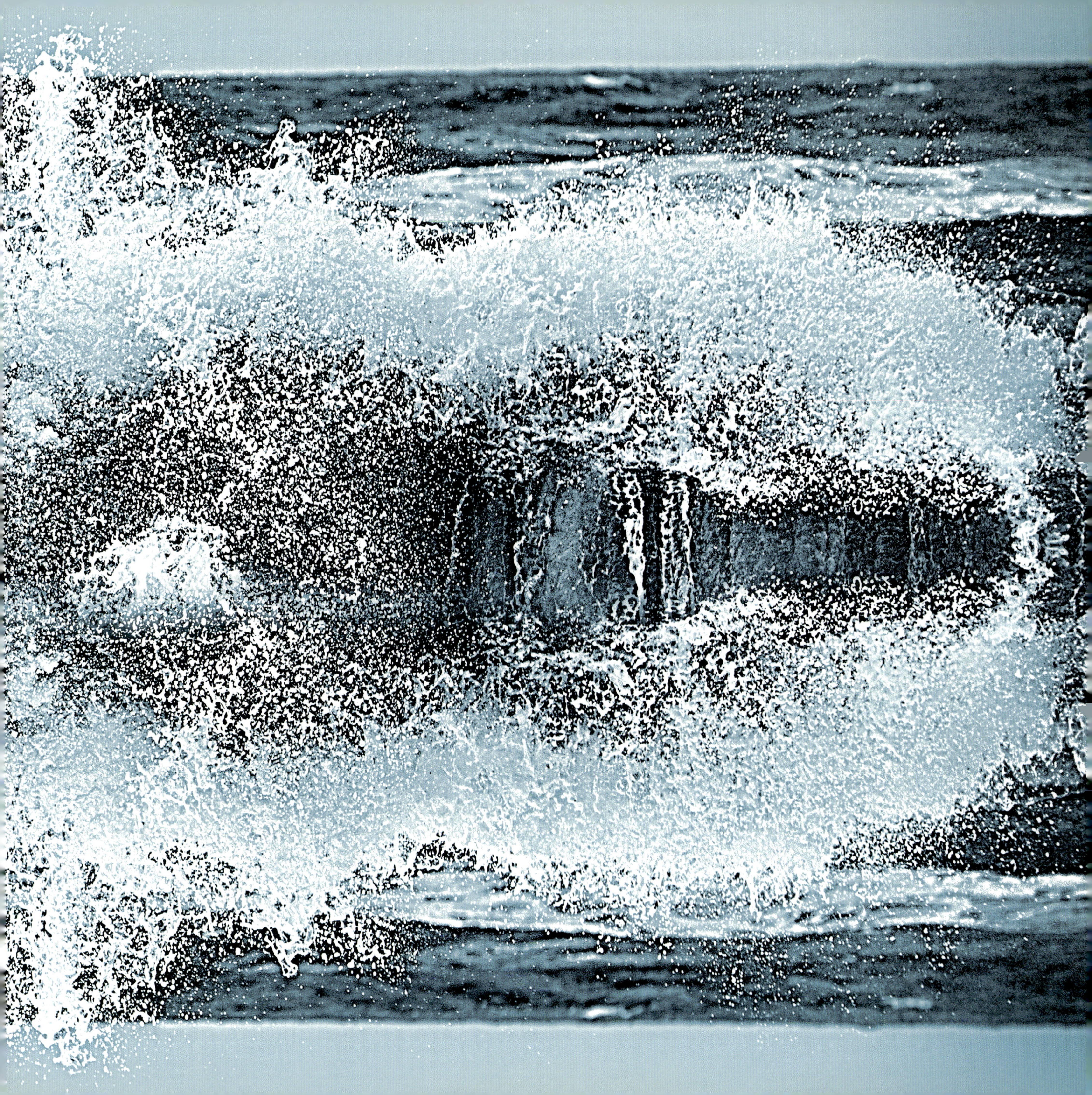

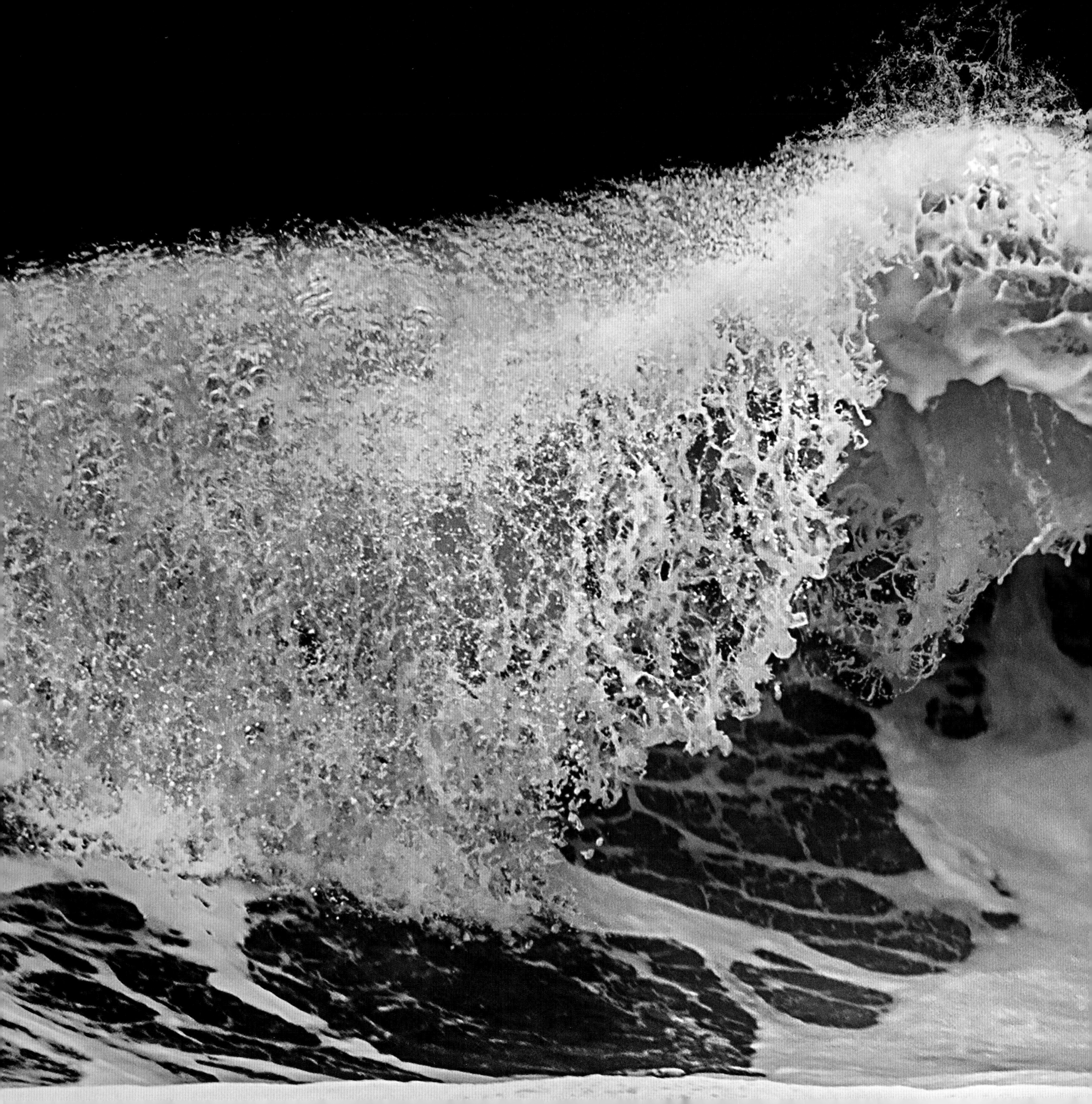

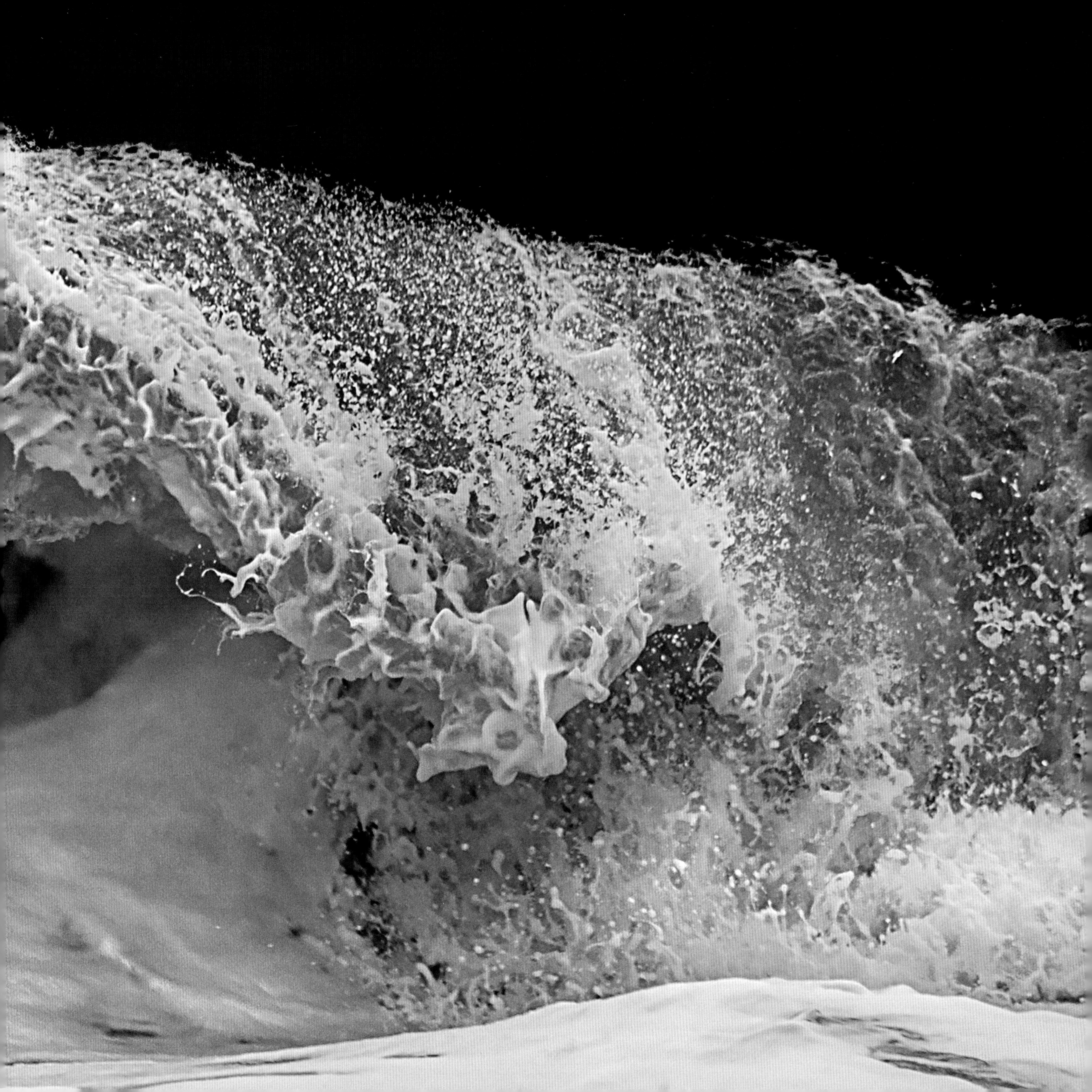

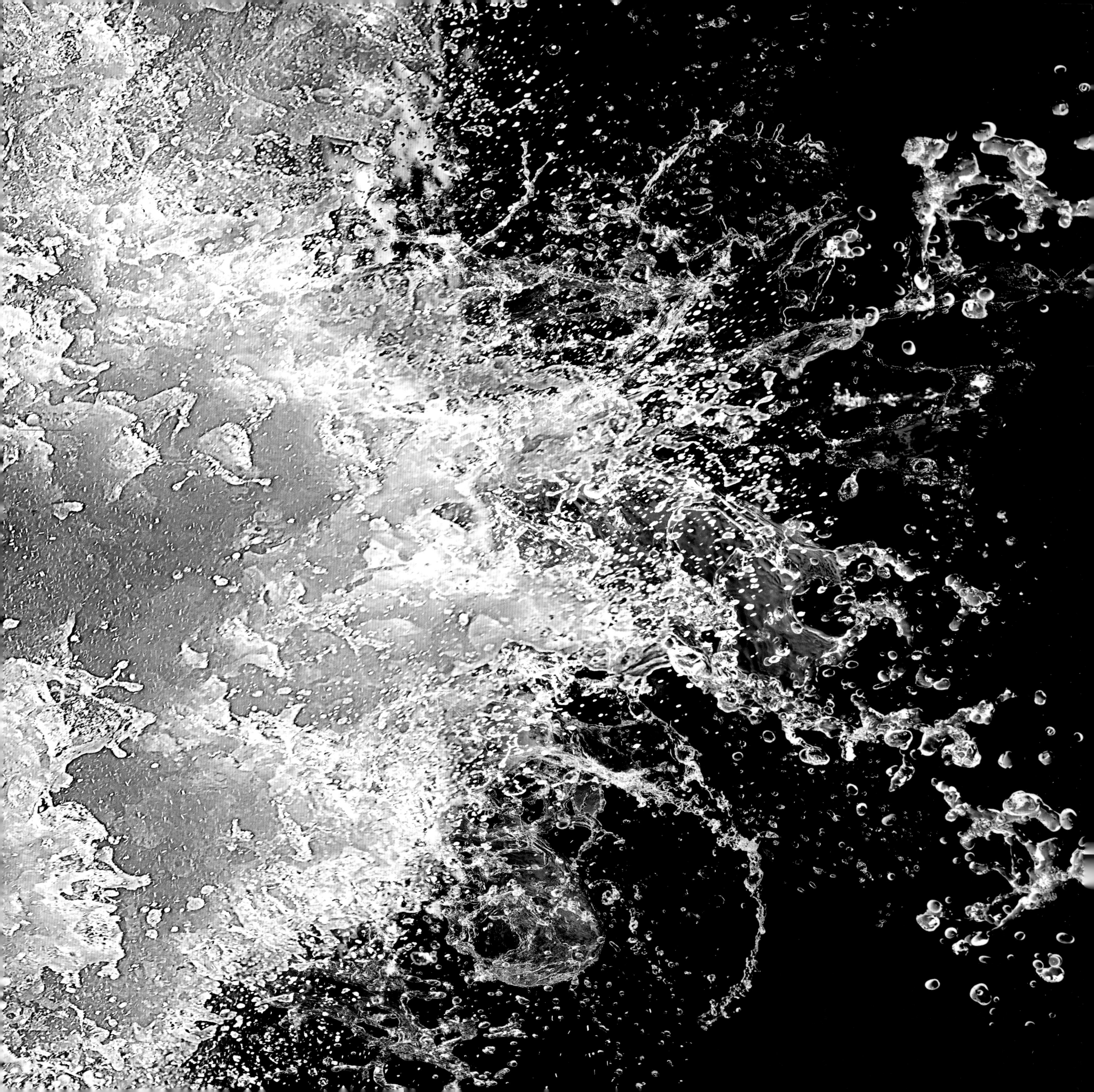

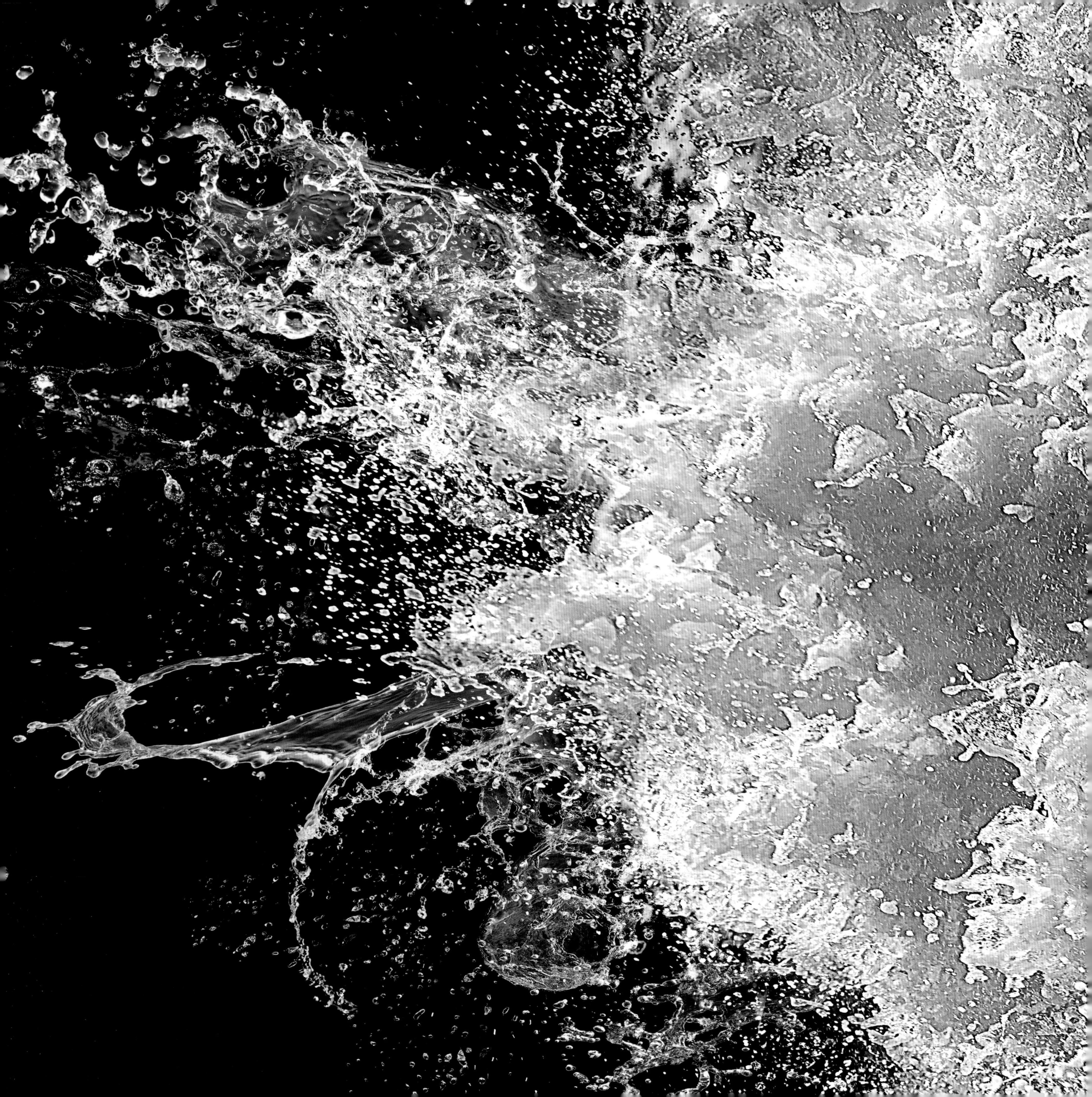

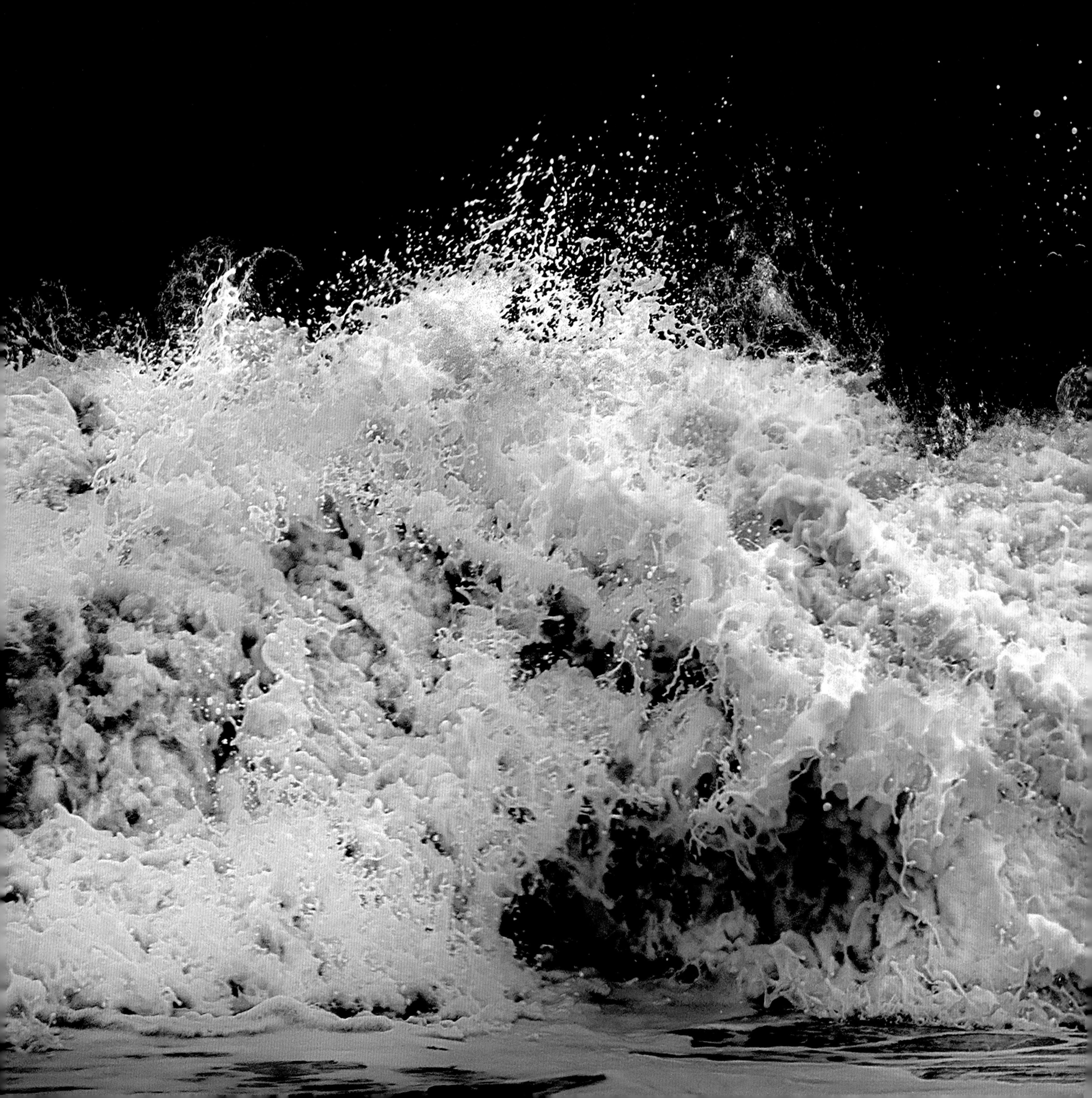

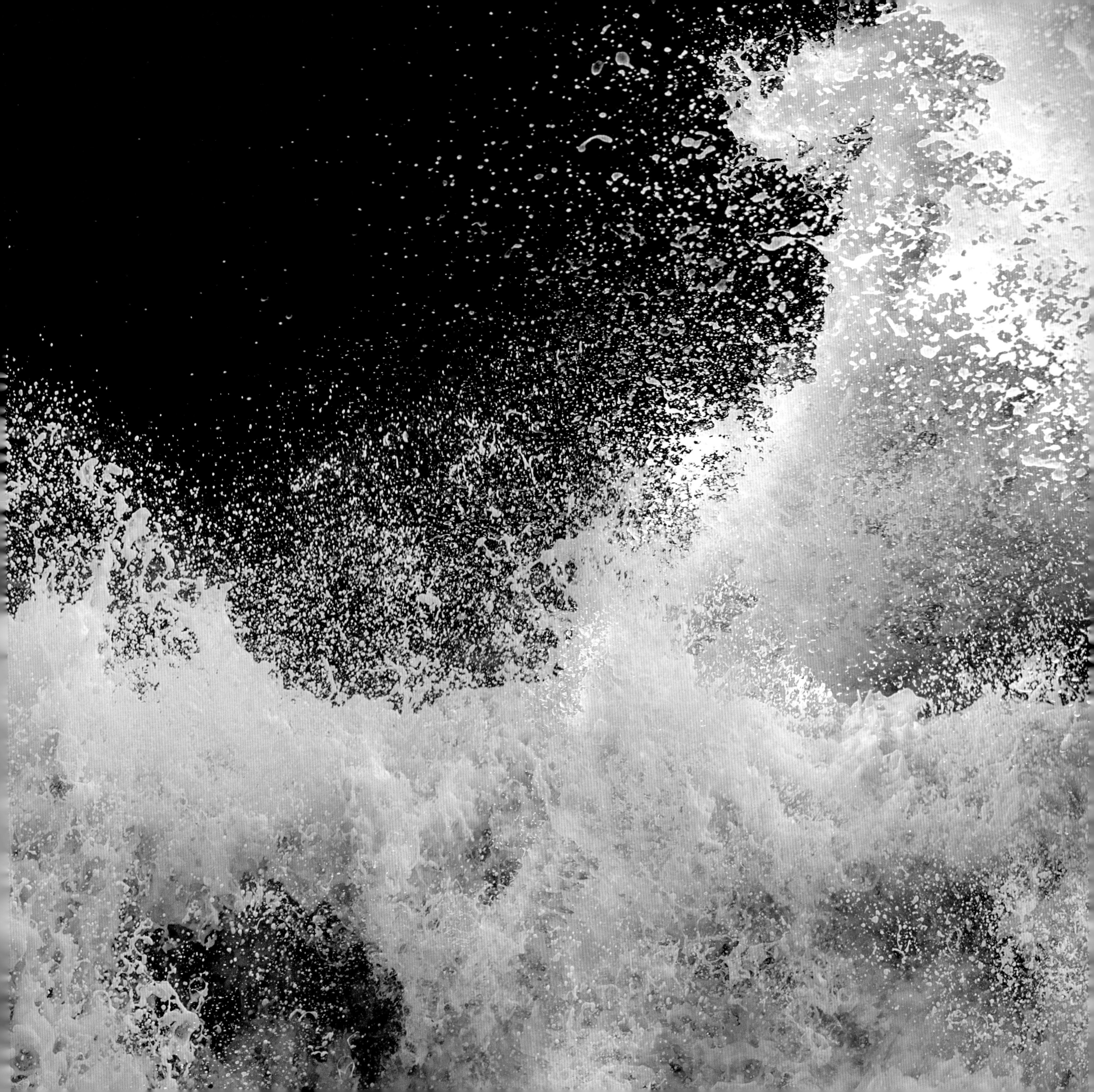

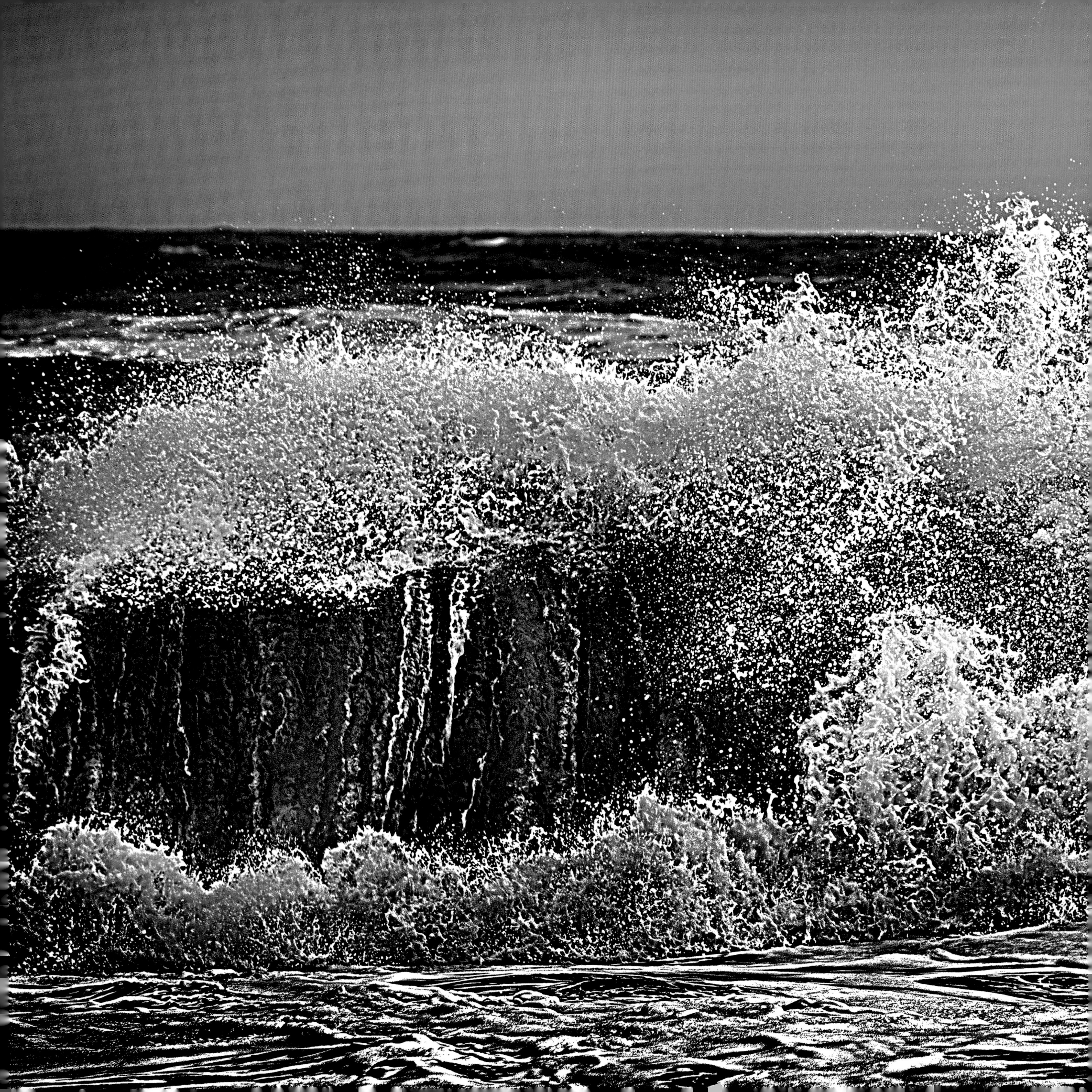

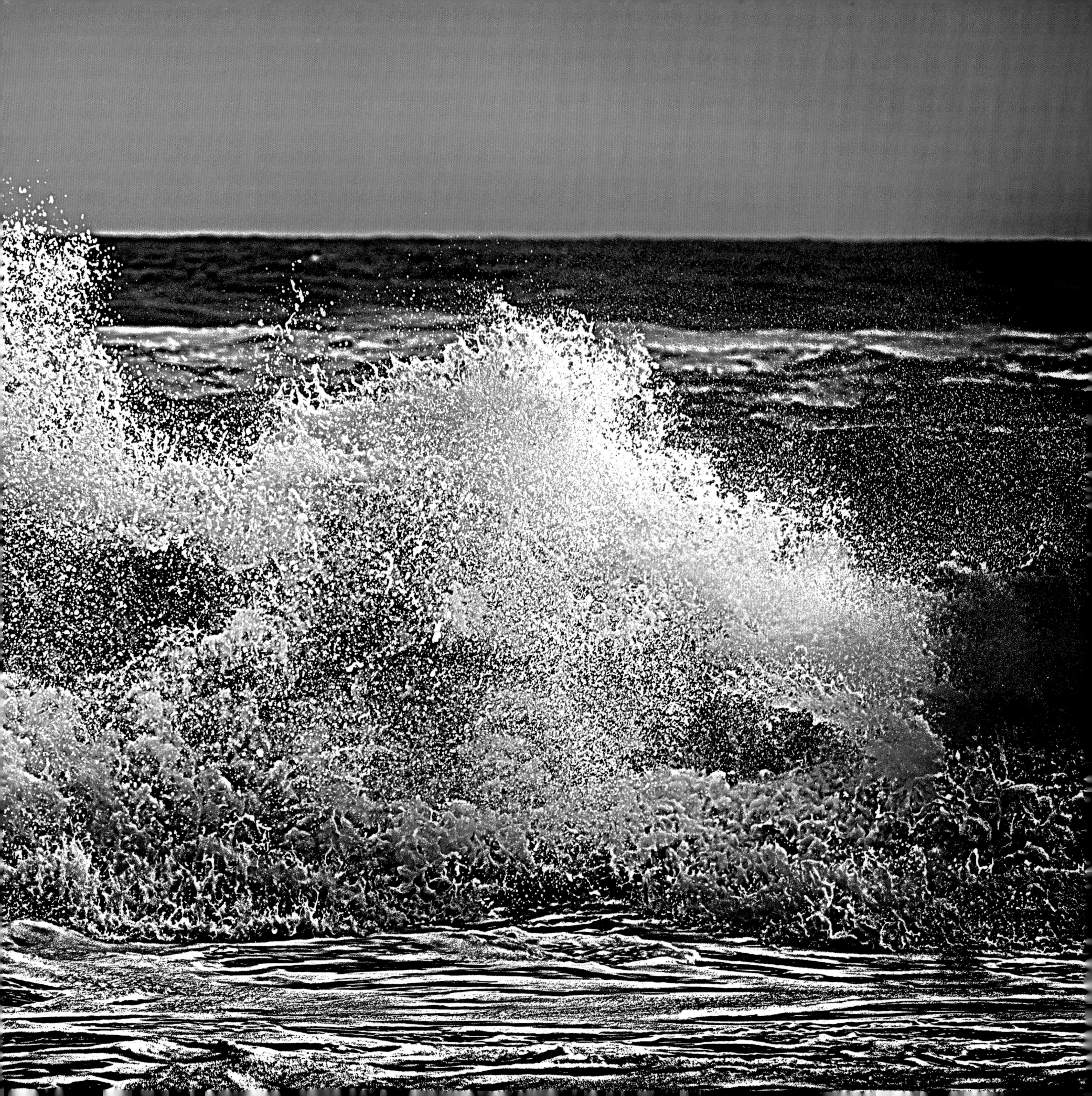

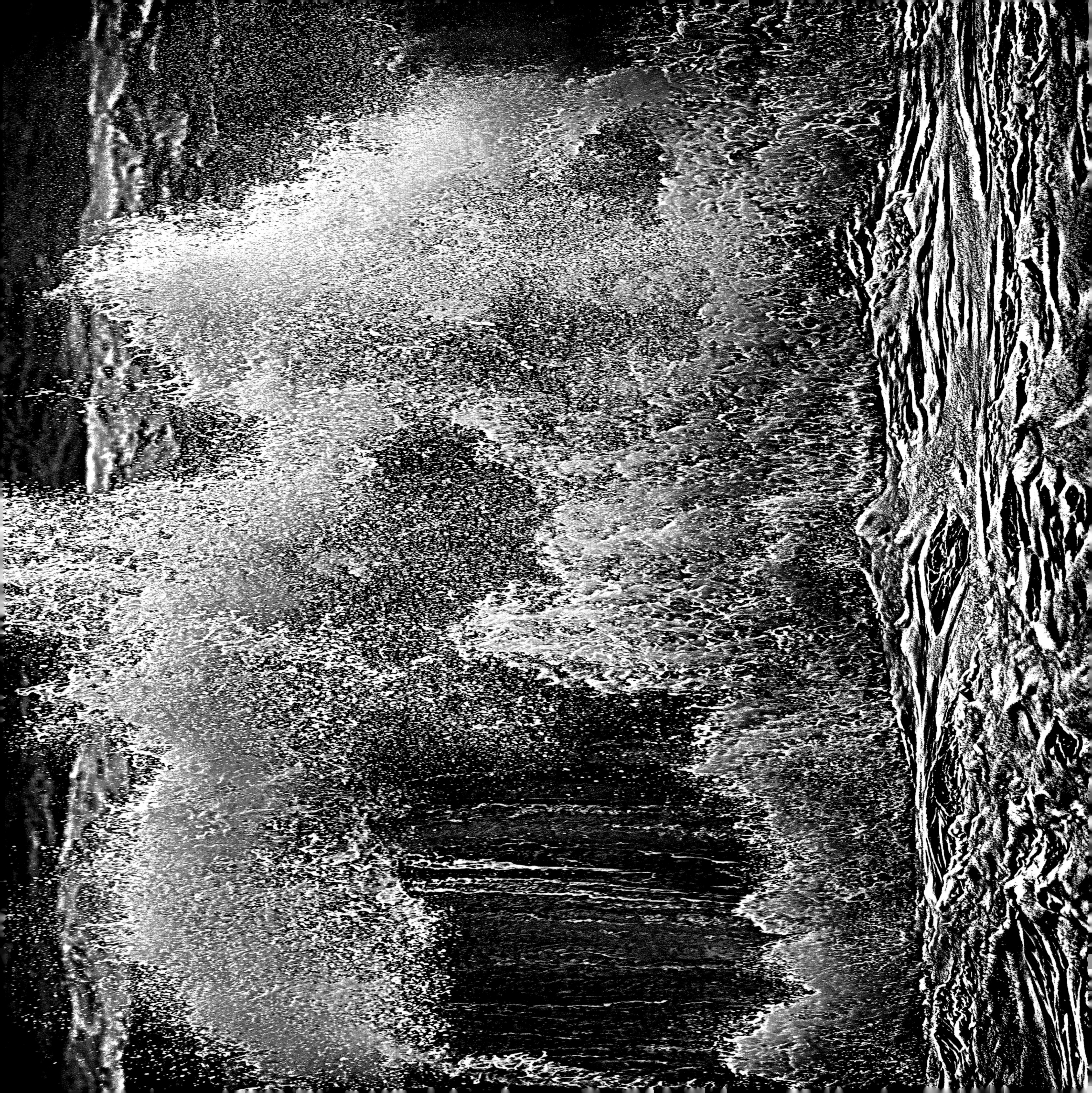

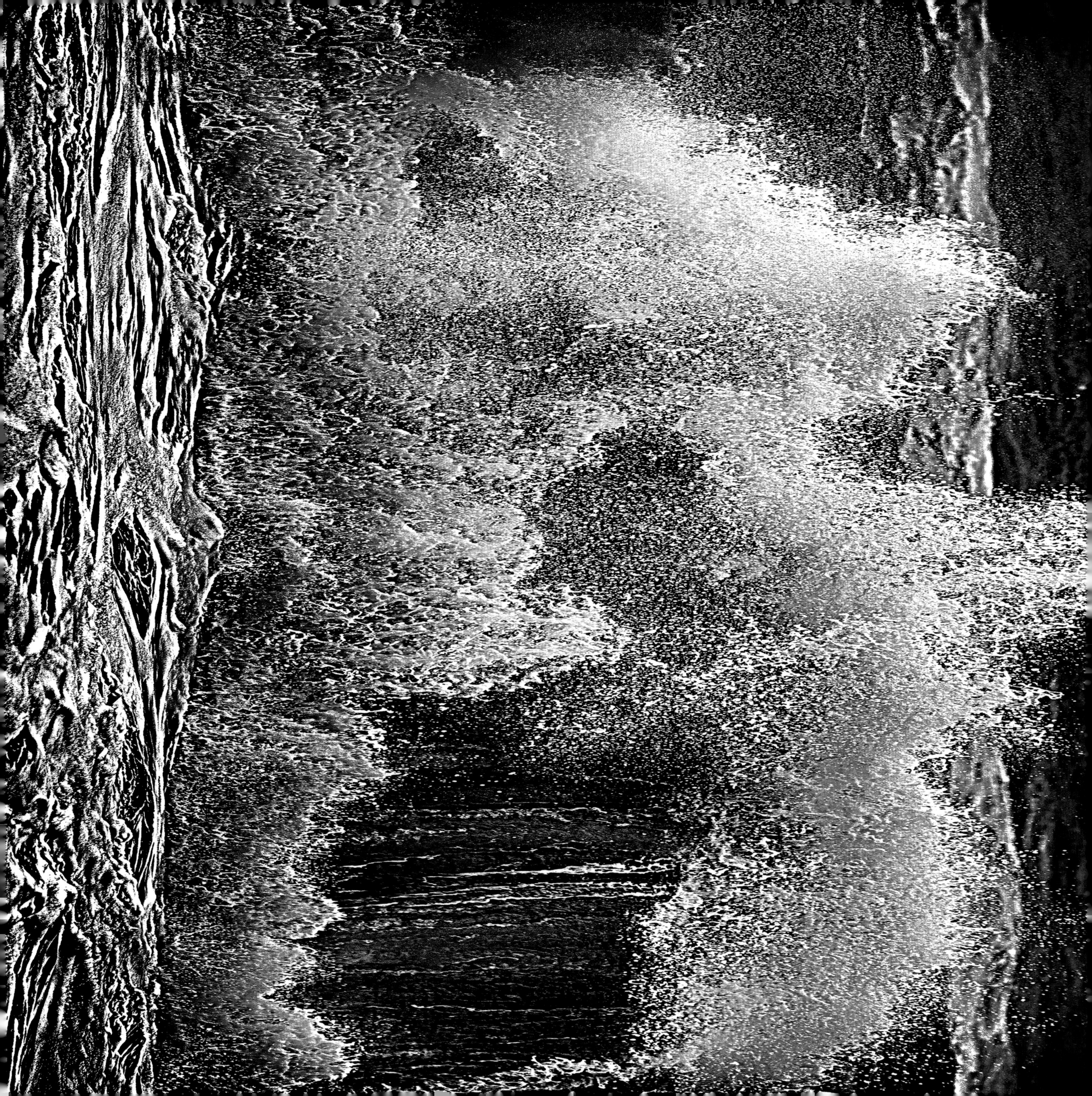

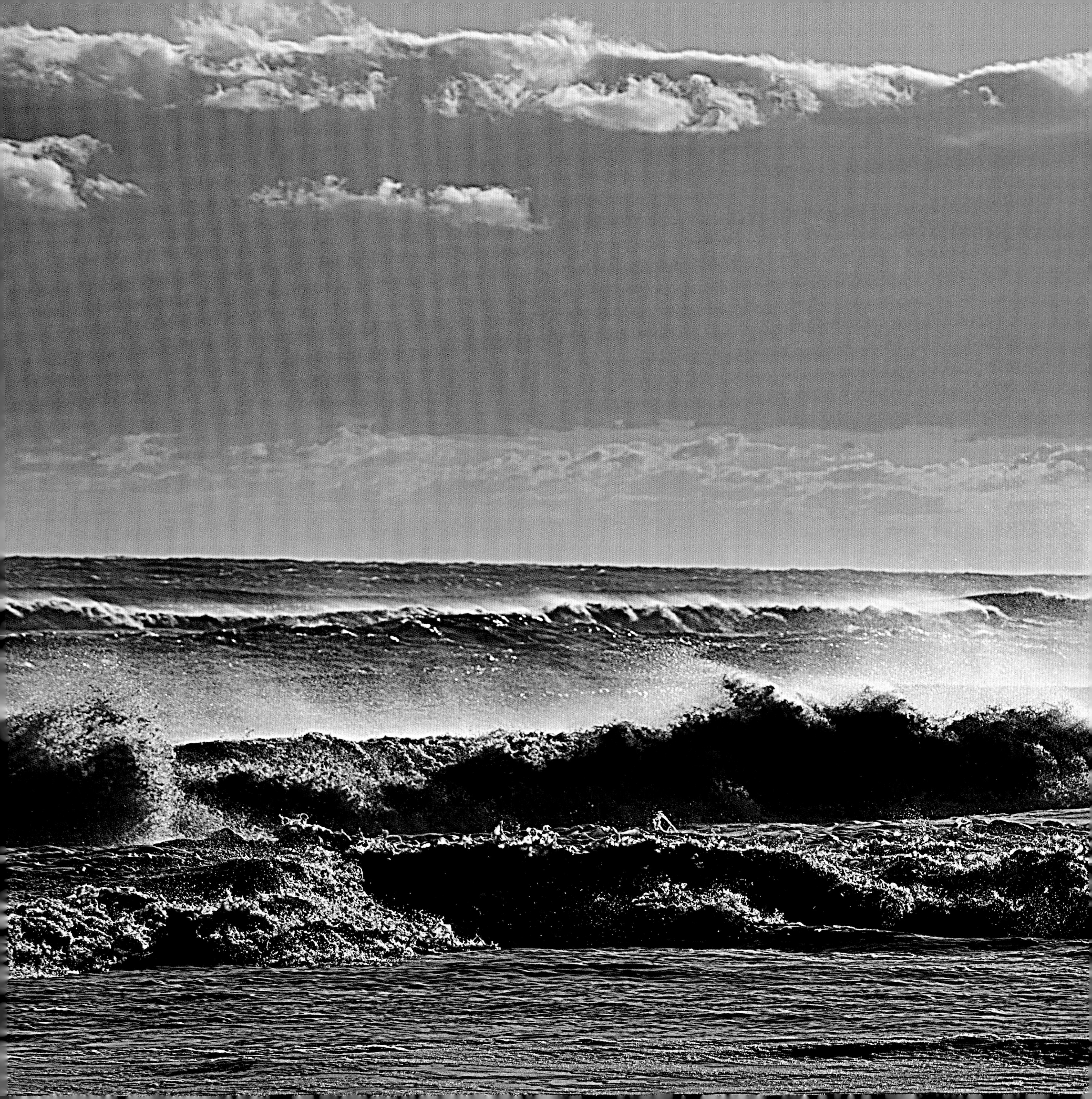

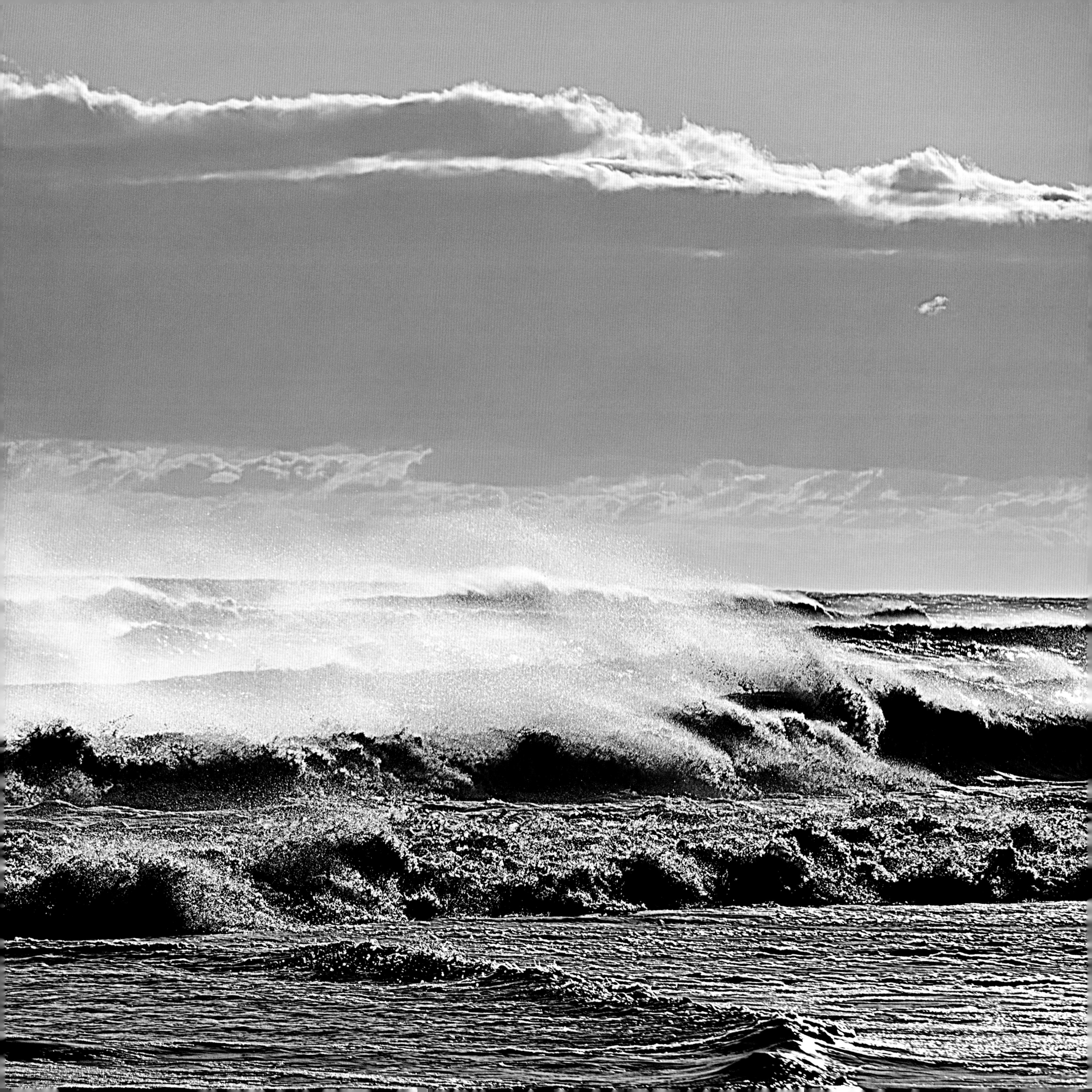

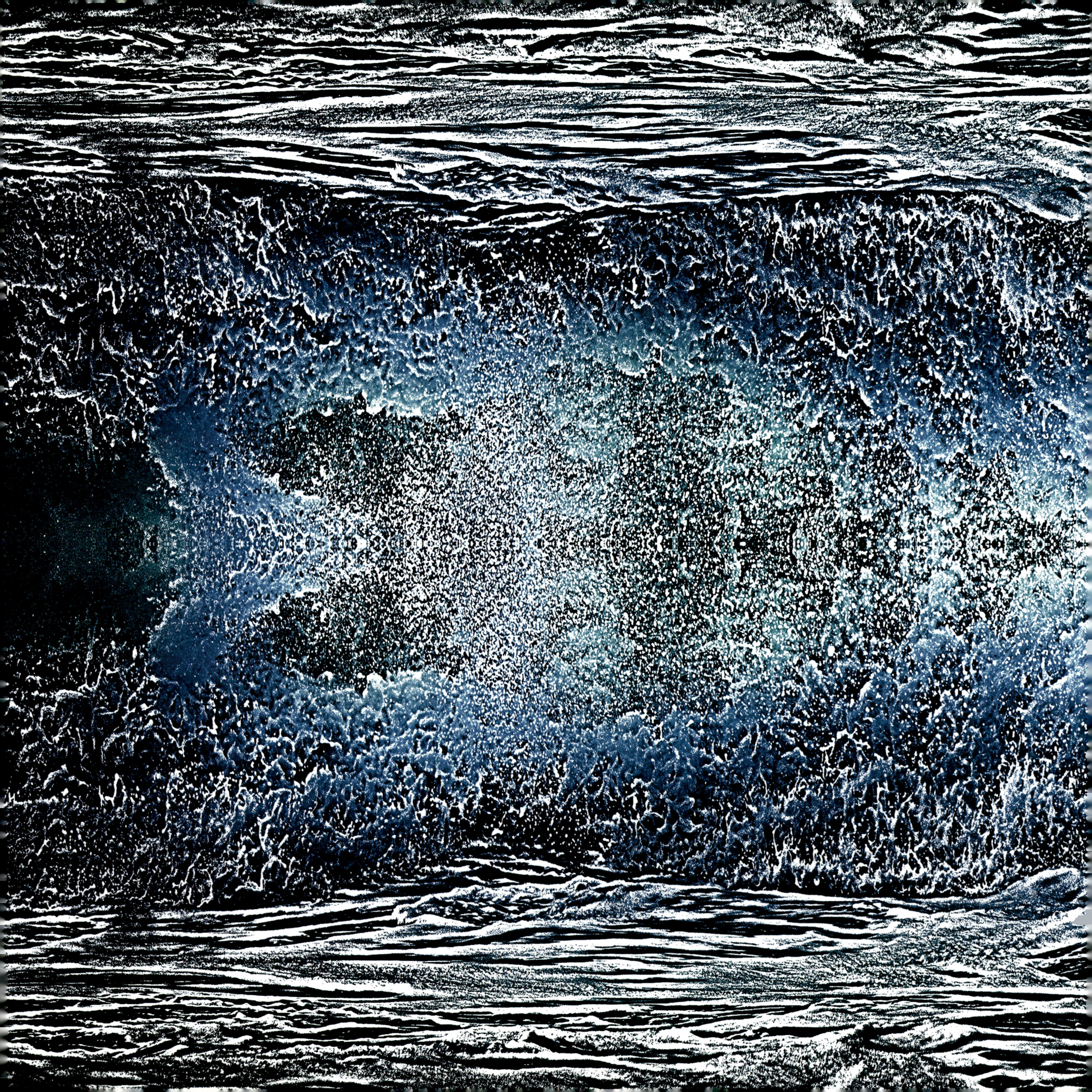

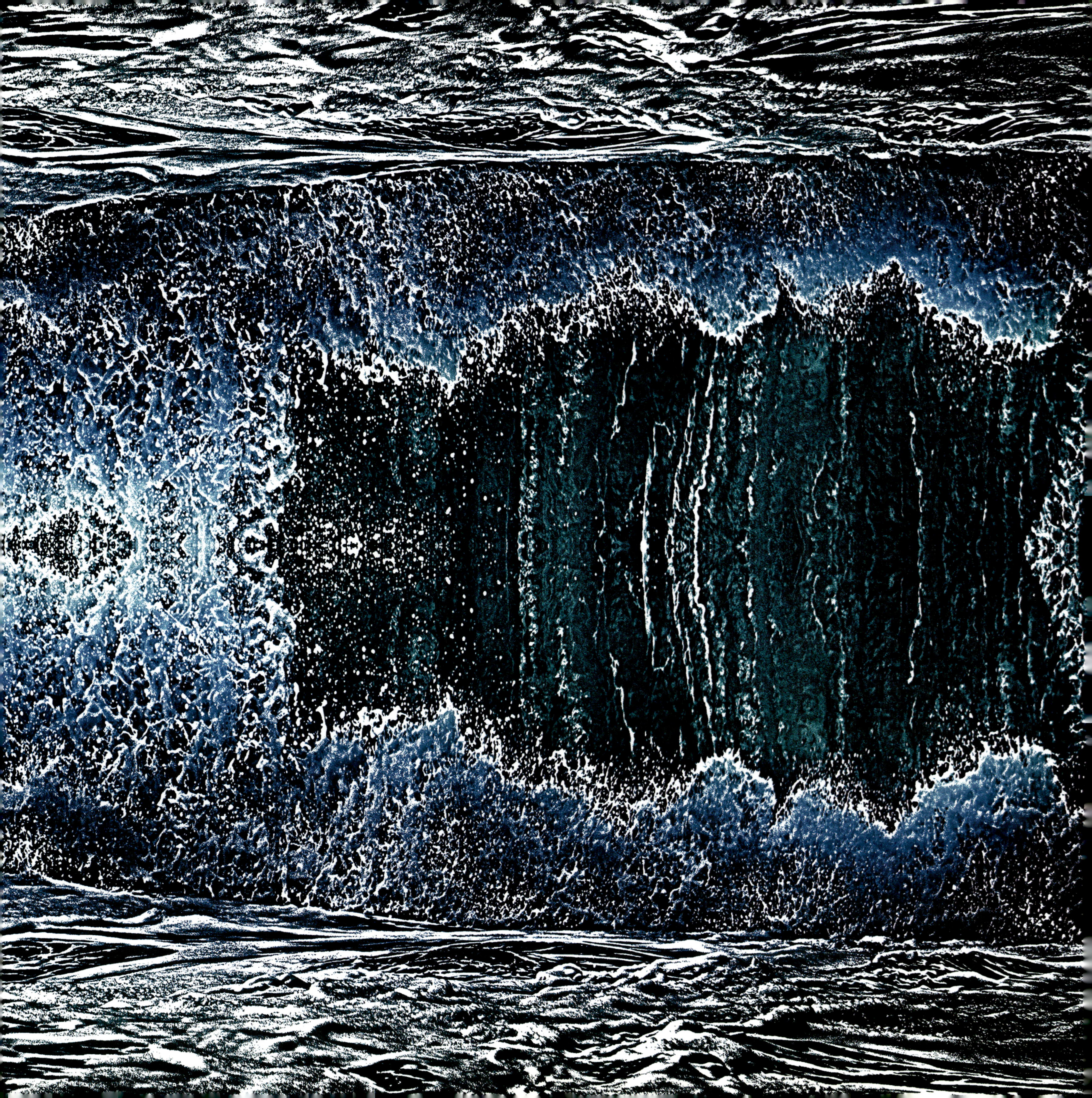

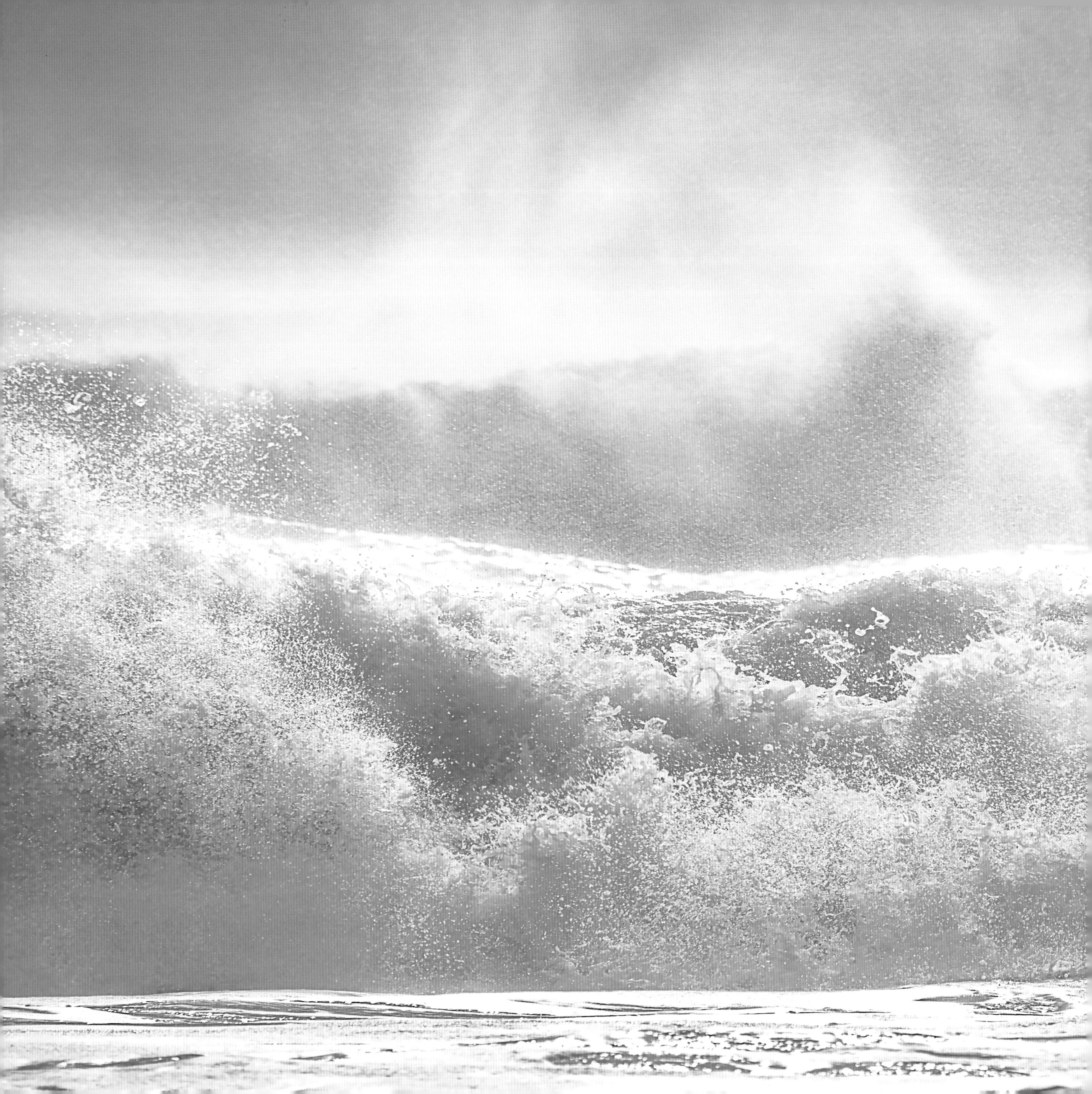

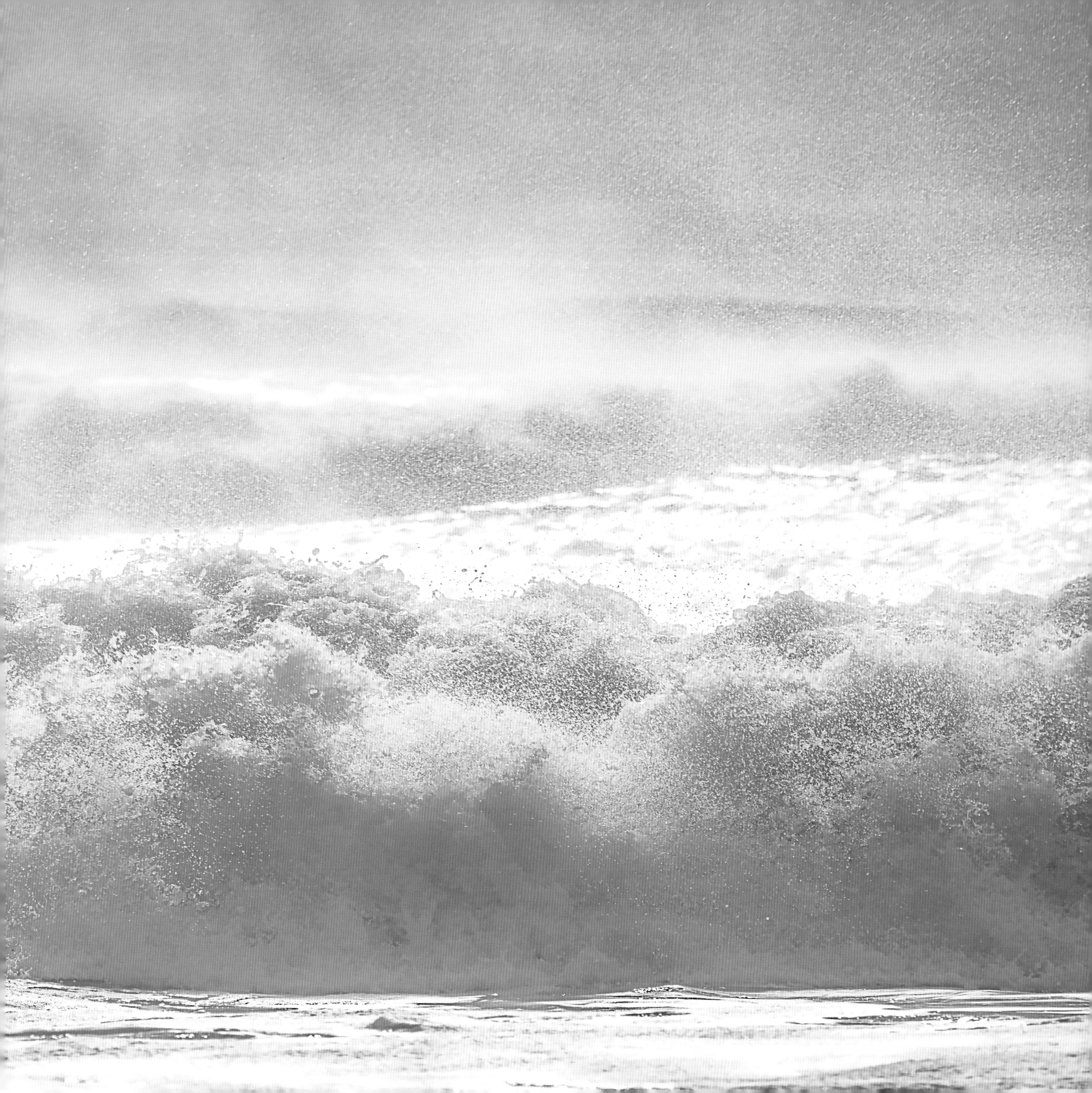

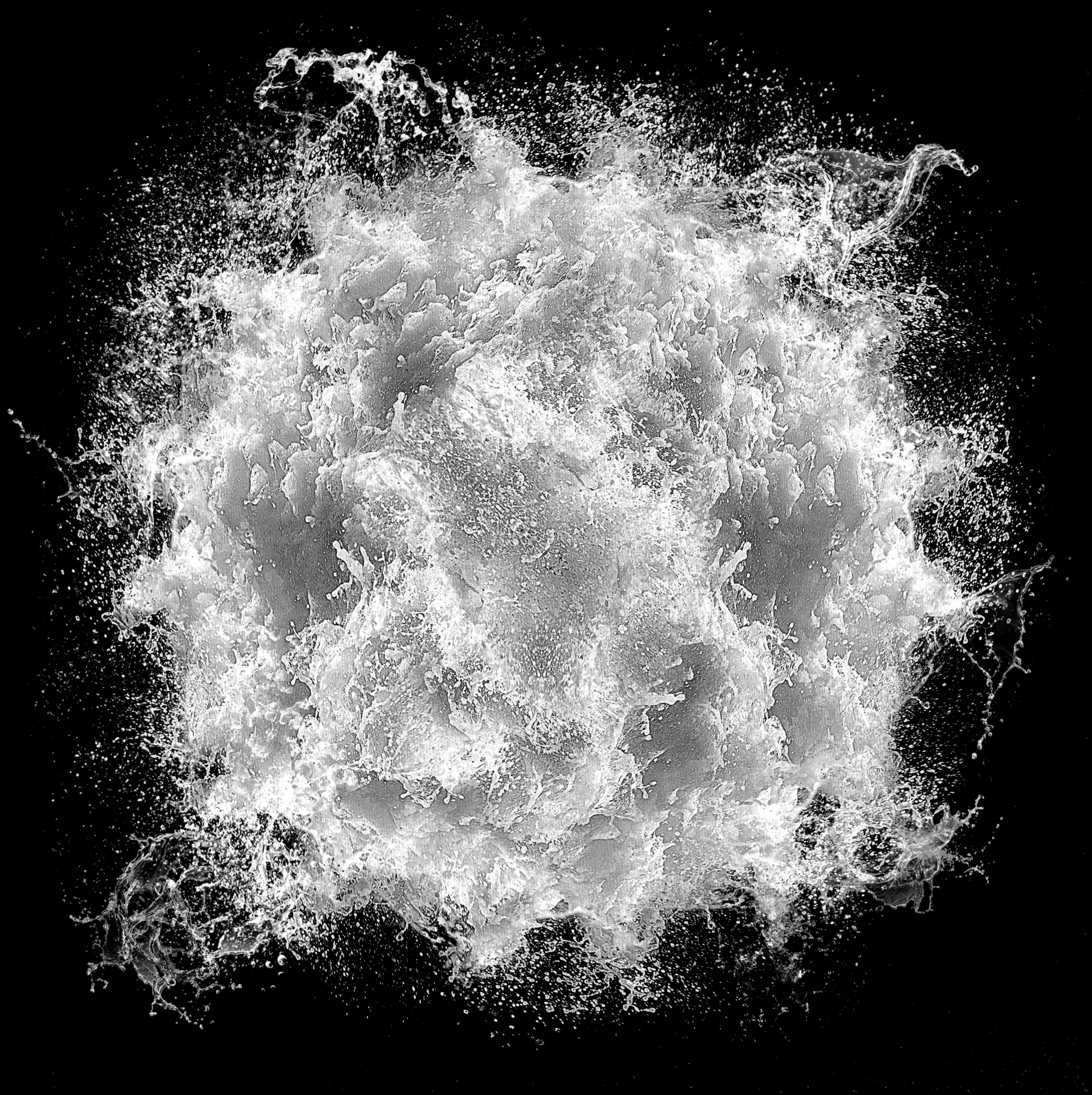

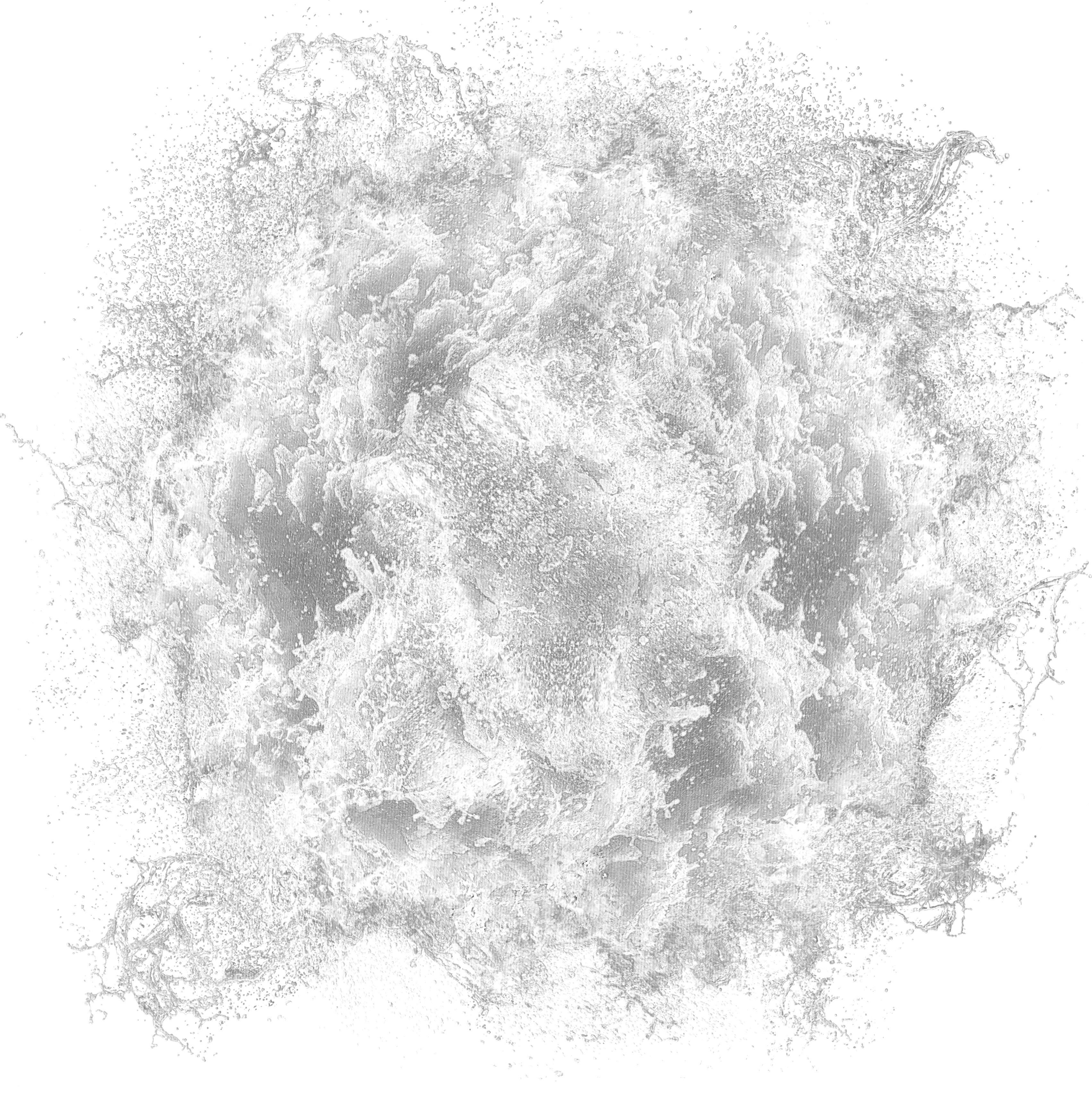

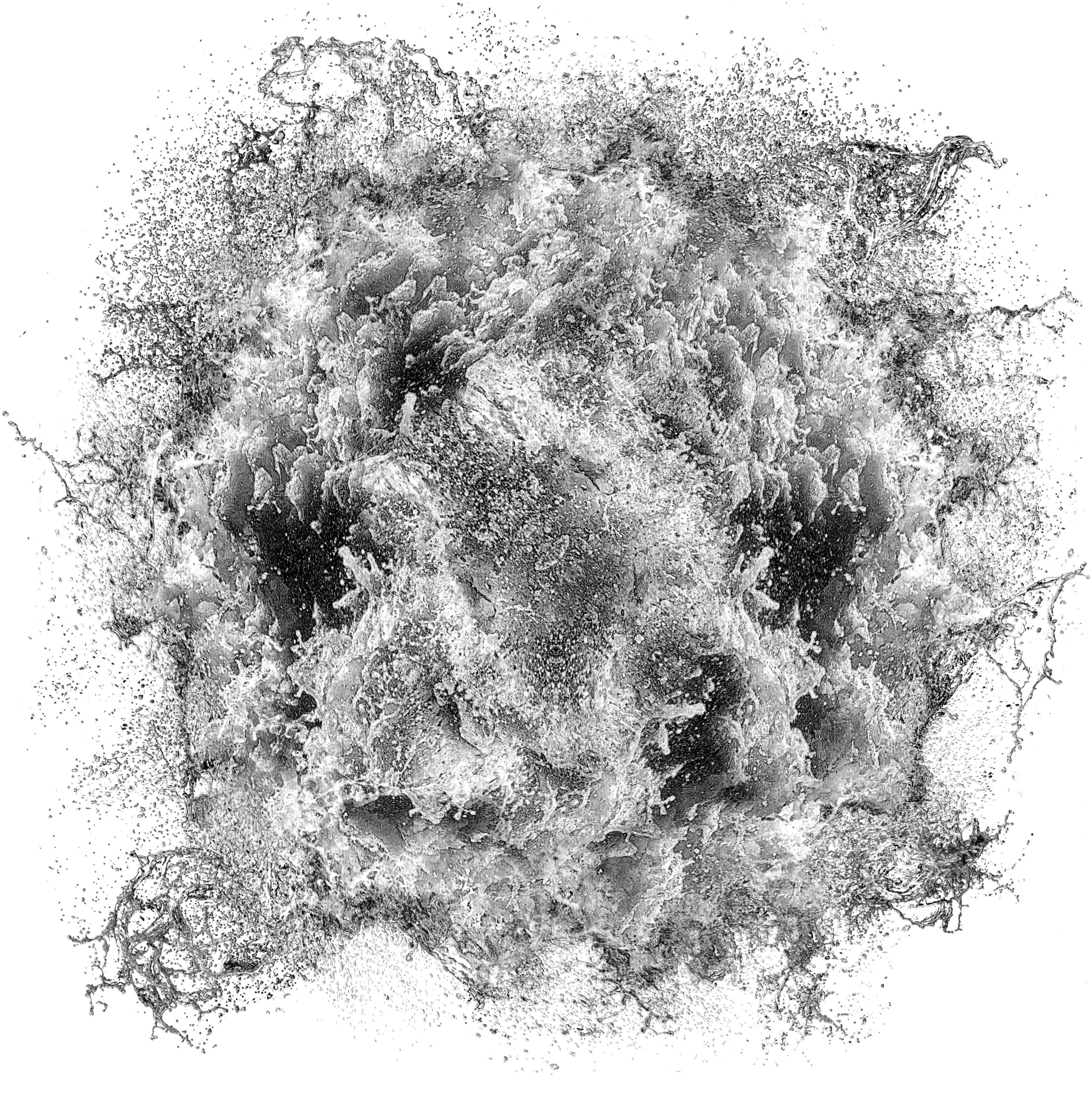

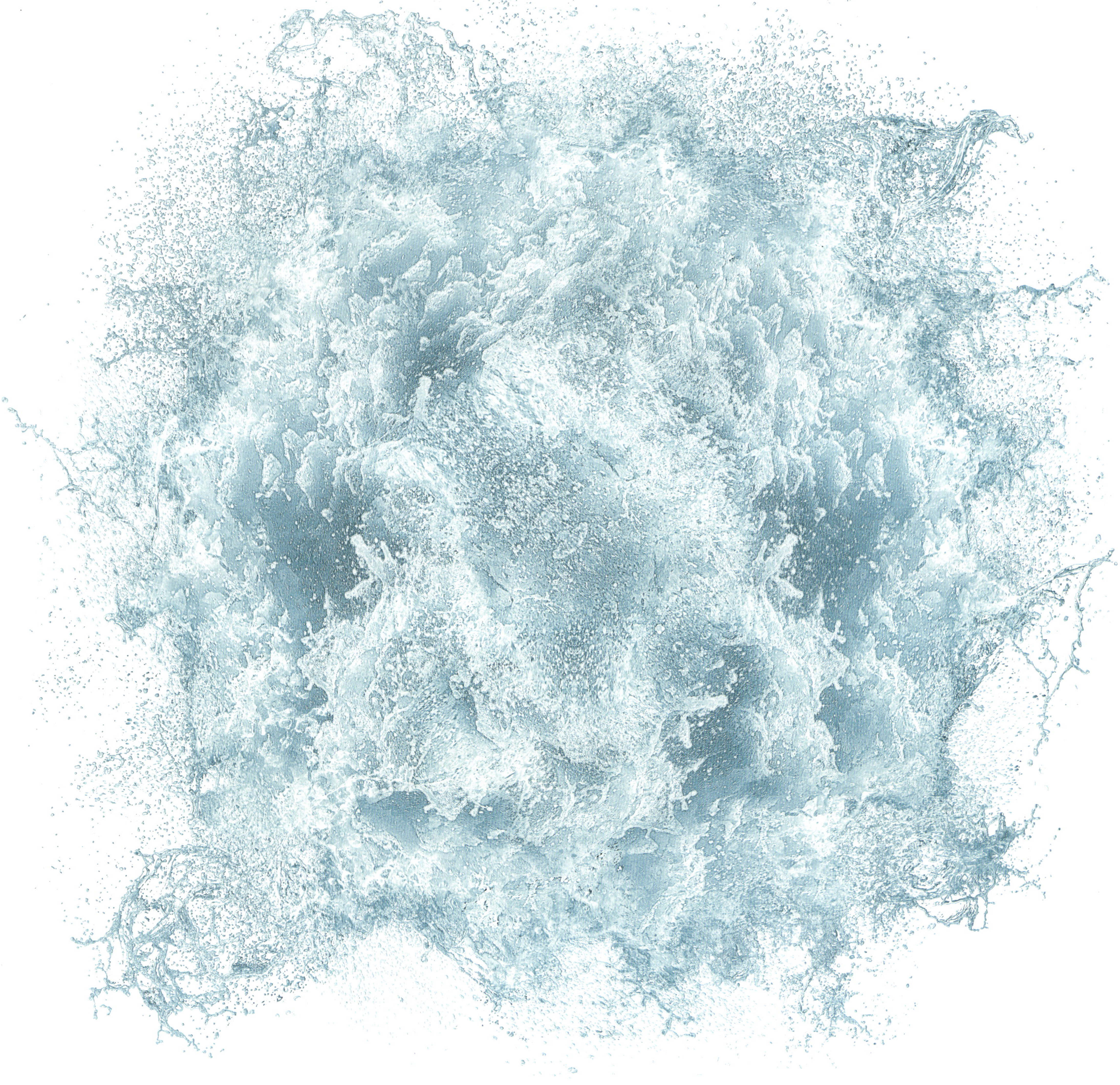

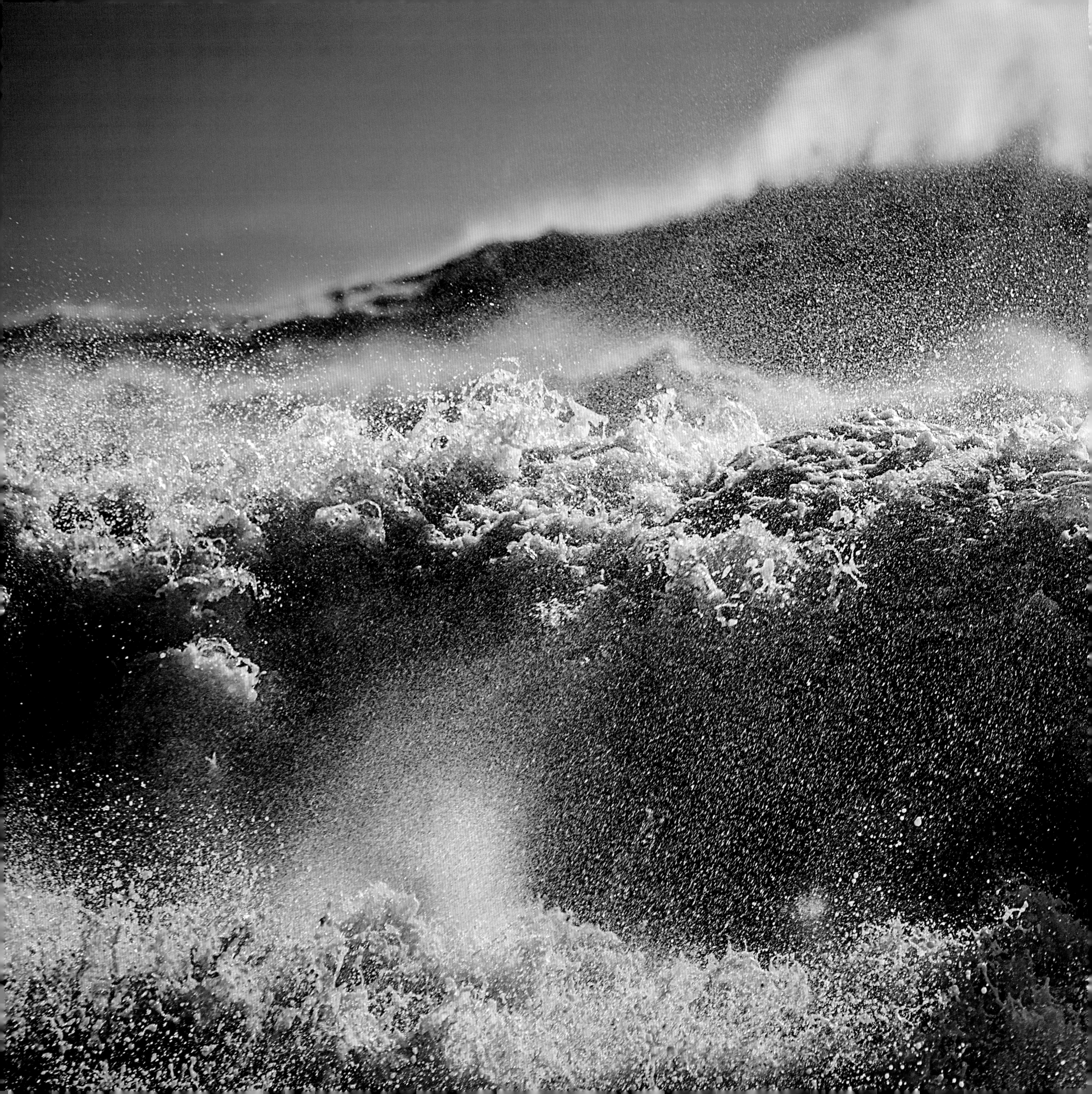

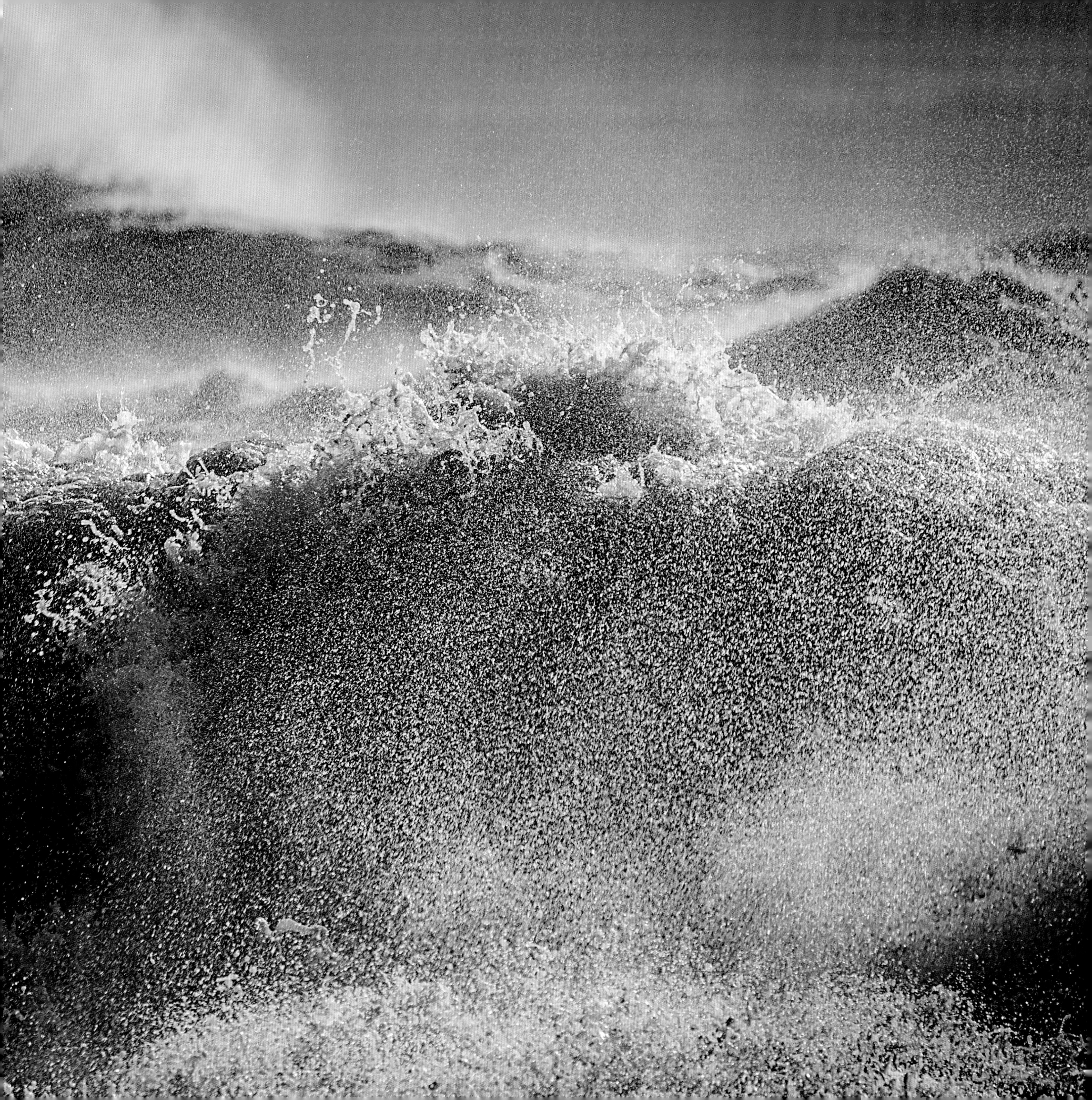

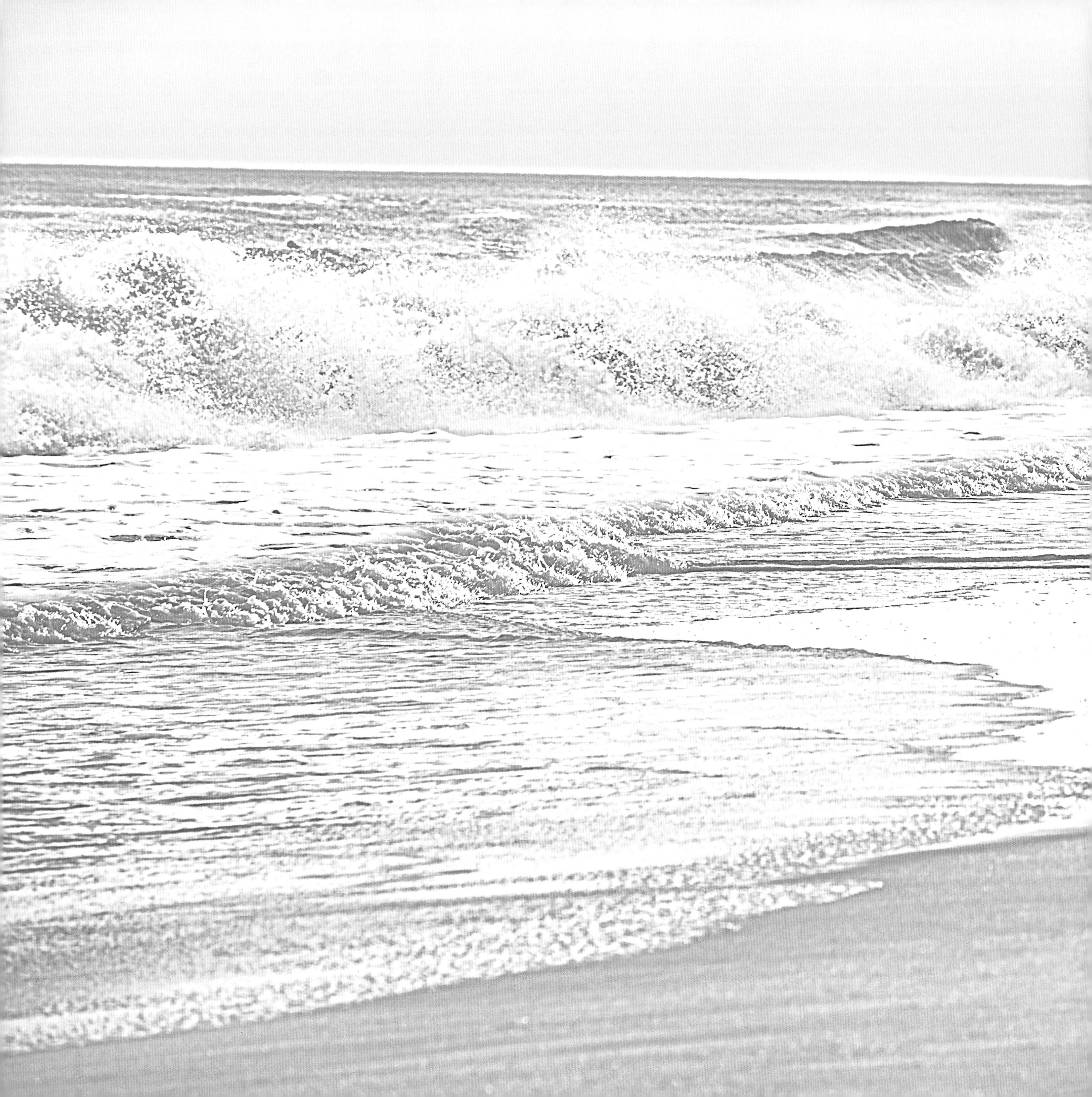

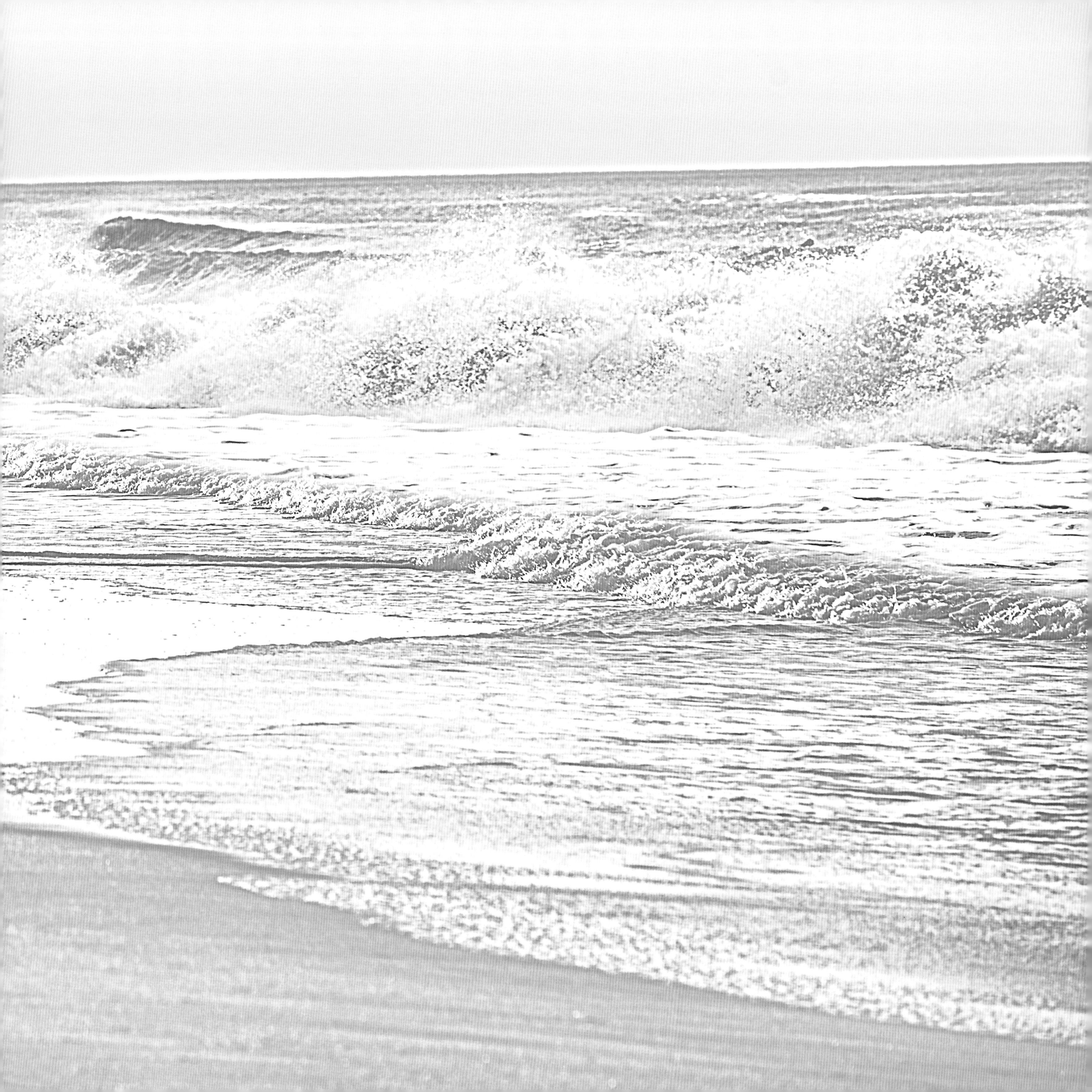

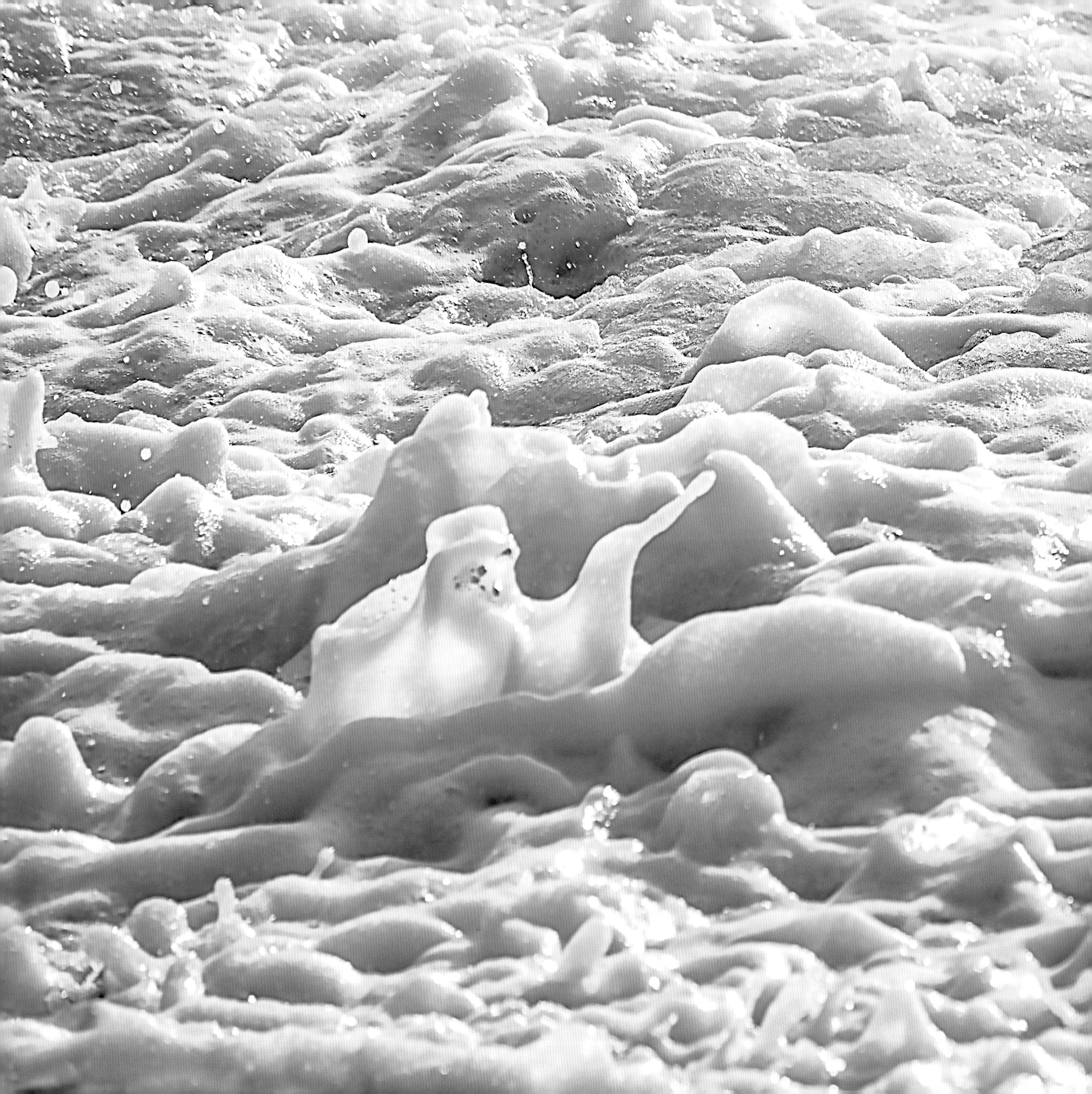

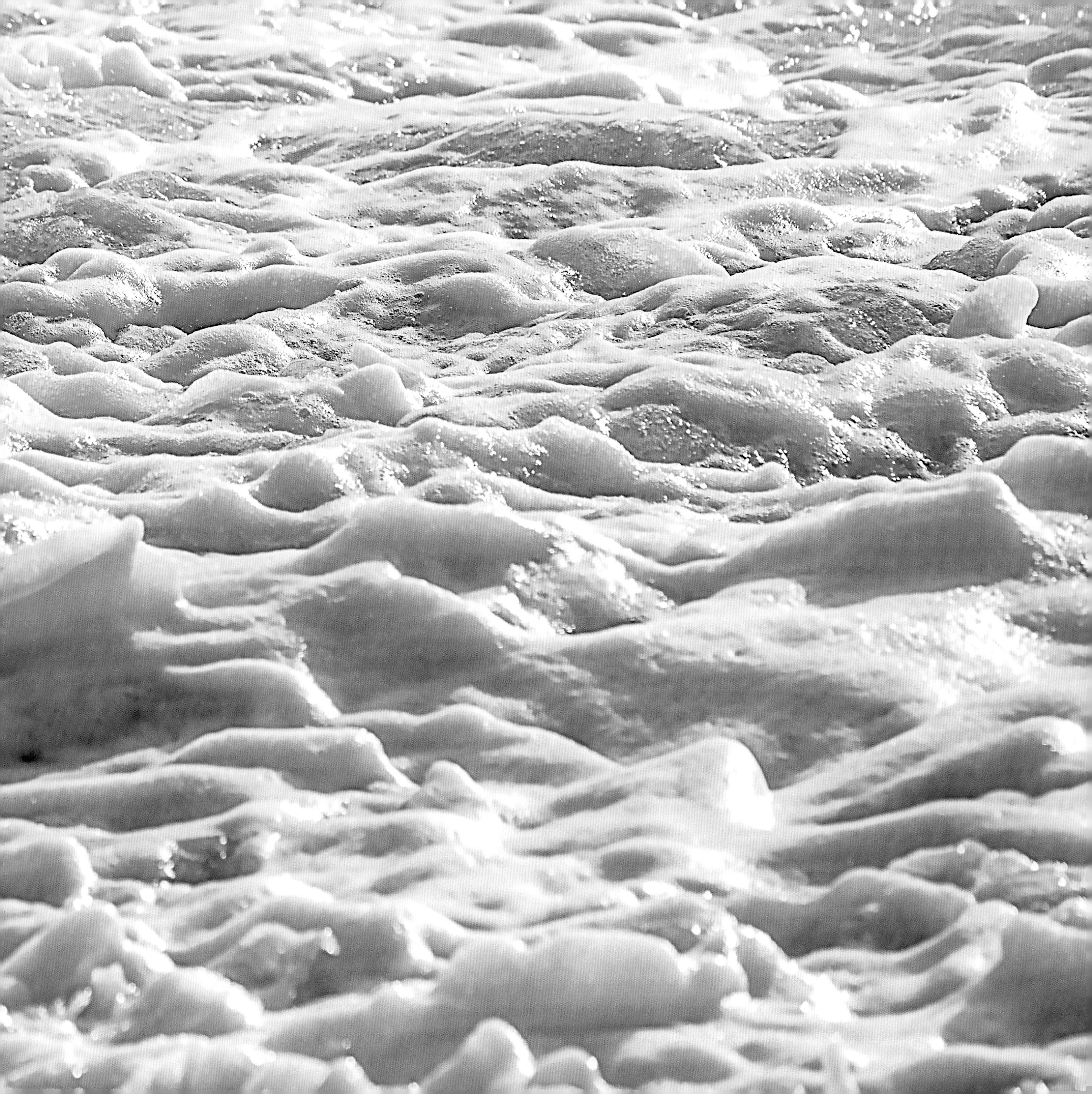

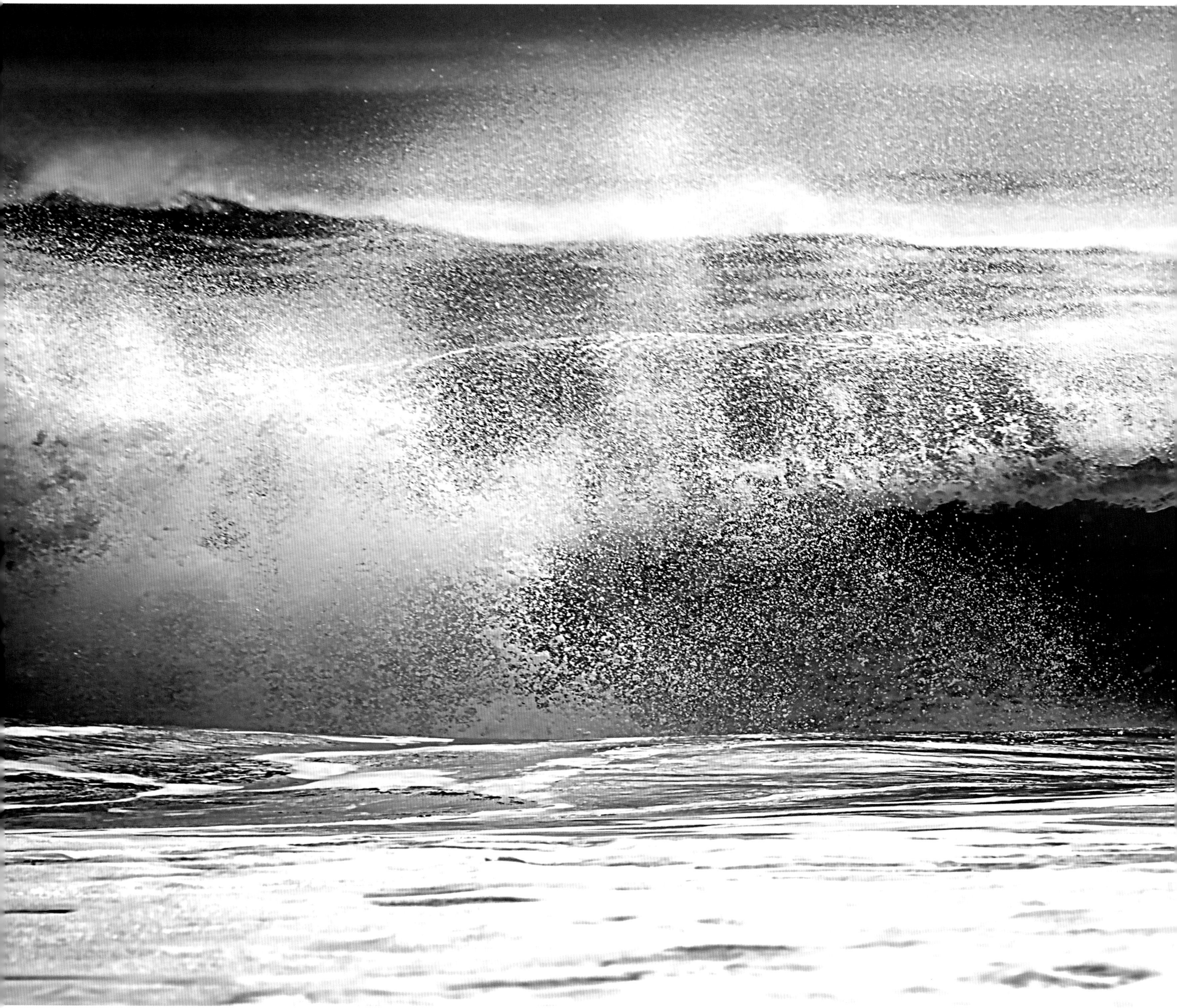

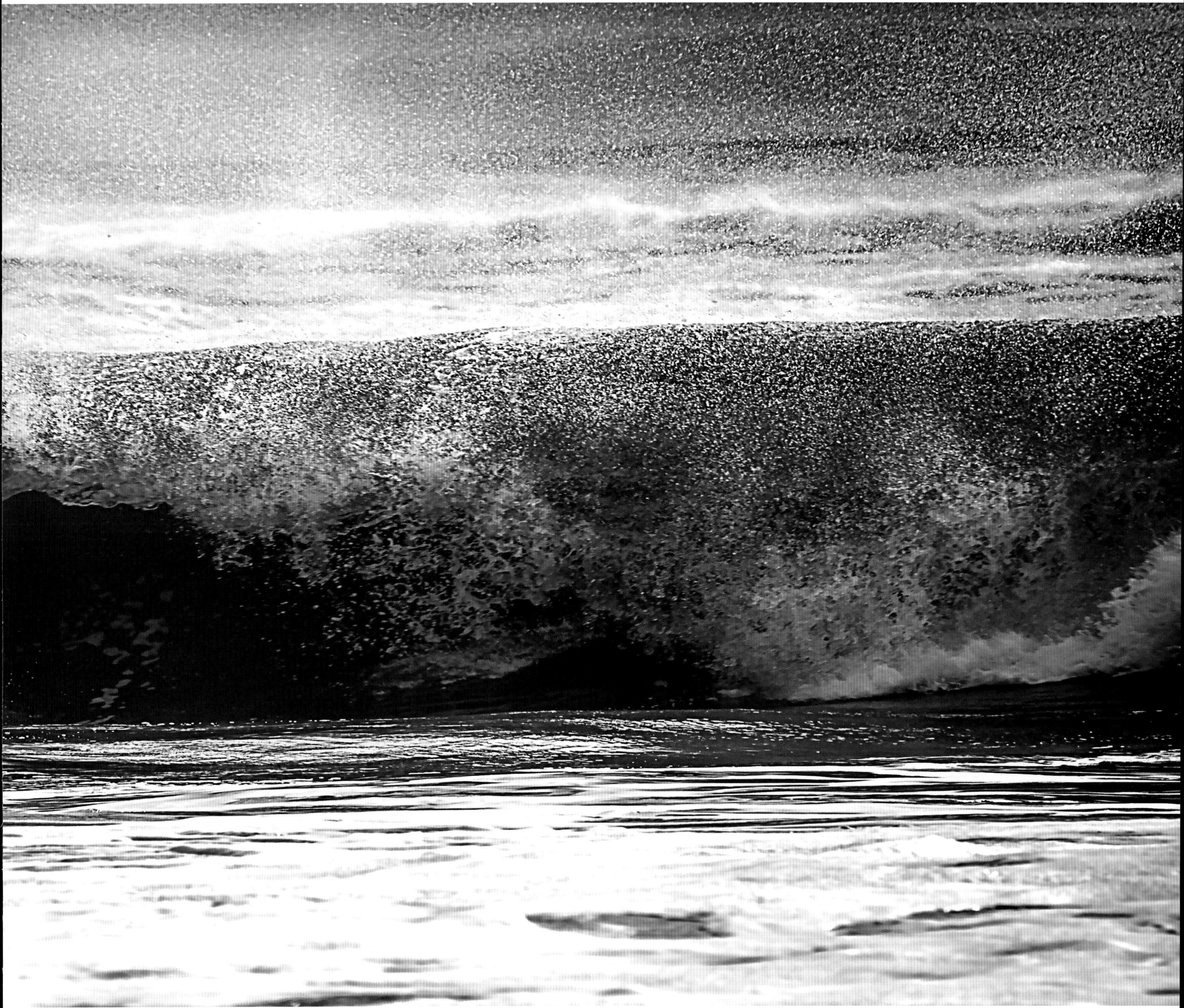

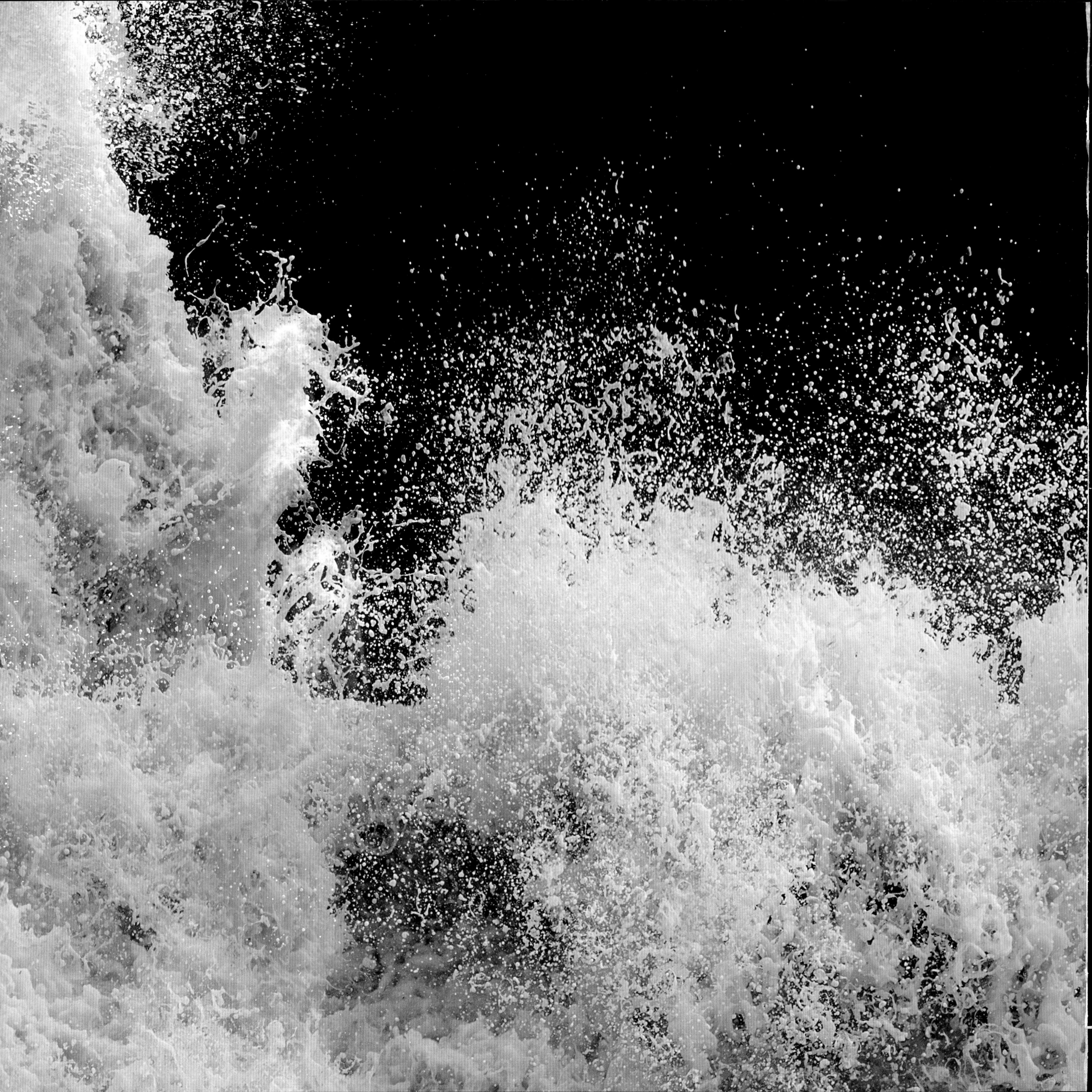

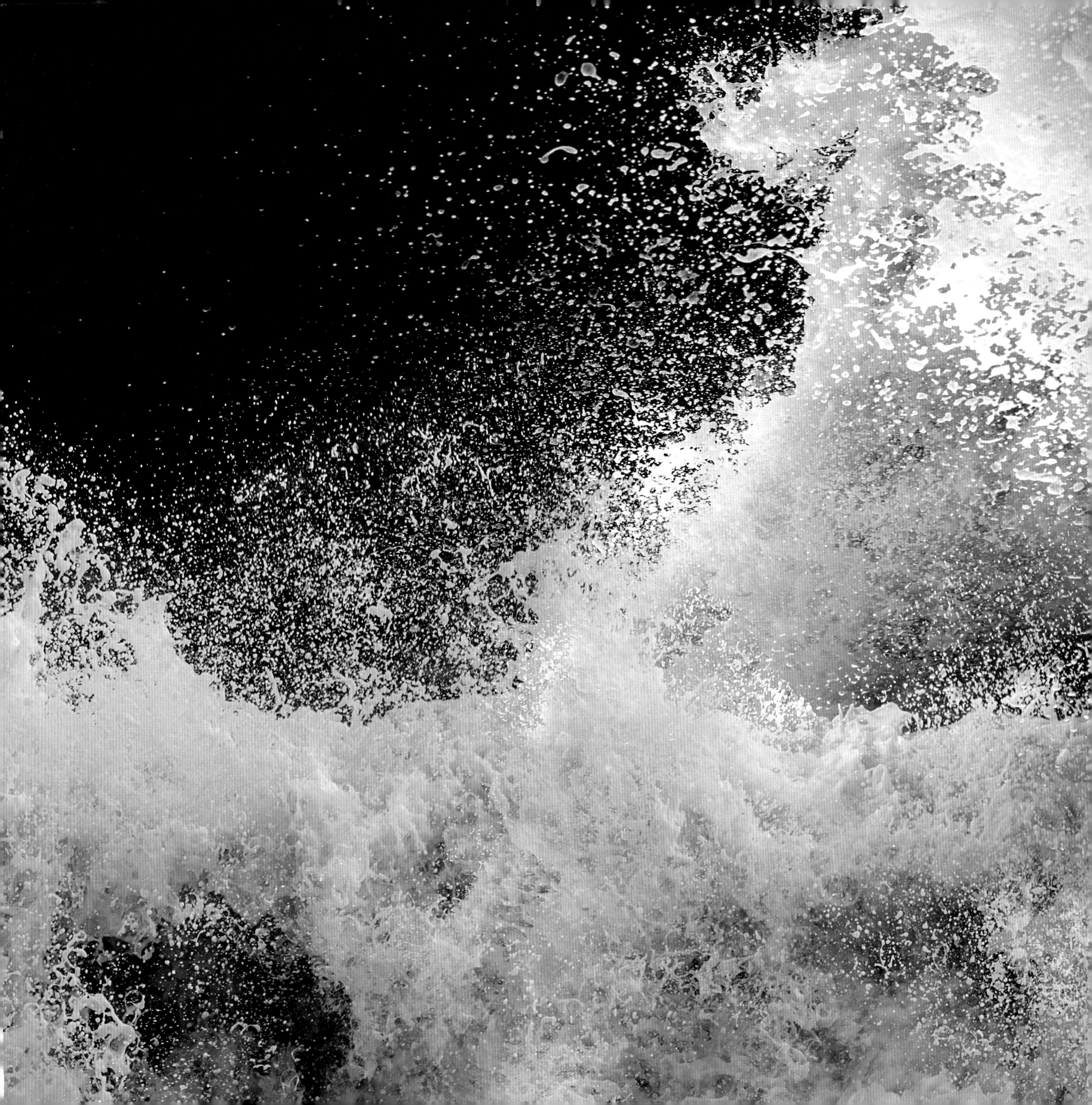

OTHER BOOKS BY BOB TABOR

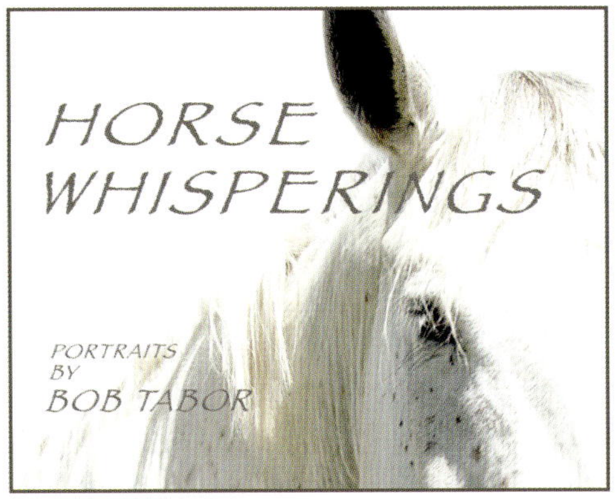

Bob's first book, *HORSE WHISPERINGS,* gave us a glimpse into exactly what was on each subject's mind when his portrait was taken. Letting the horse stay in its own environment, and using only natural light, Bob captured the unique personality of each of his regal subjects.

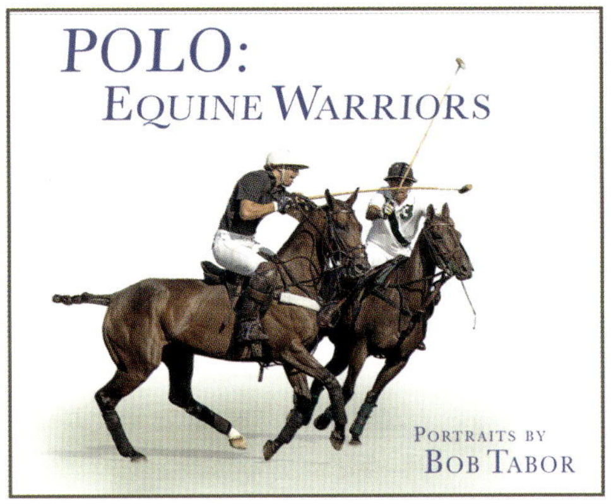

In his second book, *POLO: Equine Warriors*, Bob brought to life the inner psyche of the polo pony. An exciting, emotional experience with dramatic "in your face" images that spring from the page and put the reader right on the field.

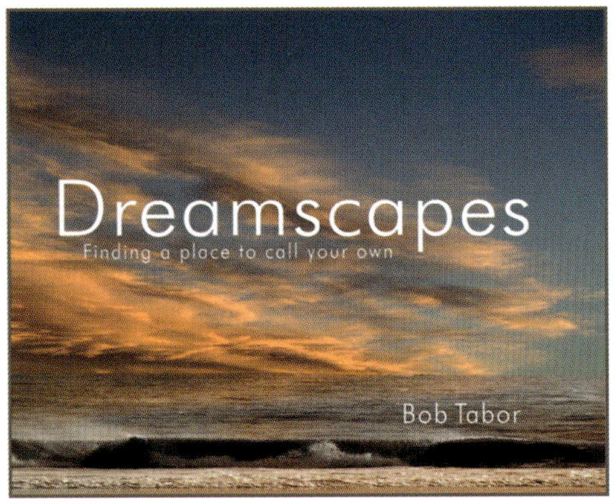

His third book, *DREAMSCAPES: Finding a place to call your own*, is a collection of images that capture the powerful effect the ocean has on all of us. Each image takes you on a visual journey that eases stress and calms inner emotions.

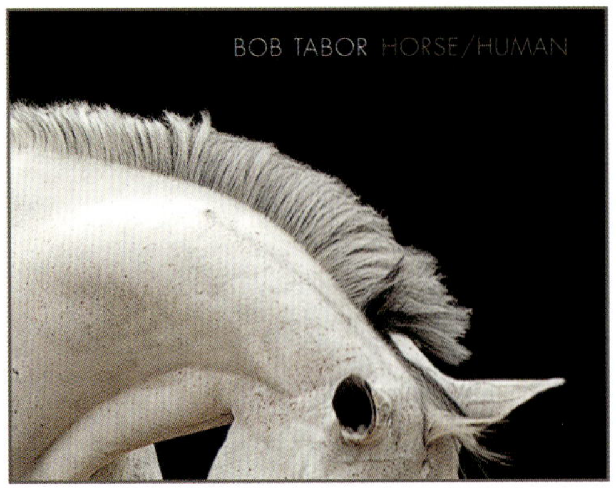

In his fourth book, *HORSE HUMAN: An Emotional Bond*, Bob continues his love affair with these beautiful and sensitive creatures. By spending countless hours photographing his subjects in their natural environment, he creates a bond that is intimate and revealing. In this relaxed atmosphere, the horses communicate through their movement, form and body language.

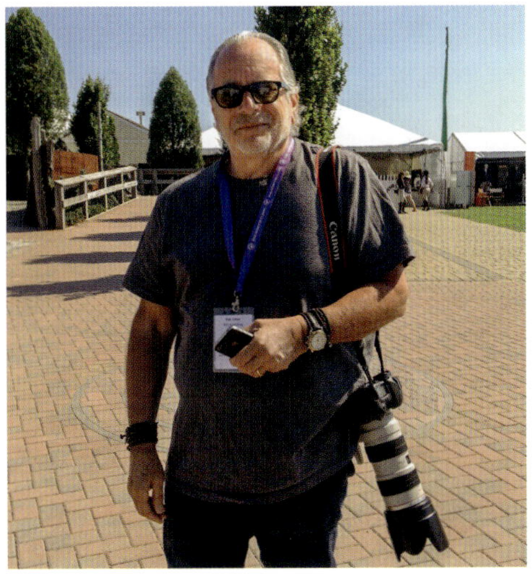
©Jessica Tabor

Bob Tabor is a celebrated photographer whose stunning horse images and seascapes are collected and admired worldwide. Bob's respect for the strength and spirit of horses combines with his technical expertise to produce images that are esteemed by art critics and animal lovers alike.

His work is a perfect combination of opposites that result in a breathtaking body of images. He juxtaposes the romantic with the practical, and a Renaissance eye with a feel for modern graphics. His work is always technically refined yet emotionally intense.

His photographs appear in galleries in the USA (New York, Southampton, Easthampton and Aspen), Hong Kong, Shanghai, England, Dubai and Peru. Bob's images may also be found in Polo Ralph Lauren boutiques on four continents: Asia, Europe, North America and South America.

In addition to galleries, Bob's work is found in private collections around the world.

Bob currently lives and works in Manhattan and Easthampton, New York.

All images are available as large format archival prints
as part of a series of 8.
Contact the artist at bobtaborimages@gmail.com

FOR MORE INFORMATION ABOUT THE AUTHOR AND HIS ART, PLEASE VISIT BOBTABORIMAGES.COM

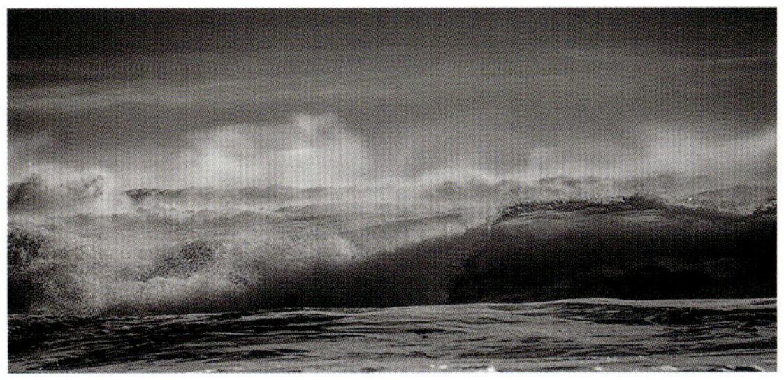

SP - 1

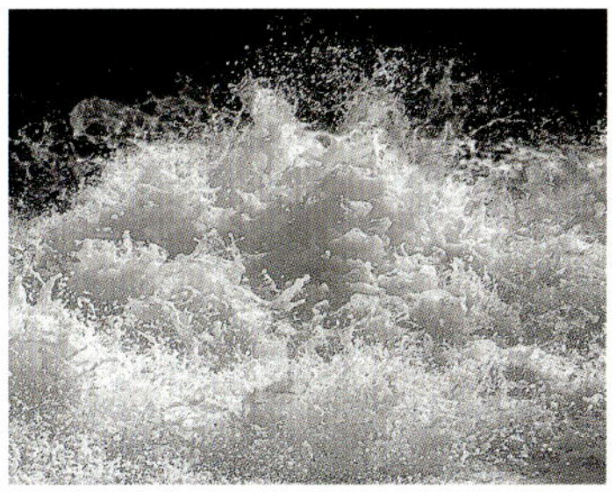

SP - 2

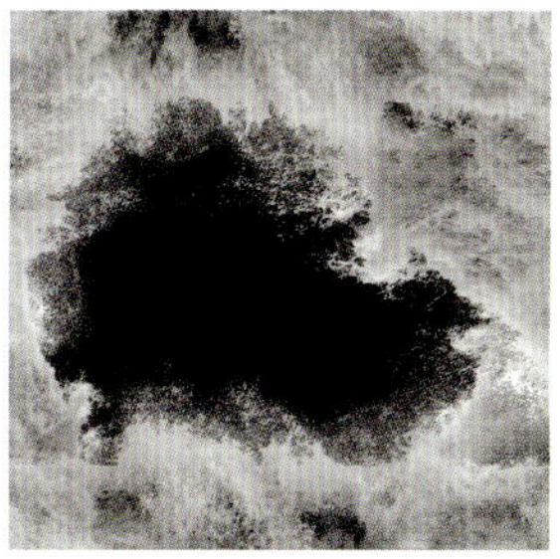

SP - 3

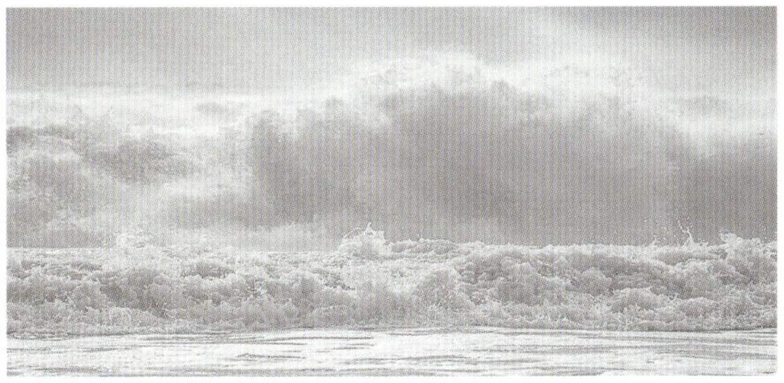

SP - 4

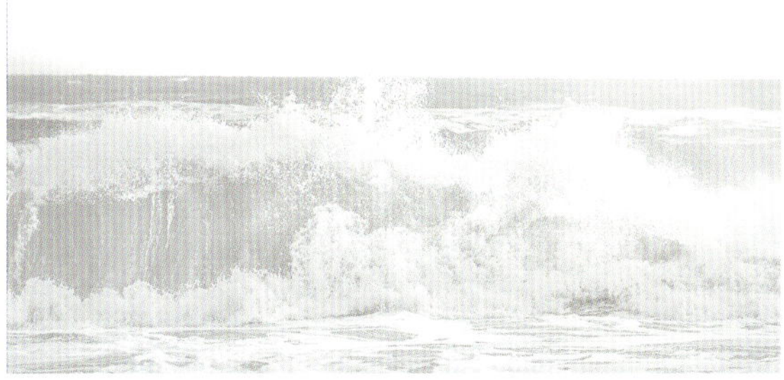

SP - 5

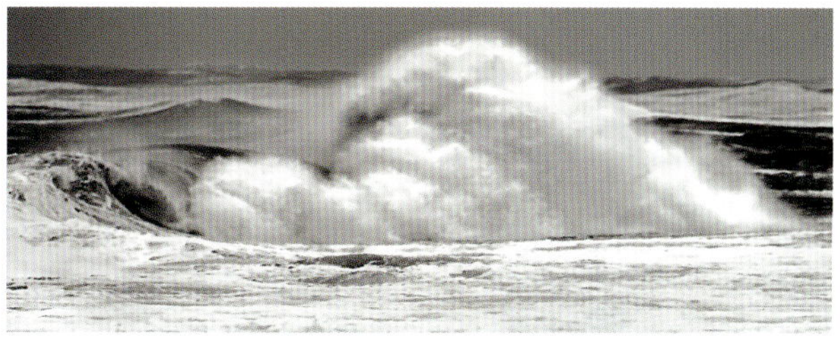

SP - 6

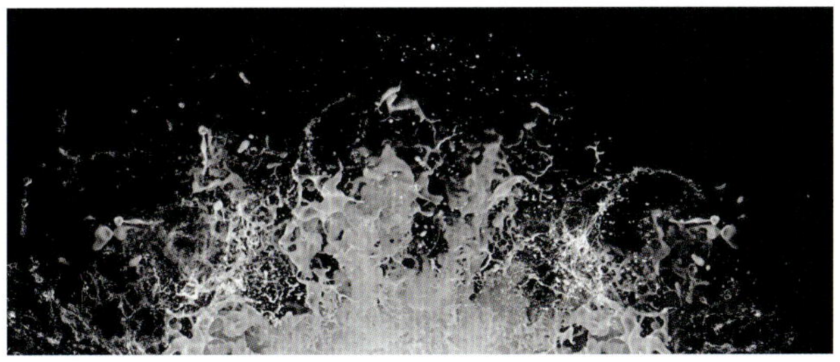

SP - 7

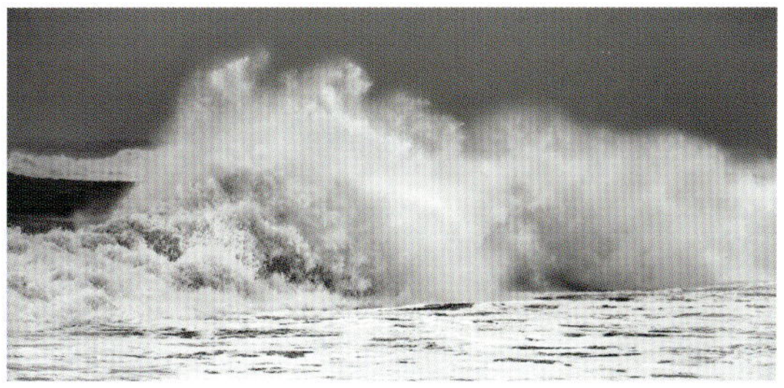

SP - 8

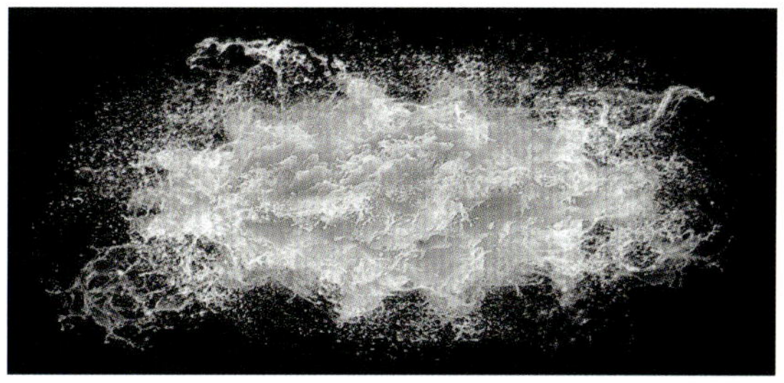

SP - 9

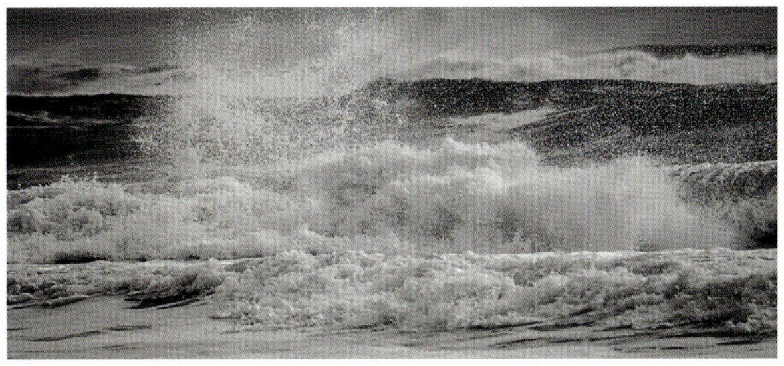

SP - 10

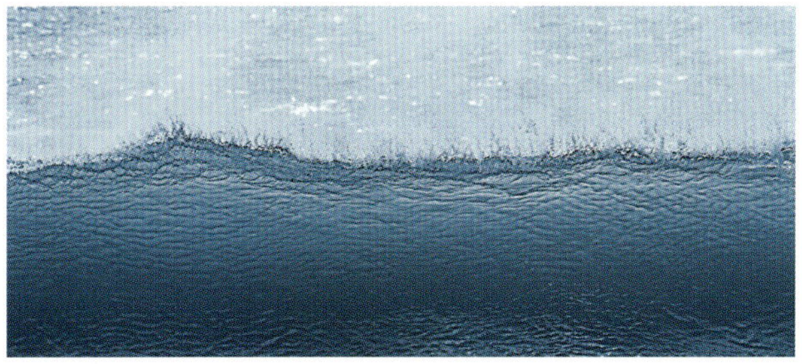

SP - 11

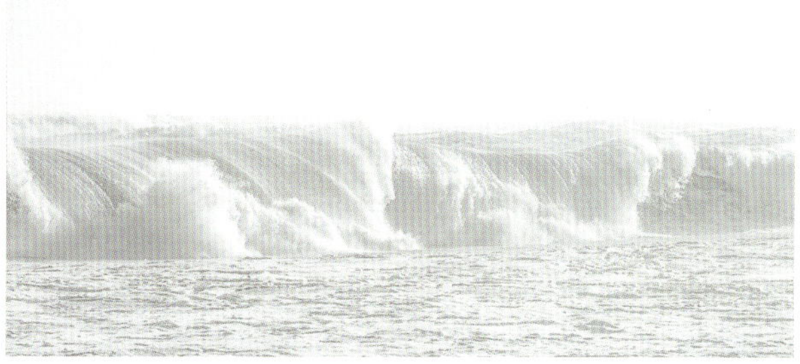

SP - 12

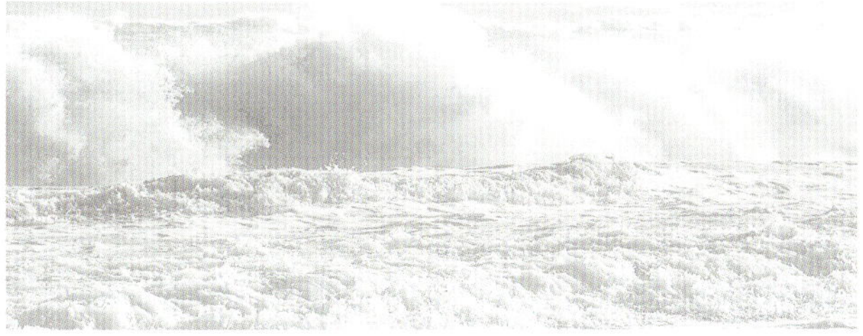

SP - 10

SP - 11

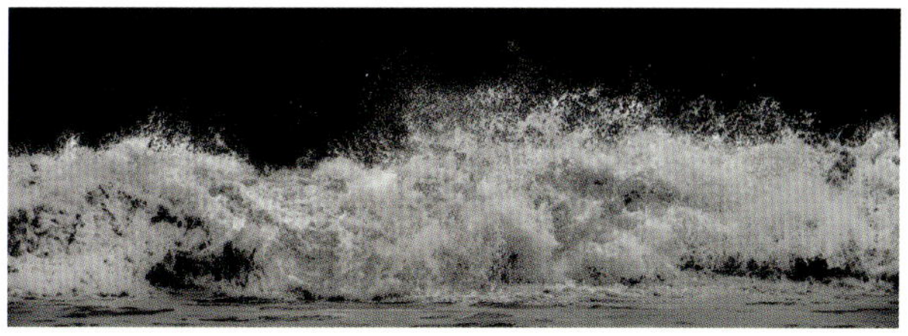

SP - 12

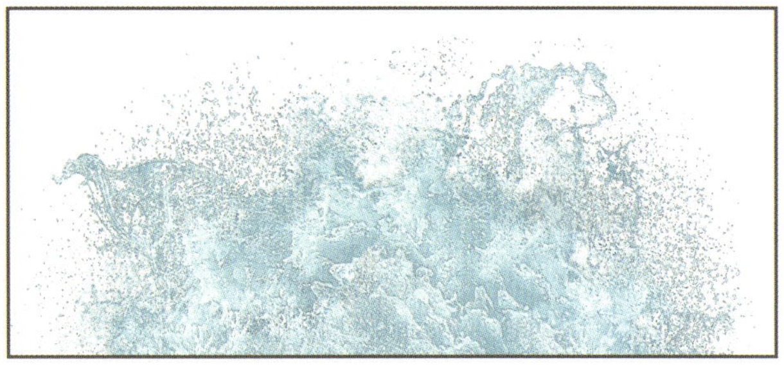

SP - 13

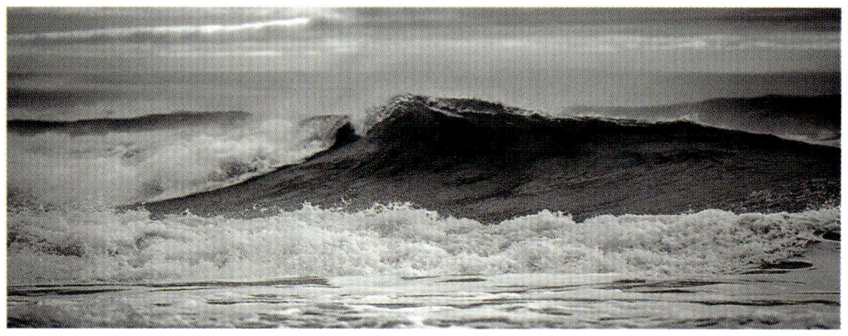

SP - 14

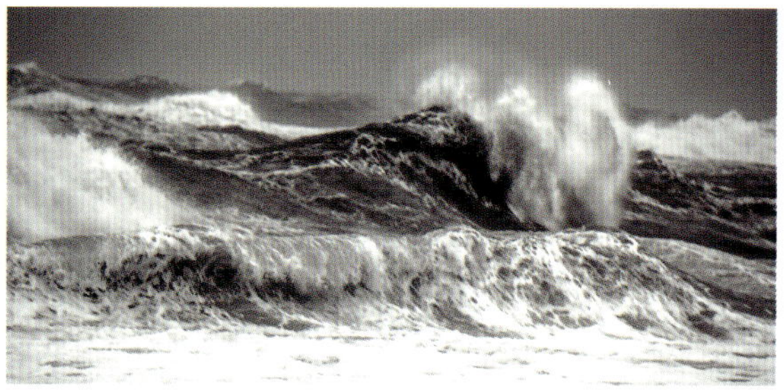

SP - 15

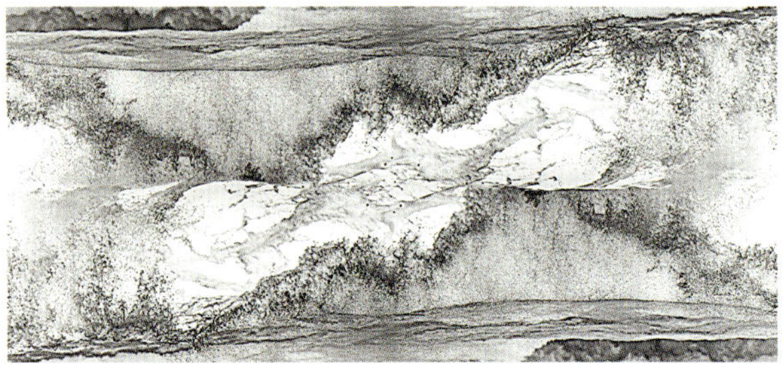

SP - 16

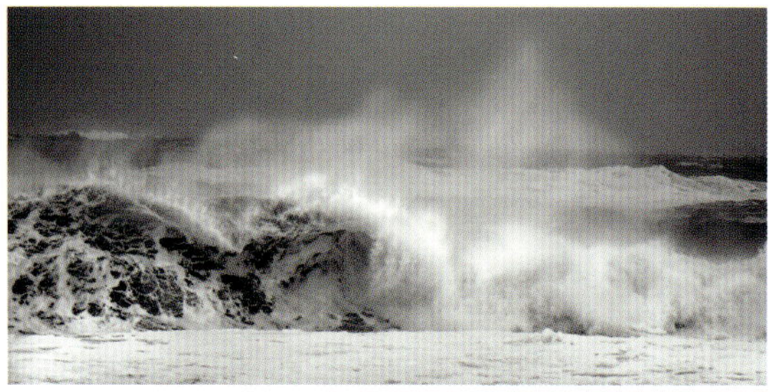

SP - 17

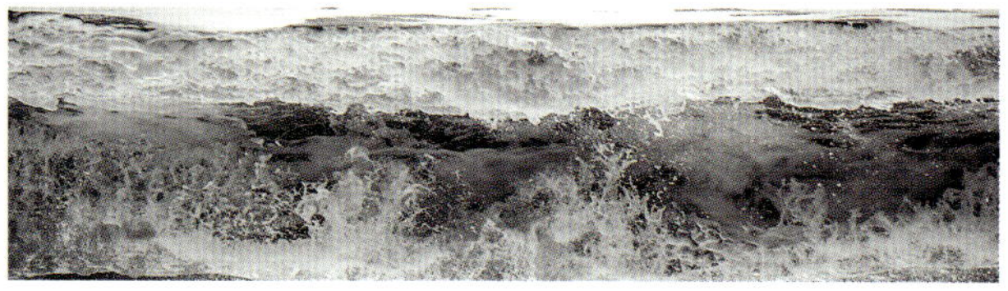

SP - 18

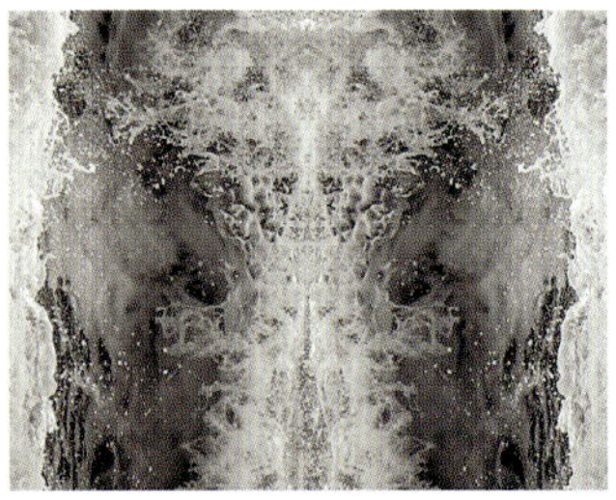

SP - 19

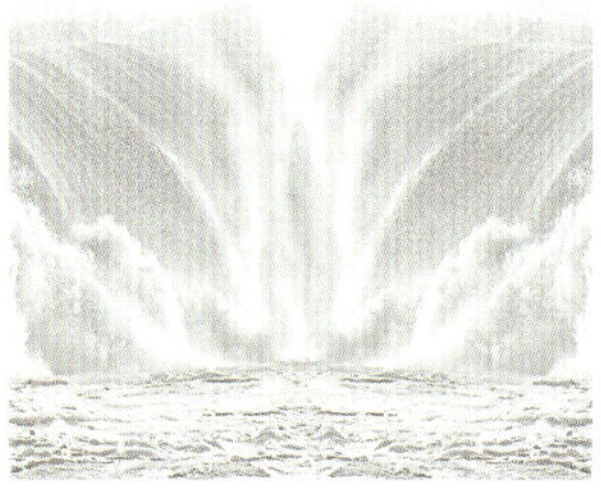

SP - 20

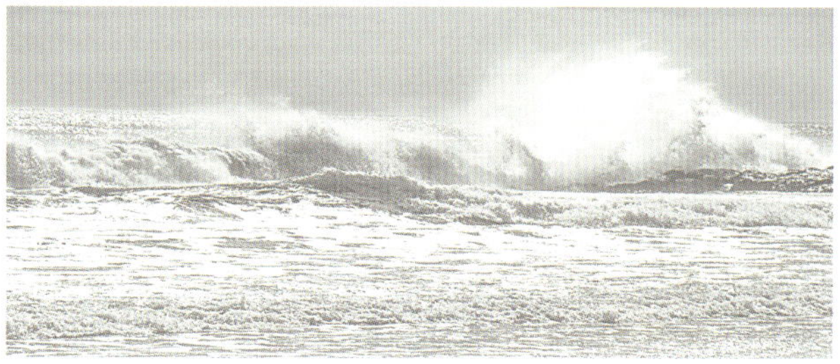

SP - 21

SP - 22

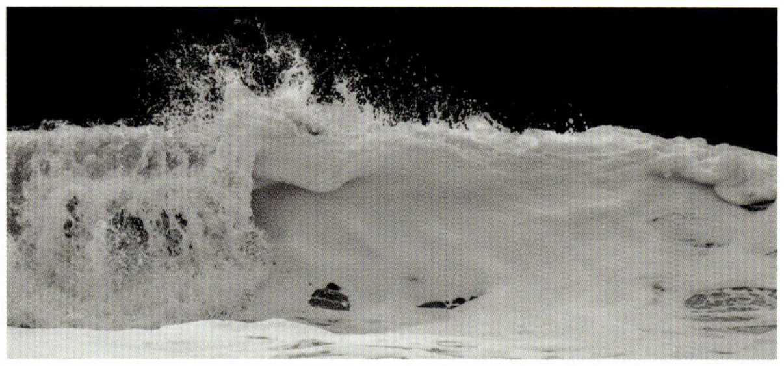

SP - 23

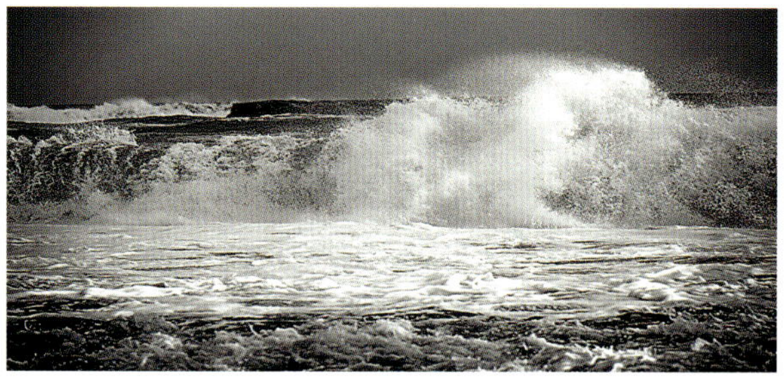

SP - 24

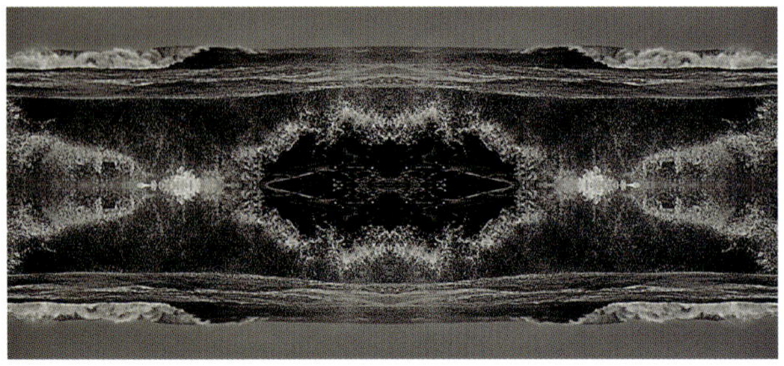

SP - 25

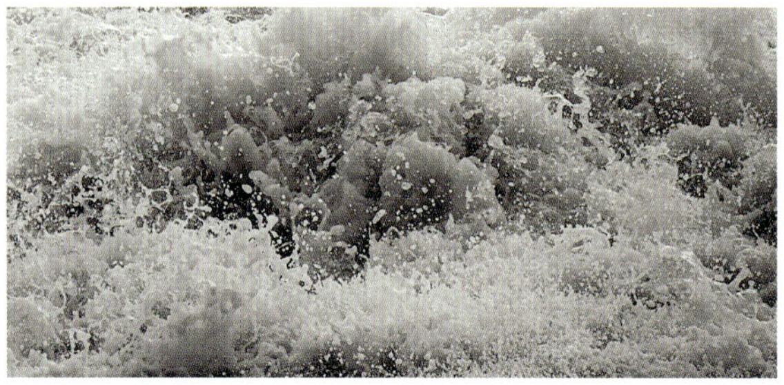

SP - 26

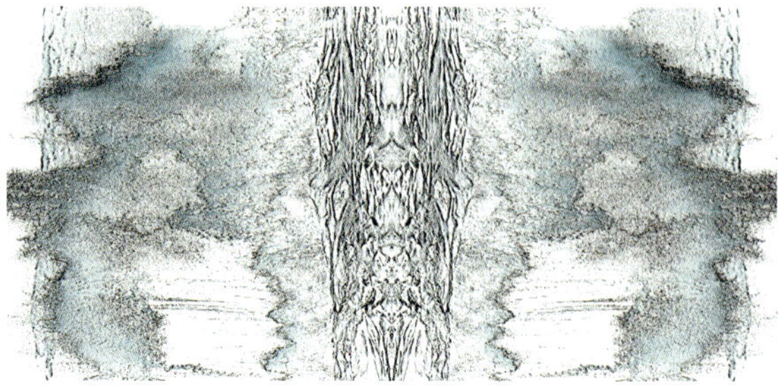

SP - 27

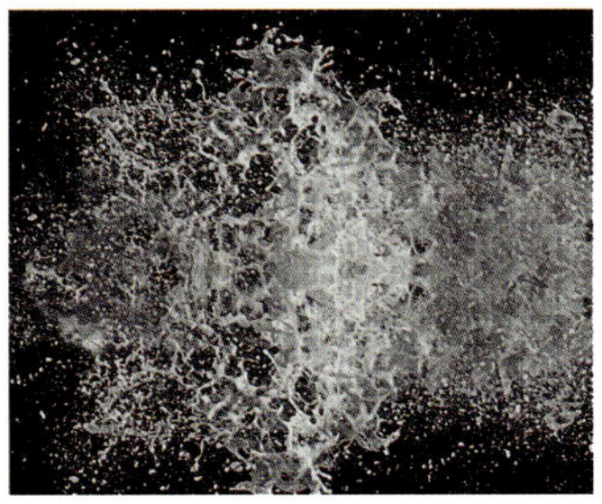

SP - 28

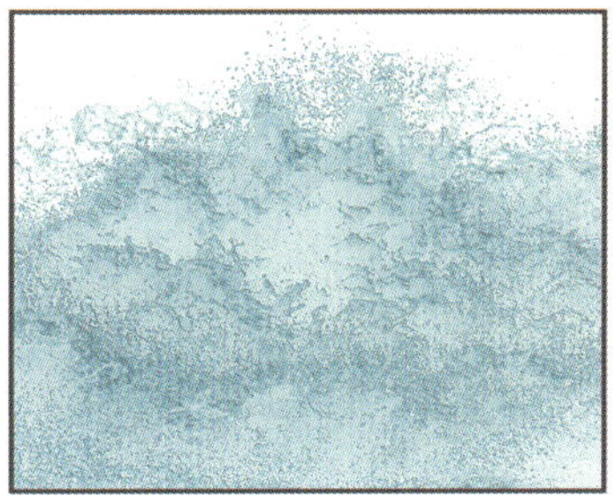

SP - 29

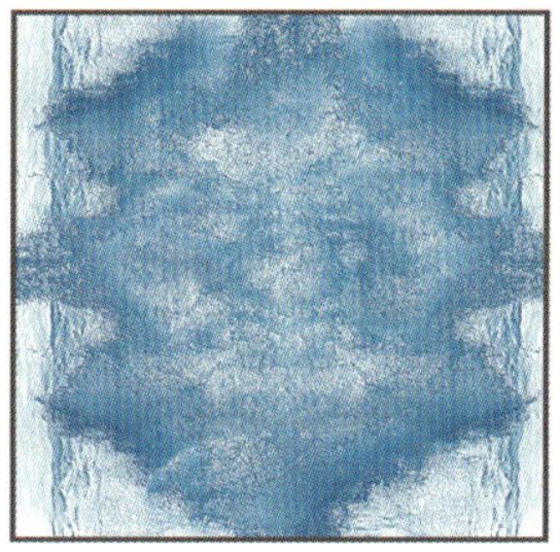

SP - 30

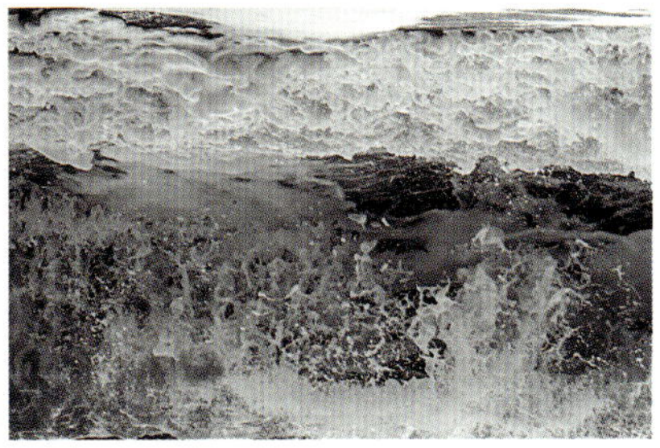

SP - 31

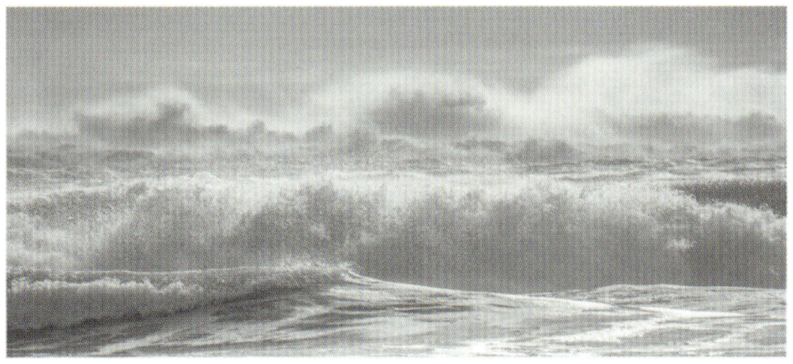

SP - 32

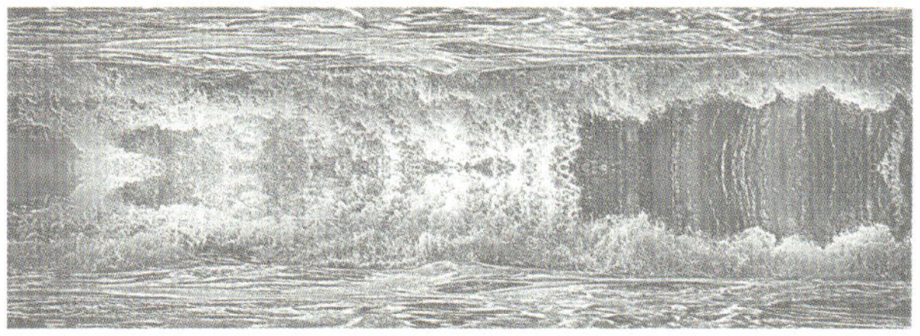

SP - 33

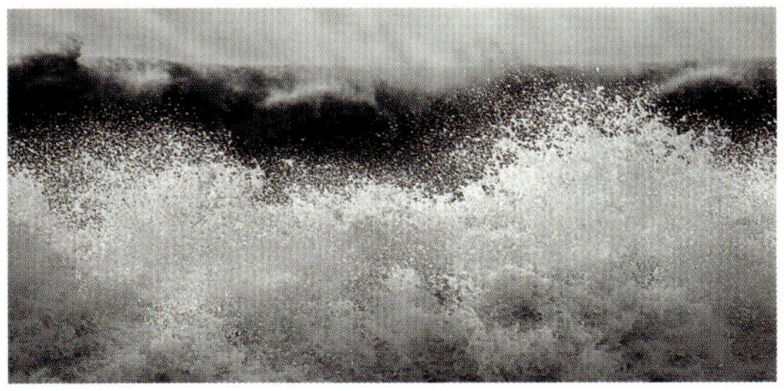

SP - 34

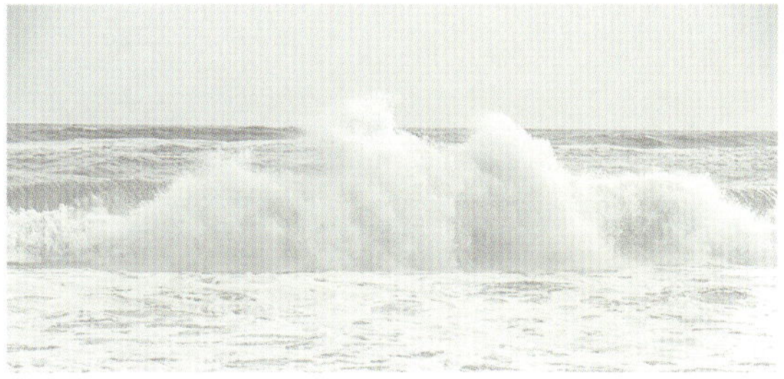

SP - 35

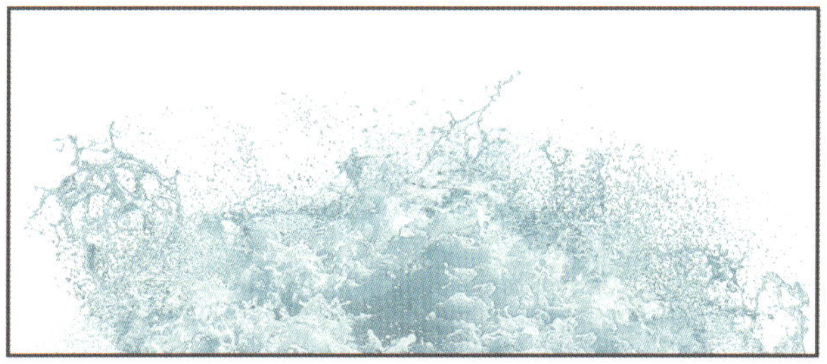

SP - 36

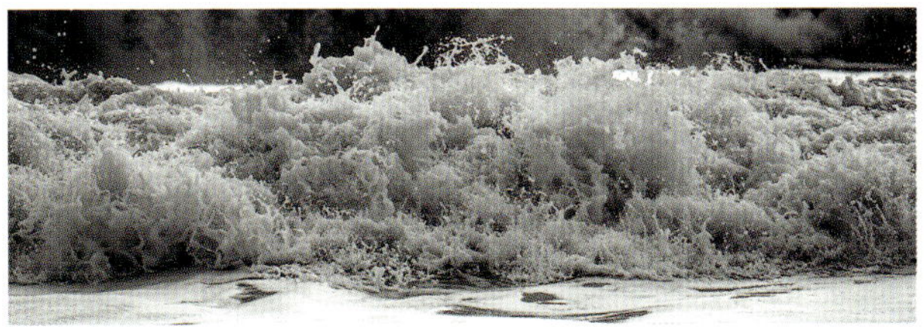

SP - 37

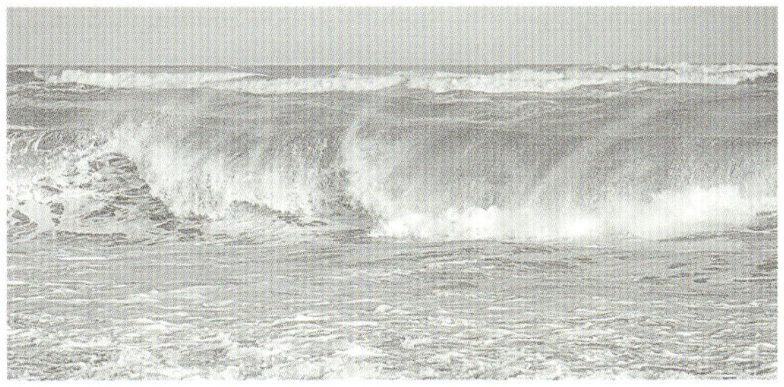

SP - 38

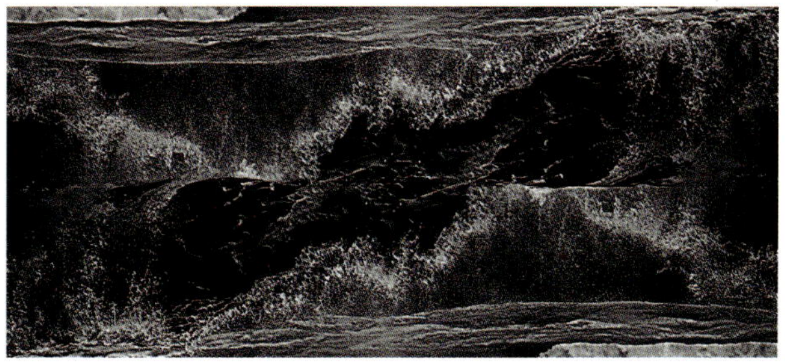

SP - 39

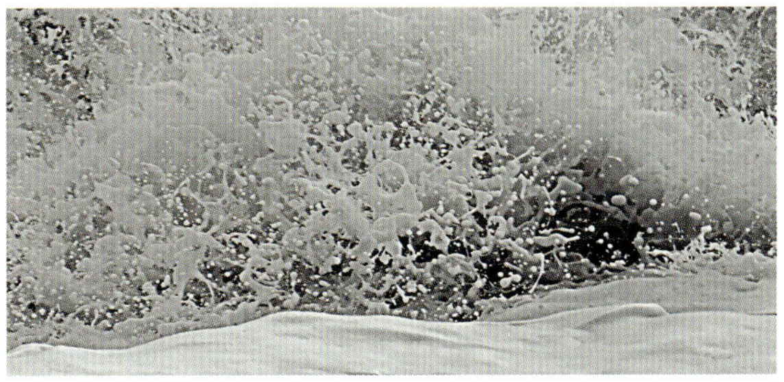

SP - 40

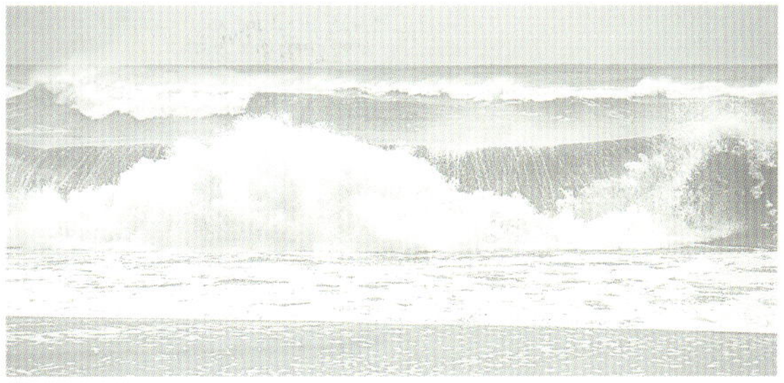

SP - 41

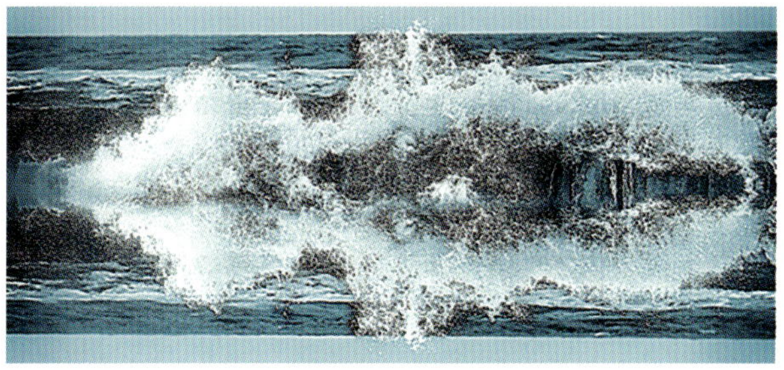

SP - 42

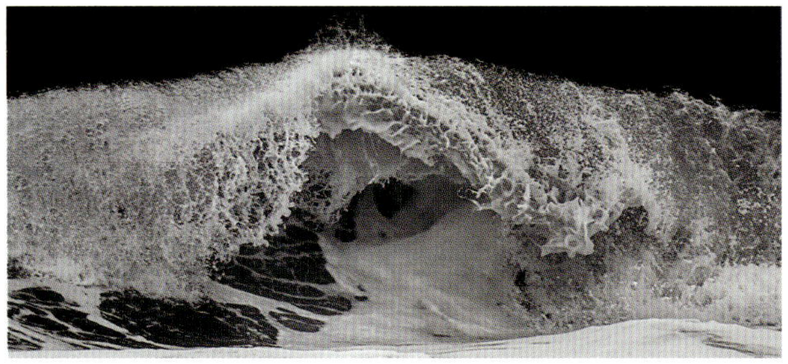

SP - 43

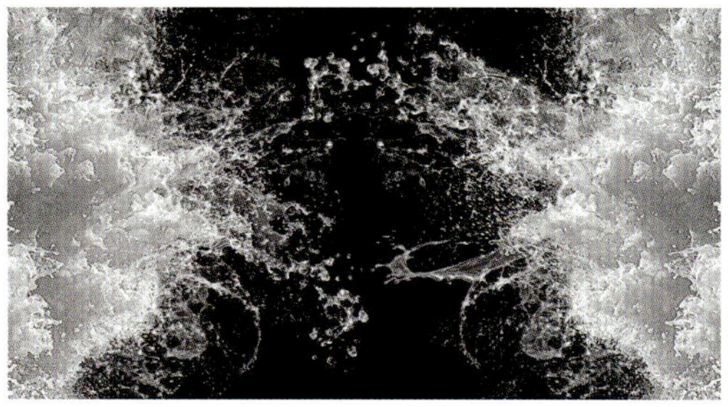

SP - 44

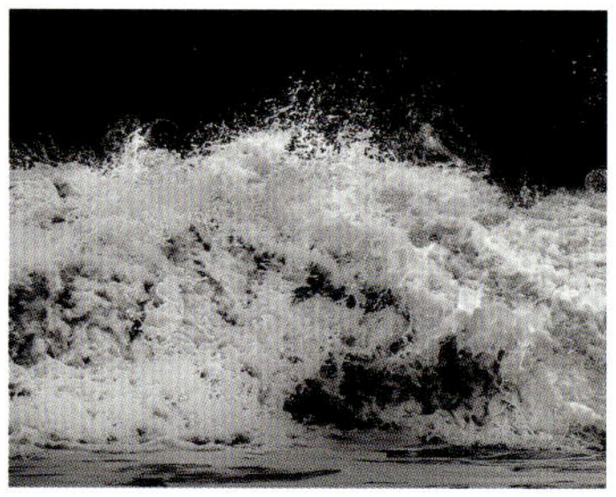

SP - 45

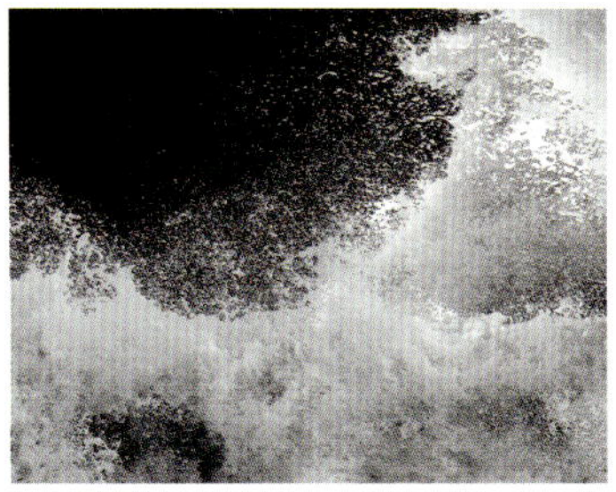

SP - 46

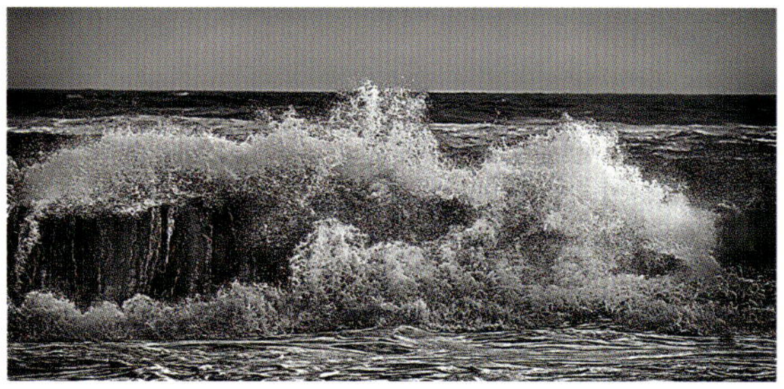

SP - 47

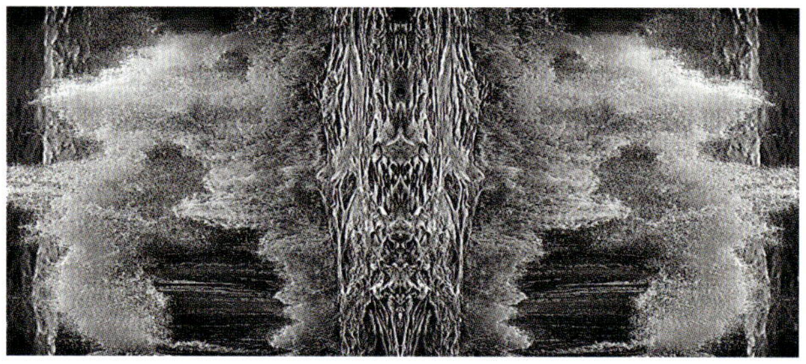

SP - 48

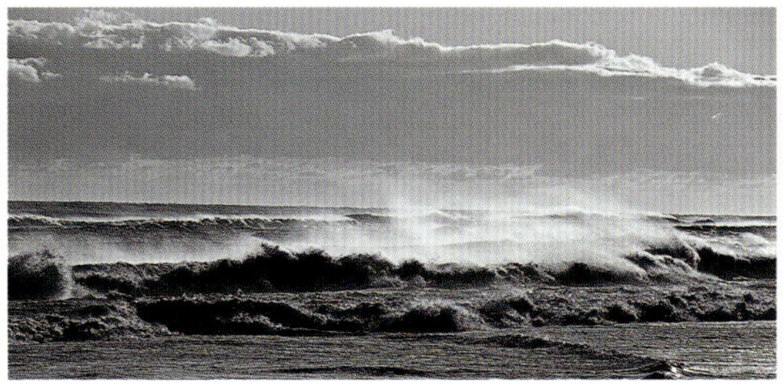

SP - 49

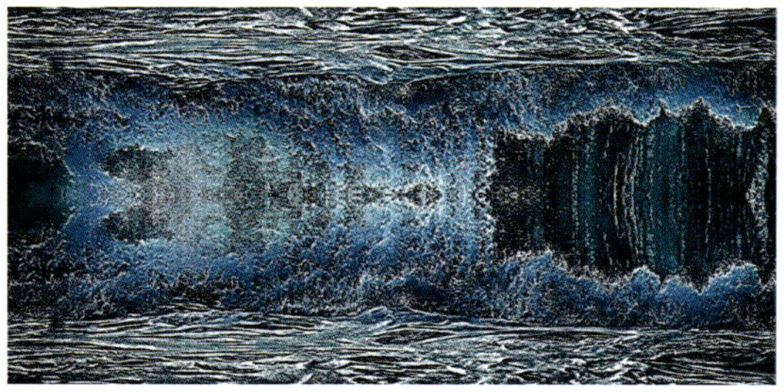

SP - 50

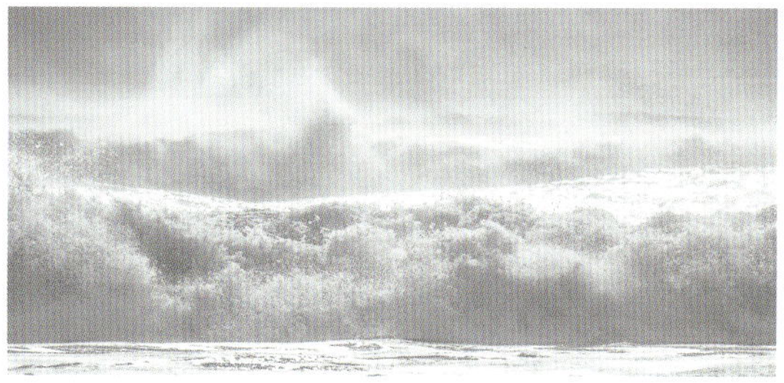

SP - 51

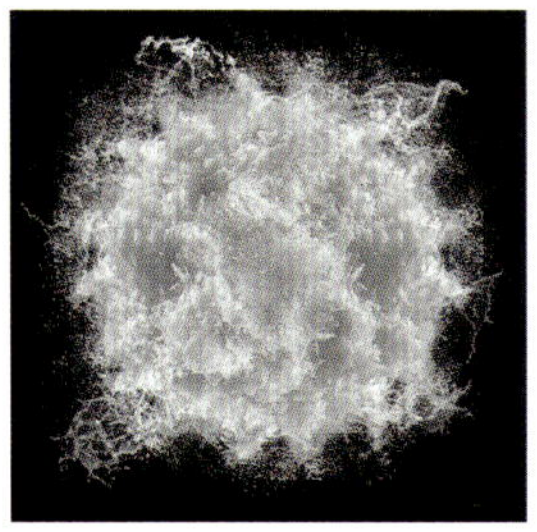

SP - 52

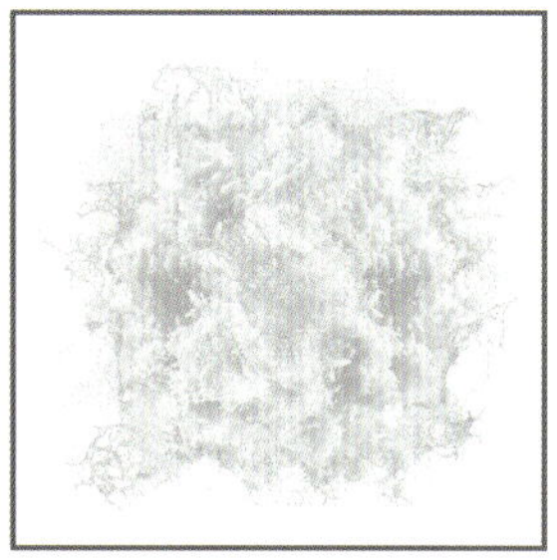

SP - 53

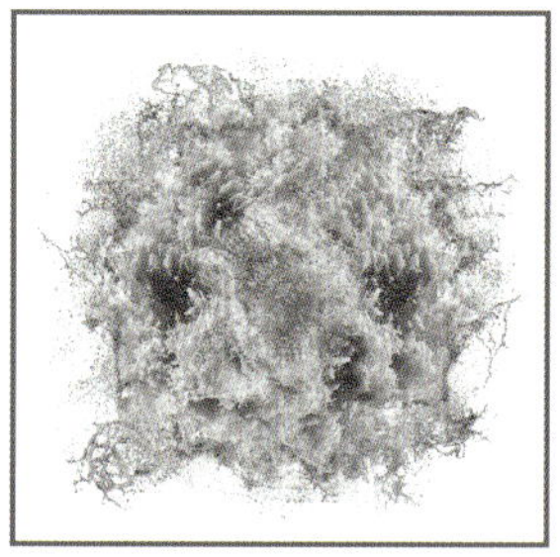

SP - 54

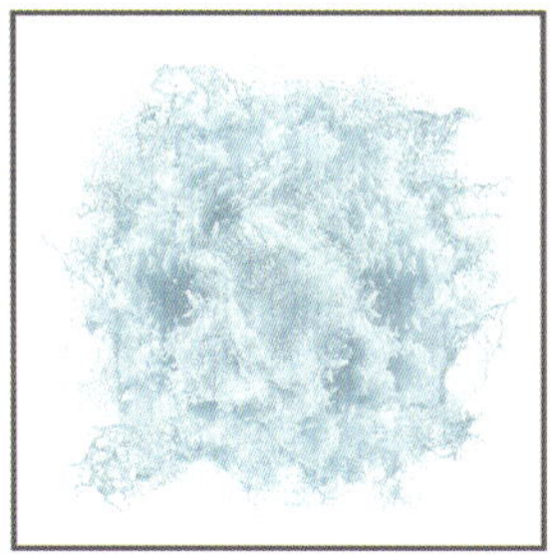

SP - 55

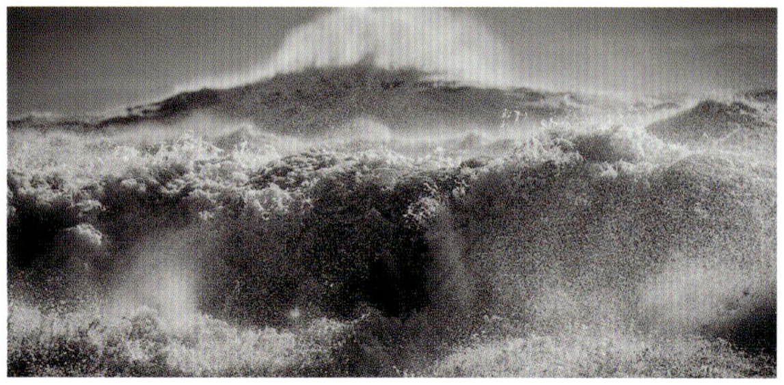

SP - 56

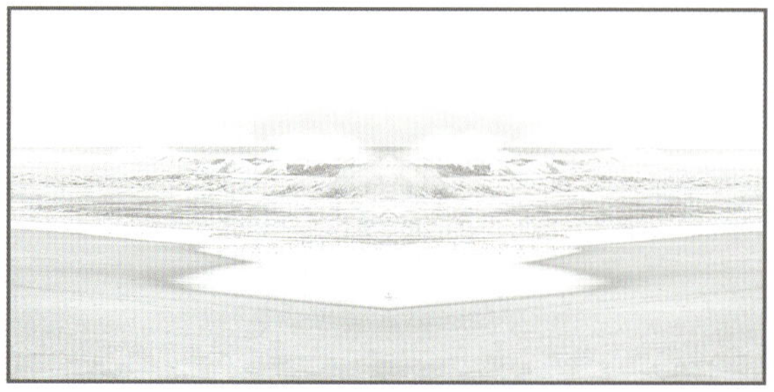

SP - 57

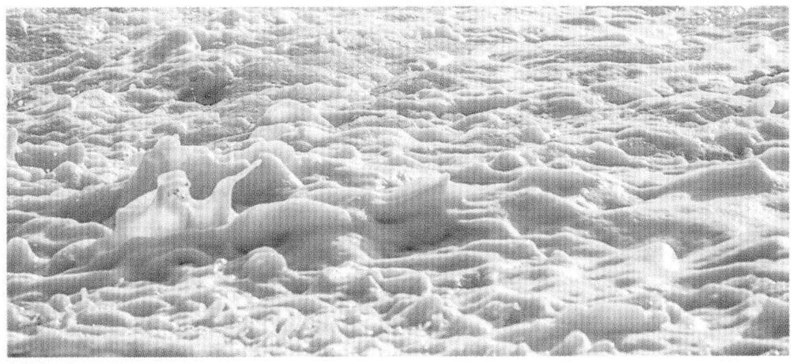

SP - 58

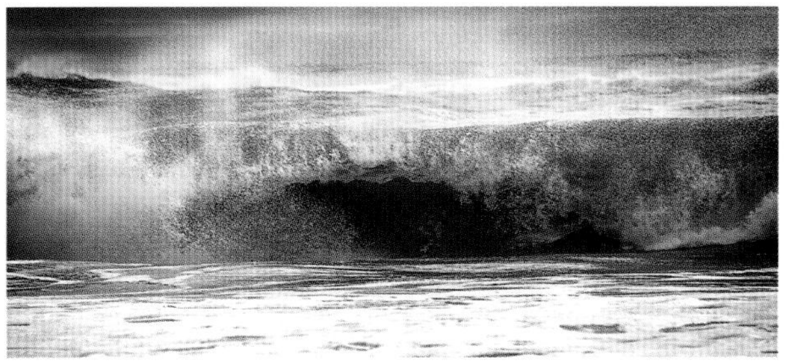

SP - 59

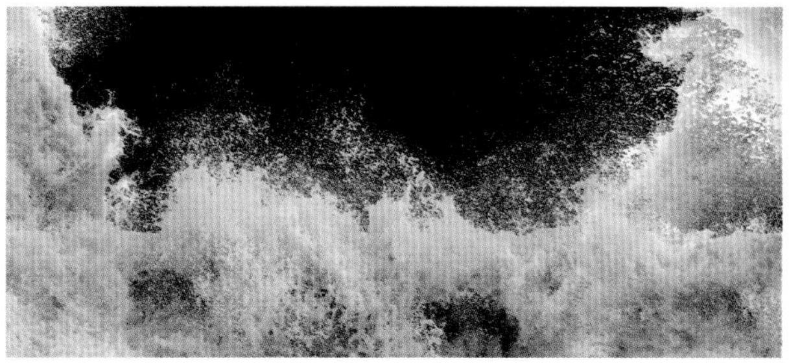

SP - 60

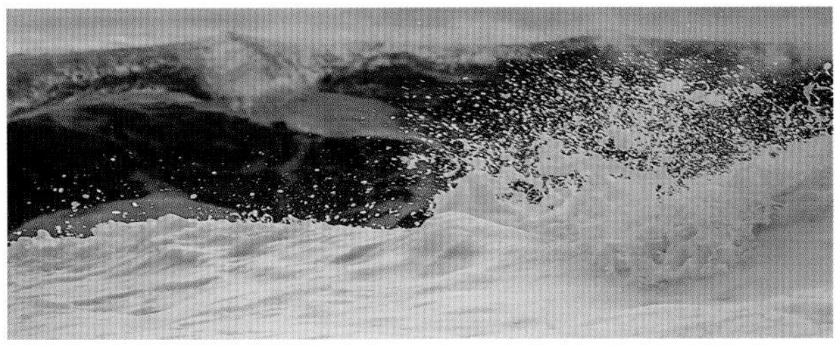

SP - 61

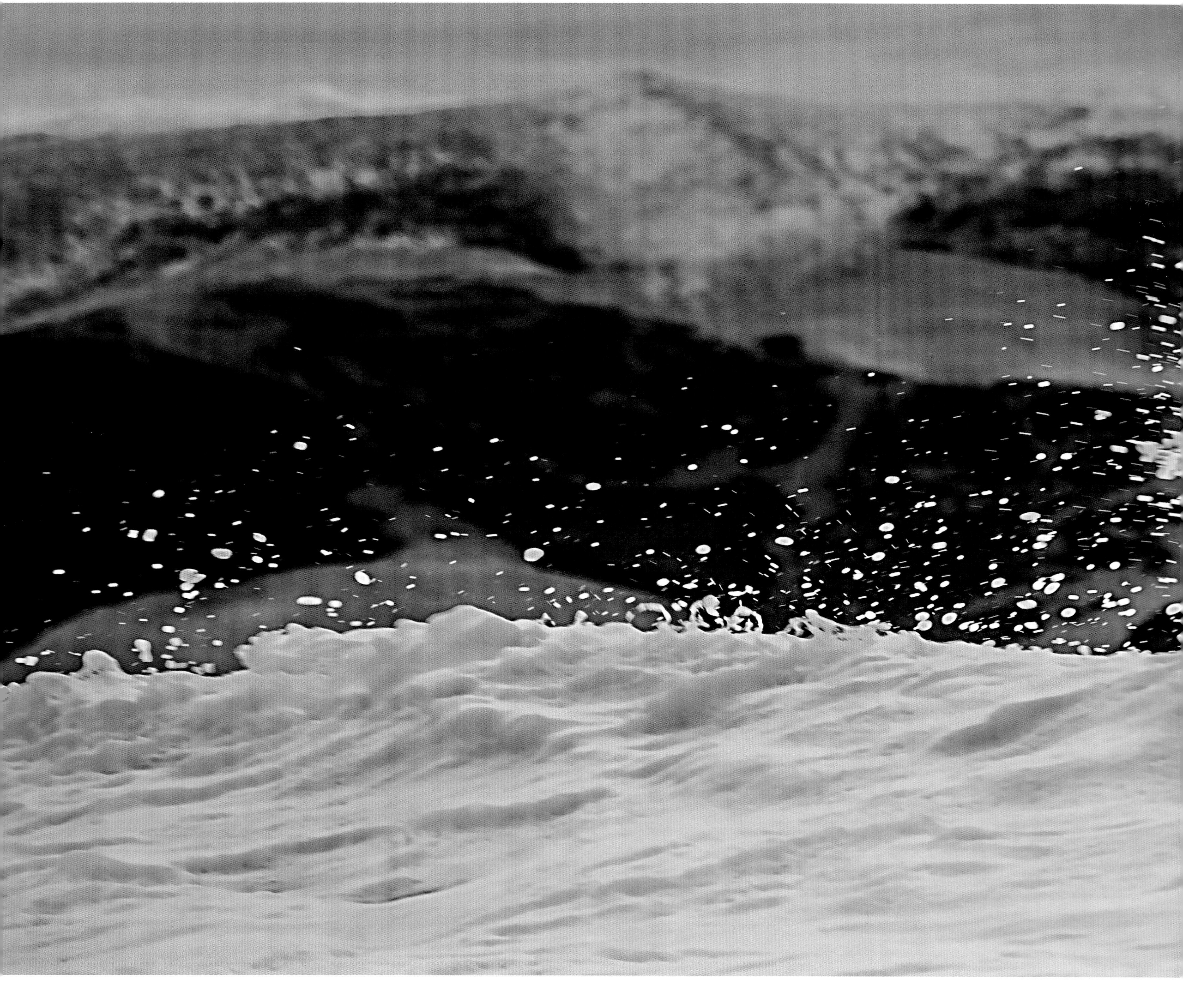

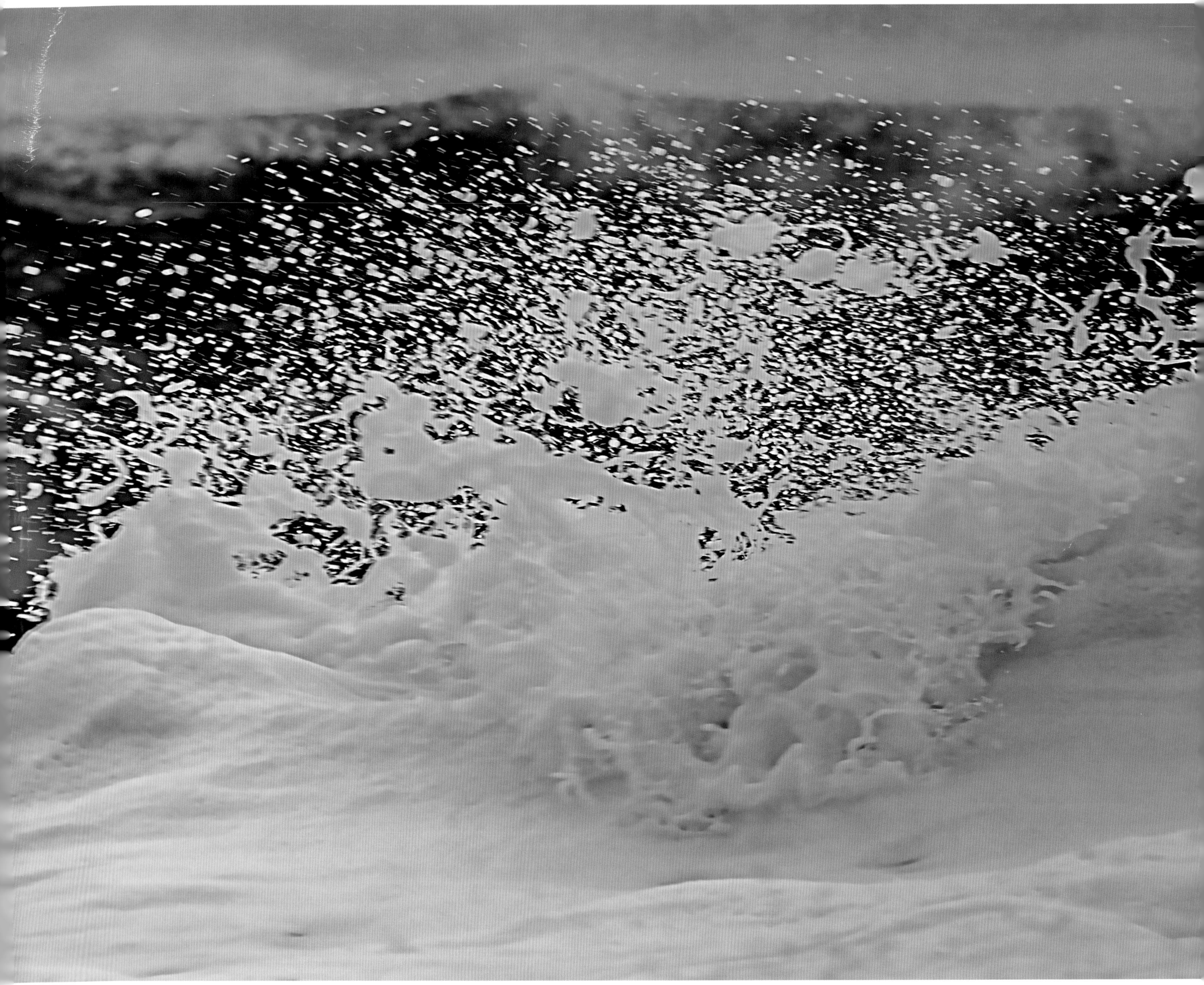